Cybernetic Systems: Recognition, Learning, Self-Organisation

ELECTRONIC & ELECTRICAL ENGINEERING RESEARCH STUDIES

PATTERN RECOGNITION & IMAGE PROCESSING SERIES

Series Editor: **Dr. Josef Kittler,**
Rutherford Appleton Laboratory, Didcot, Oxon., England

Cybernetic Systems: Recognition, Learning, Self-Organisation

Edited by:

E. R. Caianiello
Istituto di Scienze dell'Informazione, Universitá di Salerno, Italy
and
G. Musso
Elettronica San Giorgio, ELSAG S.p.A., Genova, Italy

RESEARCH STUDIES PRESS LTD.
Letchworth, Hertfordshire, England
JOHN WILEY & SONS INC.
New York · Brisbane · Chichester · Toronto · Singapore

RESEARCH STUDIES PRESS LTD.
58B Station Road, Letchworth, Herts. SG6 3BE, England

Marketing and Distribution:

Australia, New Zealand, South-east Asia:
Jacaranda-Wiley Ltd., Jacaranda Press
JOHN WILEY & SONS INC.
GPO Box 859, Brisbane, Queensland 4001, Australia

Canada:
JOHN WILEY & SONS CANADA LIMITED
22 Worcester Road, Rexdale, Ontario, Canada

Europe, Africa:
JOHN WILEY & SONS LIMITED
Baffins Lane, Chichester, West Sussex, England

North and South America and the rest of the world:
JOHN WILEY & SONS INC.
605 Third Avenue, New York, NY 10158, USA

Library of Congress Cataloging in Publication Data:

Main entry under title

Cybernetic systems.
    (Electronic & electrical engineering research studies.
    Pattern recognition and image processing series; v. 5)
    Contains papers on topics discussed at the International
    Workshop on Cybernetic Systems, organized in Salerno
    in December 1981 by the Italian Section of the
    International Association for Pattern Recognition and
    sponsored by Discoveries Italia.
    1. Artificial intelligence—Congresses.
    I. Caianiello, E. (Eduardo)   II. Musso, G.
    III. International Workshop on Cybernetic Systems
    (1981: Salerno, Italy)   IV. Discoveries Italia (Firm)
    V. Series: Electronic & electrical engineering
    research studies. Pattern recognition & image
    processing series; v. 5. [DNLM: 1. Cybernetics—
    Congresses.   2. Pattern recognition—Congresses.
    3. Computers—Congresses. Q 325 C994 1981]
    Q334.C93 1984   001.53'5   83–11095
    ISBN 0 86380 004 1
    ISBN 0 471 90219 5 (Wiley)

British Library Cataloguing in Publication Data:

Cybernetic systems.
    1. Cybernetics—Congresses
    I. Caianiello, E.   II. Musso, G.
    001.53   Q310
    ISBN 0 86380 004 1

    ISBN 0 86380 004 1 (Research Studies Press Ltd.)
    ISBN 0 471 90219 5 (John Wiley & Sons Inc.)

Printed in Great Britain

Preface

This book contains papers on topics discussed at the "International Workshop on Cybernetic systems" organized in Salerno in December 1981 by the Italian Section of the International Association for Pattern Recognition and sponsored by Discoveries Italia.

The book has been divided into five sections broadly corresponding to the themes of the Workshop, that is:

Neuron Nets and Self-organised Systems

Speech Recognition

Image Recognition

General Pattern Recognition

Natural Languages

All of these areas of research belong to the vast subject of Artificial Intelligence, which cannot be treated in depth in one book alone. The scope of this collection of papers is to describe some of the most important research currently being carried out by the international scientific community. The Workshop participants represented seven countries of North America and Europe: USA, United Kingdom, West Germany, Poland, Finland, Greece and Italy.

We would like sincerely to thank first of all the authors for their contributions, but equally well the workshop participants for the stimulating discussion which made the outcome of the workshop in terms of this volume possible.

E. R. CAIANIELLO   G. MUSSO

Contents

Neuron Nets and
Self-Organised Systems

SELF-ORGANIZED FORMATION OF FEATURE MAPS

T. Kohonen

Helsinki University of Technology,
Department of Technical Physics

ABSTRACT

It has recently been discovered that ordered (topological) maps of
observable characteristics are formed in arrays of adaptive units.
These arrays receive input signals which reflect some elementary
properties of the exterior environment, and produce output responses
which are localized in the output plane. The topological order of
output responses, after adaptation, approximates the topological
order of the corresponding input events.

INTRODUCTION

During the past forty years or so, many attempts have been made to
discover intelligent behavior in networks of formally defined neurons.
However, it seems that a central function has all the time been
missing. Although the brains are known to contain many kinds of
ordered images or maps of sensory experiences, not only in the
primary sensory areas but obviously on higher processing levels, too,
no model has previously involved such feature maps; neither has it
ever been demonstrated how the spatial order of processing units,
which obviously ought to correspond to some similarity measure or
topology of the signals, would adaptively evolve during operation.
The series of works reported in this paper is believed to be the
first which concretely proves formation of such ordered spatial
relations of processing units in different applications. These maps
are created without external supervision, by the effect of input
signals only.

ACTIVITY CLUSTERS IN A LATERALLY INTERCONNECTED ARRAY

The self-organizing ability of physical networks ensues from a couple
of simple system properties of which the first one, clustering of
activity due to local interactions, is discussed in this section.

Most neural networks in the brain, especially those in the cerebral
neocortex, are essentially two-dimensional layers of processing units

3

4

(cells or cellular modules) in which the units are densely interconnected through lateral feedback. According to some estimates, in the neocortex there are 10 000 interconnections emerging from and converging upon every principal cell. Fig. 1 delineates an array of formal neurons, each of which receives the effective primary input ϕ_i (cf. also Eq. (2)) and a great number of lateral connections from the outputs of other units. In reality, the array can be two-dimensional.

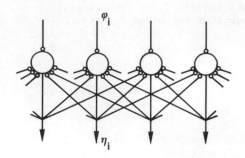

FIG. 1.   Laterally interconnected array

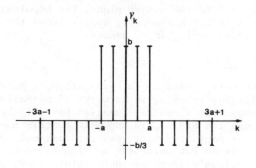

FIG. 2.   Definition of the lateral coupling function
          (a = 5, b = 0.06)

The nature of lateral coupling is a function of distance in the following way. For instance in the primate cortex, the connections up to a radius of, say 0.5 mm are excitatory and beyond that, up to about 1 mm they are inhibitory. There still exists a weaker long-range excitatory connectivity which we shall neglect in this discussion, however. In a preliminary qualitative analysis which deals with a one-dimensional array, we shall approximate the strength of lateral coupling as done in Fig. 2. Signal transfer in every unit is assumed to be described by the following expression:

$$\eta_i(t) = \sigma \left[\phi_i(t) + \sum_{k=-16}^{16} \gamma_k \; \eta_{i+k}(t - 1) \right] \qquad (1)$$

where each feedback has a small delay normalized to unity; the coeffi-
cients γ_k have been defined in Fig. 2. Here $\sigma \left[\cdot \right]$ stands for a
    nonlinearity for which we (rather arbitrarily) choose
$\sigma \left[z \right] = 0$ for $z < 0$, $\sigma \left[z \right] = z^{1.5}$ for $0 \le z \le 10$, and $\sigma \left[z \right] = 10$ for
$z > 10$. The system equation has been specified in a way in which an
interesting "avalanche" phenomenon (which seems to be the usual mode
of operation in the triggering of cortical cells, cf. Shepherd, 1974,
p. 307) is made to take place. Eq. (1), incidentally, is also a rather
realistic approximation of the transfer properties of real neurons
if $\phi_i(t)$ is the integrated afferent input.

Assume now that the input excitation $\phi_i(t)$ is some smooth function of
the array index i and it is made to last, e.g., for one unit interval
of time. The distribution $\eta_i = \eta_i(t)$ may then be plotted for subsequent instants of time as   done in Fig. 3.

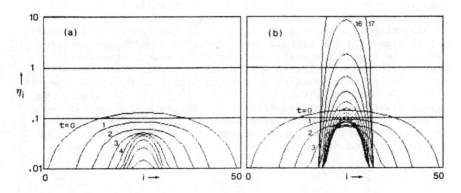

FIG. 3.   Clustering of activity in the array

There it has been taken $\phi_i(0) = A \sin (\pi i/50)$, and the excitatory
amplitude (A) was varied.[1] With A = .13 (case a) the input excitation
was below an effective "threshold" value, and with A = .14 (case b)
it was above it. In the above-threshold case the activity, due to the
lateral couplings, tends to a spatially bounded cluster, and due to
saturation it is stabilized to a "column" of constant amplitude. The
"column" is centered around the local maximum of the input excitation
$\phi_i(t)$. This phenomenon will be utilized in the adaptive process
    discussed next.

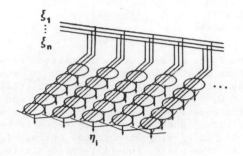

FIG. 4.   Two-dimensional adaptive array

THE LAWS OF ADAPTATION

Consider now a two-dimensional laterally coupled network shown in Fig. 4. Assume that the same set of input signals x = $(\xi_1, \xi_2, \ldots, \xi_n)$ is broadcast in parallel to all units. (Later we will also discuss a case in which each unit can receive a different set of signals.) The signals shall describe some characteristics of observable items or events, and they shall have a statistical distribution as exemplified in the next section. The units are provided with input weights $m_i = (\mu_{i1}, \mu_{i2}, \ldots, \mu_{in})$; however, it will not be necessary to assume the signal transfer properties linear. For instance, the output could be some nonlinear function like that described in the previous section. The effective input excitation is a weighted sum of input signals, defined by the inner product (similarity) of x and m_i,

$$\phi_i = < x, m_i > . \tag{2}$$

The dynamic process, exemplified earlier in the one-dimensional case, is now directly generalizable for a two-dimensional network, and it will be obvious that a circular cluster of activity around the maximum of ϕ_i is then obtained.

The input weights are assumed to change adaptively. In many learning models, the so-called *conjunction hypothesis* is applied: the input weights are modified in proportion to input signals values, but the magnitude of changes is further proportional to the output activity of the neuron. If this principle is applied to the present case, only those neurons which are situated within the activity cluster (concentrated around the maximum of ϕ_i) will change.

Many simulations performed so far have indicated that if the system behavior, in an idealized form, is describable by the following rules, self-organization always takes place, and the details underlying the implementation of these rules are then immaterial.

Self-organizing rules:

1. Find the maximum of $< x, m_i >$, and define a cluster of units around the maximum.

2. Change the input weights m_i of those units lying within the cluster *towards* x.

In practice, it has turned out advantageous to choose a larger dimension for the cluster in the beginning, and then let it shrink with time.

One possible simple simulation formula for Rule 2 might be

$$m_i(t + 1) = m_i(t) + \alpha(t) \cdot \left[x - m_i(t) \right] \qquad (3)$$

where $\alpha(t)$ is a slowly decreasing positive scalar, a "gain parameter". Many other laws have also been tested. For details, see previous publications (Kohonen, 1981a-d).

DEMONSTRATIONS OF ADAPTIVE FORMATION OF ORDERED MAPS

Computer simulations of self-organization have been performed on artificial and natural data. A common feature in the various experiments is that the input signal set x has a statistical distribution with a complex structure. Samples of input representations are drawn from the distribution at random.

Example 1:

Assume a two-dimensional array of processing units of the type shown in Fig. 4. Let the input signals and the weight parameters form three-dimensional vectors $x = (\xi_1, \xi_2, \xi_3) \in R^3$ and $m_i = (\mu_{i1}, \mu_{i2}, \mu_{i3}) \in R^3$, respectively.
For convenience, every x is normalized to unit length whereby its end point lies on the surface of the unit sphere in R^3. Let the x vectors have a structured distribution depicted in Fig. 5a.

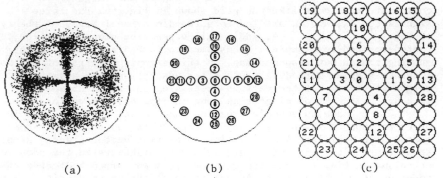

FIG. 5.   Ordered mapping in Example 1. (a) Distribution of training vectors, (b) Test vectors, (c) Output map

The input weights $\mu_{ij}(0)$ are initially defined as random numbers. After a sufficiently large number of training steps which depends on the "gain parameter" $\alpha(t)$ of Eq. (3), the processing units become specifically sensitized to different x in a particular order. To test that this order corresponds to that of the input signal distribution, a set of labelled test vectors can be chosen as shown in Fig. 5b. When each of them is applied at the inputs in turn, it causes output responses in the array. That unit which gives the maximum response, i.e., which has the maximum inner product $< x, m_i >$, is defined to be the *image* of x on the array. As can be seen from Fig. 5c, the spatial order of the images corresponds to the topological order of the test vectors. A couple of comments ought to be made. To the first, although the output map on the array were topologically correct, its branches can be bent in different ways. This deformation, however, serves a useful purpose. It can be seen that the *scale* of the image is optimal (a common property of these mappings) since the map tends to be aligned along the borders. To the second, there are many equally probable symmetrical alternatives in which the final map may be realized. In order to break the symmetry and to define a particular orientation, some extra control information is necessary. For instance, some of the units could have fixed input weights to force the image into a wanted place.

Example 2:

A somewhat more concrete demonstration deals with elementary visual perception of objects which have a variable position and size. A one-dimensional object is represented by a line of light which has the width of W and displacement D with respect of origin (Fig. 6a.). Both of these parameters are distributed at random over a support $(0 \leq D \leq 1, 1 \leq W \leq 2)$. The perceiver consists of three light-sensitive detectors upon which the line falls. Each of the detectors produces a signal ξ_i (i = 1, 2, 3) which is directly proportional to the incident light flux. For efficiency of representation, a constant background has been subtracted from all signals. The D-W coordinate net which is rectangular is then represented by corresponding vectors $x = (\xi_1, \xi_2, \xi_3) \in R^3$ (normalized to unity length). On the surface of the unit sphere the image of the coordinate net looks like the grid shown in Fig. 6b. The three signals ξ_1, ξ_2, and ξ_3 are led to a two-dimensional array of the type of Fig. 4, and a self-organizing process similar to that described in Example 1 is assumed to take place. In stead of showing the output response map, in this example a different and more accurate display method is used. After adaptation, the asymptotic weight vectors m_i of the various processing units are drawn in (μ_1, μ_2, μ_3)- coordinates as done in Fig. 6c. All vectors are made to emanate from the same point of origin, and in order to show to which unit they belong, their end points are connected with auxiliary lines: a line connecting vector i and j simply shows that unit i and unit j are adjacent neighbours in the same row or column in Fig. 4. Thus the grid of lines so formed indicates the topology of weight vectors. As can be seen, the point density of the m_i vectors tends to imitate the distribution of x vectors. In other words, an almost rectangular map, corresponding to the D-W coordinates, is formed onto the processing unit array.

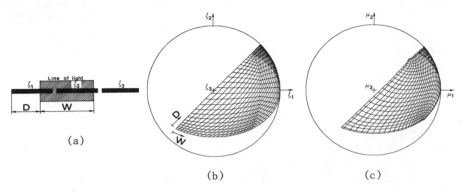

FIG. 6.   Independent mapping of position and size.
(a) Three light detectors, (b) Training vectors,
(c) Weight vectors

Example 3:

The purpose of this experiment is to show that the inputs can be non-identical as long as the signals preserve their original topological order. Consider Fig. 7 which depicts a one-dimensional array of processing units. This system will receive sinusoidal signals and become ordered according to their *frequency*. Assume a set of resonators of bandpass filters tuned at random. They may have a rather shallow resonance curve. The inputs to the array units are now picked up at random from the resonator outputs, different samples for different array units, so that there is no order in any structure or initial weight parameters. Next a series of adaptation operations is carried out, every time generating a new sinusoidal signal with a randomly chosen frequency. After a number of iteration steps the units start to become sensitized to different frequencies in an ascending or descending order. Final results of two experiments are shown in Table 1.

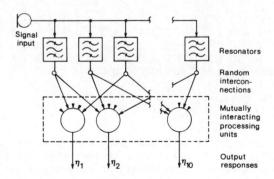

FIG. 7.   Adaptive system which forms a frequency map

There were twenty second-order filters with quality factor Q=2.5 and resonant frequencies distributed at random over the range $[1,2]$. The training frequencies were drawn at random from the range $[.5,1]$. The numbers in the table indicate those test frequencies to which each processing unit became most sensitive.

TABLE 1. Formation of frequency maps

Unit	1	2	3	4	5	6	7	8	9	10
Experiment 1, 2000 training steps	.55	.60	.67	.70	.77	.82	.83	.94	.98	.83
Experiment 2, 3500 training steps	.99	.98	.98	.97	.90	.81	.73	.69	.62	.59

Example 4:

This demonstration shows that the same process is able to organize hierarchically related data, e.g., representations for which the similarity relations between items are defined in the form of a classification tree. A similar problem is met in empirical or numerical taxonomy: one is looking for the best relational structure between a set of operational taxonomic units, based on their mutual similarity.

Consider Table 2 which represents an input data matrix. The columns, labelled "A" through "6", are hypothetical recordings of observable items, and each row position indicates the numerical value of a characteristic. Only ξ_1 through ξ_5 are given characteristics whereas the sixth component ξ_0 has been introduced to normalize the item vectors. Normalization is not necessary for self-organization but it makes the process smoother and faster.

TABLE 2. Input data matrix

```
       Item
       A B C D E F G H I J K L M N O P Q R S T U V W X Y Z 1 2 3 4 5 6
Char.
ξ₁     1 2 3 4 5 3 3 3 3 3 3 3 3 3 3 3 3 3 3 3 3 3 3 3 3 3 3 3 3 3 3 3
ξ₂     0 0 0 0 0 1 2 3 4 5 3 3 3 3 3 3 3 3 3 3 3 3 3 3 3 3 3 3 3 3 3 3
ξ₃     0 0 0 0 0 0 0 0 0 1 2 3 4 5 6 7 8 3 3 3 3 6 6 6 6 6 6 6 6 6 6 6
ξ₄     0 0 0 0 0 0 0 0 0 0 0 0 0 0 0 0 0 1 2 3 4 1 2 3 4 2 2 2 2 2 2 2
ξ₅     0 0 0 0 0 0 0 0 0 0 0 0 0 0 0 0 0 0 0 0 0 0 0 0 0 1 2 3 4 5 6
```

$$\xi_0 = (100 - \sum_{i=1}^{5} \xi_i^2)^{1/2}$$

The data given in Table 2 have been chosen according to a principle which defines a *data structure*. If the items are chained in a similar way as the so-called dendrograms or cladograms are formed in taxonomy, i.e., by linking those pairs of items which have the smallest mutual distance, then Table 2 corresponds to the binary tree shown in Fig. 8a.

The array was otherwise similar to that of Fig. 4 except that each
unit had six inputs, and the units were arranged in a hexagonal
lattice. The input vectors used in training were now picked up from
the columns of Table 1 at random. After self-organization, the output
map usually reflected similar topological relations as the binary
tree, as seen from the case depicted in Fig. 8b.

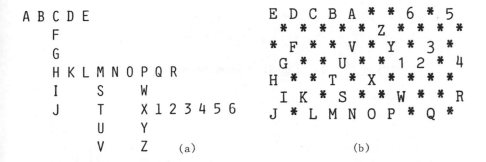

```
A B C D E                          E D C B A * * 6 * 5
    F                               * * * * * Z * * * *
    G                              *  F * * V * Y * 3 *
    H K L M N O P Q R               G * * U * * 1 2 * 4
    I     S     W                  H * * T * X * * * *
    J     T     X 1 2 3 4 5 6       I K * S * * * W * * R
          U     Y                  J * L M N O P * Q *
          V     Z      (a)                    (b)
```

FIG. 8.   Hierarchical ordering. (a) Binary tree of the data
           matrix, (b) Ordering result (output map)

Example 5:

Finally the above process was applied to natural data, viz. samples
of speech waveforms of the Finnish language. The purpose was to find
an ordered map of phonemes. For this experiment, 30 samples of each
of the eight vowels /u o a æ ∅ y e i/   and ten consonants
/s m n ŋ l r j v h d/   were used; these phonemes are adequately
characterized by their frequency spectra.

The spectral decomposition of 4 kHz lowpass-filtered speech waveforms
was made by a programmed DFT algorithm, using a 25.6 ms Hamming window
and 10 kHz sampling rate. Of a 128-point logarithmic power spectrum,
15 sample points with 12 equally spaced points were selected from the
frequency range ⌈200 Hz, 3 kHz⌉, and three points from the range
⌈3 kHz, 5 kHz⌉. From these spectra, samples were chosen at those instants of time which corresponded to stationary phonemes. These
samples thus constituted the 15-component input pattern vectors.

After self-organization, it was tested to which phoneme each unit
became most sensitive, giving the maximum response; the unit was
labelled by this phoneme. Fig. 9 is an example of ordering results.

In the evaluation of experimental results, one has to realize that
the phonemic samples used in training are only believed to be
correct; in principle, there is a possibility that the speaker did
not really pronounce them in the same way. It is plausible that
different utterances of, say, /h/ represent different phonemes if
they occur in different context. For instance, between two /a/ or
/æ/, /h/ is probably voiced.

FIG. 9.   Self-organized phoneme map

CONCLUSIONS

In this discussion, experimental results from many different experiments on self-organization have been represented. In a short discussion it is beyond possibilities to carry out a mathematical analysis which would clarify the reasons for ordering; let it be referred to other publications (e.g., Kohonen, 1981c). One may only intuitively understand that some kind of continuous order must follow from the "chaining" property of the Self-Organizing Rules stated in the beginning.

There can be twofold implications of the above findings; to the first, this principle might be applied in a similar way as *clustering algorithms* are used for the organization of experimental data. Another, perhaps even more fundamental impact would be if this principle helped to understand the formation of *internal representations of information in the central nervous system.*

REFERENCES

Kohonen, T., 1981a. Automatic formation of topological maps of patterns in a self-organizing system, in Proc. 2nd Scandinavian Conference on Image Analysis (Eds. Oja and Simula), pp 214-220. Pattern Recognition Society of Finland, Espoo, Finland.
Kohonen, T., 1981b-d. Helsinki University of Technology Technical Reports Nos. TKK-F-A461, 462, 463.
Kohonen, T., 1982. Self-organized formation of topologically correct feature maps. Biological Cybernetics, 43, 59-69.

COMPUTING WITH NEURAL NETS:
DESIGN AND TECHNOLOGY

J. Becker and I. Eisele

Federal Armed Forces University Munich
Department of Electrical Engineering
Werner-Heisenberg-Weg 39
D - 8014 Neubiberg - FRG

ABSTRACT

Due to its serial operation the present-day computer faces severe
drawbacks. It is suggested that neural nets may overcome some of these
difficulties.

For an optimal realization of such nets the mutual influence of net
design and modern technology has to be taken into account.

As a practical example we show how to design a net for solving the
diffusion equation in a parallel way.

Finally we look into the possibilities of realizing such a net with
integrated circuitry.

INTRODUCTION

In this talk we shall try to discuss the mutual influence between the
design of neural nets and the available technologies. We shall investigate the question how technology restricts the design of neural
nets, and we shall look into the possibilities of developing new technologies to make more powerful nets.

DATA PROCESSING WITH NEURAL NETS

A substantial amount of hard physical work is nowadays done by man-
made machines. It is now the aim of mankind to make machines which may
take over a substantial amount of hard mental work. Since computers
for many tasks show a poor performance when compared to the brain, a
better understanding of the latter may be necessary to design a
thinking machine.

A famous mathematical model for the activities of a neural system is
given by the set of equations

$$U_h(t+\tau) = \theta[\sum_k a_{hk} U_k(t) - S_k] \, , \tag{1}$$

where U_h is a Boolean variable describing the state of the neuron h (U_h = 0: inactive, U_h = 1: active). Time is quantized in this model; all neurons are synchronized.

The properties and solutions of the system (1) have been studied in detail by Caianiello and coworkers [1].

Clearly, two important features of the brain are mirrored in these equations: parallel processing and learning. (Learning may be achieved by a slow variation of the couplings a_{hk} and the thresholds s_k.)

The equations (1) are purely deterministic. However, stochastic processes seem to play an important rôle in the brain (like in any other self-organizing system). Noise may help a system to find its optimal order parameters (i.e., working conditions); it may even create order (noise induced transitions) [2]. Regrettably, noise has mainly been considered as something disturbing to engineering. Thus, there is no technology of noise. Furthermore, even the theoretical foundations of stochastic processes are not yet completely laid, in particular for systems which are not in equilibrium.

Therefore it seems premature to incorporate noise into a thinking machine, and we shall stick to the model (1) described above.

HOW TO MATERIALIZE NEURONS

It is obvious that connecting twenty neurons (each of the size of a biscuit box with an electric bulb to indicate activity) will not make an intelligent machine. We need a very large number of neurons for a useful net, which means that the individual neuron must be very small.

Let us therefore discuss which materials resp. material properties may be useful for making neurons.

First, one might think of <u>chemical</u> reactions (enzyme reactions, cycles, hypercycles) in which concentrations, modes of operation, or molecular structures may be used to code data. However, since we need many neurons we would probably have to introduce an additional spatial (i.e., cellular) structure which takes us to the next point already.

Second, and closest to the brain, we may use <u>biological</u> systems, both artificial or natural. An artificial system may be attainable, since membrane physics and chemistry have recently made a substantial progress, but still there is no technology to make sufficiently correlated structures for our purpose.

As for natural systems, to grow a real brain in a glass aquarium is an extremely appealing idea; but problems start with the fact that usually nervous tissues have lost the ability to grow.

Third, we look at <u>optical</u> effects. Here the main problems are diffraction (which limits miniaturization), scattering, and high power losses, so that it seems unlikely that optical properties will be used to make nets.

Fourth, and already more promising, we may use <u>magnetic</u> or <u>dielectric</u> properties. For example, magnetic bubbles have been used in memories. As an application of dielectric properties we quote the MNOS (Metal-Nitride-Oxide-Semiconductor) structure, which can be used for logic or memories.

Fifth, and probably most realistic, one can exploit <u>electric</u> properties, in particular, of semiconductors and superconductors. For both types of materials there is a well developed technology. Since the technology for superconducting circuitry (e.g., Josephson junctions) is similar to the one for semiconductors we shall stick to these for the rest of this paper.

TECHNOLOGICAL RESTRICTIONS FOR NEURAL NETS ON INTEGRATED CIRCUITS (IC)

Logical values may be represented by voltages, currents, or charges, where charges can only be kept for about 1 ms (without refreshing). There are various techniques to make logical elements with semiconducting materials, like bipolar (in particular, Integrated Injection Logic (I^2L), MOS (Metal-Oxide-Semiconductor), or a combination of them.

The basic unit to be considered for making a neural net with integrated circuits is a single chip. At present, a chip contains typically 10^5 elements (diodes, transistors, etc.) on an area of 5 by 5 mm.

However, on the average only 20 % of the area of the chip are covered by these elements. Some 70 % are needed for the wiring between the elements; some 10 % serve to insulate the connections against each other. To connect the net on the chip to the outside world, there is a rather limited number of "legs" which hardly exceeds 60.

The power loss of a chip has to be less than 500 mW, otherwise it becomes too warm. This is the main obstacle against further miniaturization, because if one wants to have more transistors on a chip the power loss per transistor has to be lowered. This implies e.g. that the oxide should become thinner which is difficult to achieve.

It is the characteristic feature of a neuron that it consists of a <u>processor</u> with one or several inputs and one output and a <u>memory</u>. (Of course, several neurons may share a processor with several outputs.) The processor is nothing else than a map from a set of Boolean variables $\{X_1, \ldots, X_N\}$ into the set $\{Y\}$ of one Boolean variable.

How can we represent this map in hardware?

Because of the tolerance of the single electronic elements (typically a few percent), only 4-5 different voltage levels may be distinguished because errors may be weighed and summed with the data (cf.eq.(1)).

Furthermore one has to allow for longer switching times as compared to binary logic. Hence the use of threshold or multi-valued logic does not offer an advantage.

On the other hand, designing and making a processor with an arbitrary mapping is not a big problem for binary logic, apart from the fact that a complicated mapping requires many elements. One may use

- ROMs (Read Only Memories) for a big number of inputs and a good mixture of "ones" and "zeroes" in the output;
- PLAs (Programmable Logic Arrays) for a big number of inputs, but relatively few "ones" in the output;
- Logic Gates for a small number of inputs.

The memories will in general be realized by flipflops, even if there may be more elegant methods (see below).

In any case, because of the technological data mentioned above, the possibilities of designing a neural net with IC's are rather restricted. We have to minimize the number of connections to the outside world, the number of connections between the neurons, the number of elements of each neuron, and the number of neurons itself. It will turn out that these requirements lead to a loss in the organizational structure of the net and consequently in speed.

A POSSIBLE APPLICATION FOR "STUPID" NETS

A neural net may store information, process data in a parallel way, evolve in time, and learn.

A "stupid" net, in our terminology, is a net which is not able to learn. It just follows a given algorithm, very much like a computer, though in a parallel way.

In principle a net may store an enormous amount of information. One may thus think of using nets as memories. However, since technology limits the number of connections between the neurons, information can only grow linearly with the number of neurons, such that a general use of nets as memories seems ruled out at present.

We are now left with parallel processing and time evolution. Hence it is an alluring idea to use nets to calculate the time evolution of complex systems.

Suppose a system may be described by a set of variables, $\vec{u}: = \{u_k;$ $k=1, \ldots, N\}$, $\vec{u} = \vec{u}(t)$, which of course may depend on certain parameters. Suppose that the time evolution of the system is given by the set of differential equations,

$$\frac{d}{dt} \vec{u}(t) = H(\vec{u}(t)). \tag{2}$$

Following Euler, we replace the differential quotient by a difference quotient and obtain

$$\vec{u}(t+\tau) = \vec{u}(t) + \tau \cdot H(\vec{u}(t)). \qquad (3)$$

By representing each variable u_k by a set of binary digits it is now easy to design a neural net the time evolution of which follows precisely eq. (3).

Also a computer would use this equation to solve the problem. Yet a neural net shows two striking advantages:

First, a neuron is a memory and a processor at the same time (whereas memory and CPU are separated in computers, so that data have to be transferred all the time).

Second, each variable u_k has its own processor allowing for a truly parallel processing.

There is a wide range of problems of this type, from weather forecast via world econometric models to spin dynamics. To be more specific, we now choose a particular system.

One of the simplest examples is certainly the diffusion equation for one space dimension,

$$\frac{\partial n}{\partial t} = D \frac{\partial^2 n}{\partial x^2} , \qquad (4)$$

or, in discretized form,

$$n_k(t+\tau) = n_k(t) + \kappa[n_{k+1}(t) - 2n_k(t) + n_{k-1}(t)] \qquad (5)$$

with

$$\kappa := \frac{\tau \cdot D}{(\Delta x)^2} \qquad (6)$$

where Δx is the spatial lattice spacing. This problem is particularly simple since eq. (5) is linear and each variable is only coupled to its nearest neighbours.

κ is restricted by the inequality

$$\kappa \leq \frac{1}{2} ; \qquad (7)$$

otherwise the procedure (5) becomes numerically unstable. Eq. (5) reduces to a particularly simple form if we choose $\kappa := \frac{1}{2}$:

$$n_k(t+\tau) = \frac{1}{2}(n_{k+1}(t) + n_{k-1}(t)) , \qquad (8)$$

i.e. the value of a variable at time $t+\tau$ is simply the mean of its nearest neighbours at time t.

18

Remark: Instead of using Euler's method, cf.eq.(3), it has many advantages to use the time reversal invariant discretization ("central difference quotient") [3]:

$$u(t+\tau) = u(t-\tau) + 2\tau \cdot H(u(t)).\tag{9}$$

This method is always numerically stable, and the discretization error is proportional τ^2.

In this scheme the neurons have a certain short-term "memory". However, it requires more storage space, and therefore we disregard it in this paper. (More advanced numerical techniques, like implicit methods, τ^2 extrapolation, or variable τ control, would still be more complicated to be realized in a net).

ANATOMY OF A NET FOR SOLVING THE DIFFUSION EQUATION

We represent each variable u_k in the binary code; each digit is then realized as a neuron.

Each lattice site receives inputs from other lattice sites which have to be weighed and added. In principle there are logical networks that do this job in a parallel way; but these nets naturally are quite big.

A simpler net which adds several numbers in a semiparallel way is the accumulation register (cf.fig.1). It consists of "data neurons" made

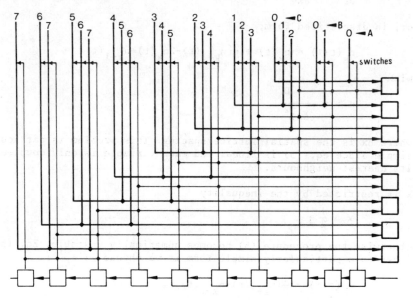

FIG 1. Adding three numbers A, B, and C to
an accumulation register (schematic)
Thick lines: data net, thin lines: control net

from a full adder and two flipflops per bit, and a set of "control neurons" (which, in this case, is simply a chain of delay neurons combined with appropriate switches).

Yet this solution still requires too many elements and too many connections. In the case of eq. (8) one can further reduce their numbers. The simplest case in a shift register and a full adder per lattice site; it still allows for parallel processing with respect to the lattice, but processing at each lattice site is how purely serial (cf.fig.2 and 3). (This is the concept of array processors, cf.[4].)

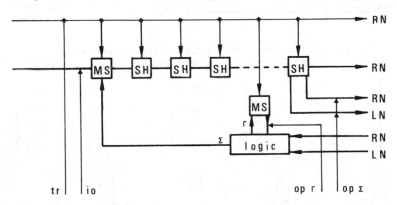

FIG 2.   Memory and logic for one lattice site (simple net)
MS: master–slave flipflop, SH: sample-hold flipflop,
Σ: sum, Γ: carry out, RN: right neighbour, LN: left
neighbour, tr: trigger, io: IN/OUT switches, op Σ/Γ:
switches to operate sum and carry out

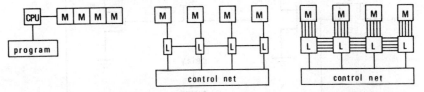

FIG 3.   Serial versus parallel treatment of the diffusion
equation. M: memory, CPU: central processing unit,
L: logic.
Left: computer,time step parallel, space step serial
Center: simple net, time step serial, space step
          parallel
Right: net with accumulation register, time step
          quasi-parallel, space step parallel

The details of the full adder and the elements of the shift register may be seen from figures 4 and 5 [5]. To set the initial data and to read out the results, one closes the switches IN/OUT which connect all the shift registers. Data are then serially transfered to and from the net.

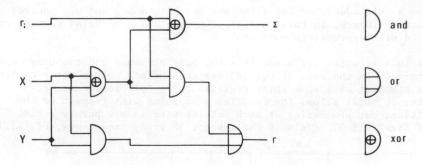

FIG 4. Full adder: construction from basic gates.
X, Y: inputs, Γ_i: carry in, Σ: sum, Γ: carry out

Truth
tables:

X Y	$\Gamma_i = 0$ 1		X Y	$\Gamma_i = 0$ 1	
0 0	0 1		0 0	0 0	
1 0	1 0	$\Big\} = \Sigma$	1 0	0 1	$\Big\} = \Gamma$
0 1	1 0		0 1	0 1	
1 1	0 1		1 1	1 1	

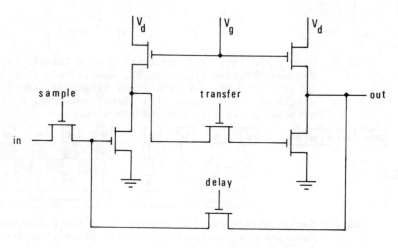

FIG 5. Quasistatic sample and hold flipflop

Let us now calculate how many elements we need for each lattice site.
Let N be the number of bits, i.e. the accuracy. The full adder requires 4 inverters and 9 AND resp. OR gates. If we use diodes for the
gates we need 33 elements altogether. (In practice one would make the
gates from transistors to reduce power losses.)

For a static shift register we need N-1 sample-hold (SH) flipflops, 2
master-slave (MS) flipflops, and 4 switches. Each SH flipflop requires

7 transistors, each MS flipflop requires 18. The total number of elements per lattice site is listed in the following table.

Accuracy (bits)	N = 8	N = 16	N = 32
Memory	89	145	257
Logic	33	33	33
Total	122	178	290
Number of Lattice Sites per Chip	$\sim$ 1000	$\sim$ 700	$\sim$ 400

TABLE. Number of elements per lattice site and number of lattice sites per chip as a function of the accuracy for solving the diffusion equation with a simple net.

These figures look fine if we are satisfied with the one dimensional diffusion equation. Each chip would have 6 data lines and 7 control lines connected to the outside world, and it is easy to couple 100 chips to reach 10^5 lattice points, a number which is a reasonable upper bound for today's serial computers.

Things get much worse if we look at the case of two dimensions. Because the number of "legs" of a chip is restricted to $\sim$ 60, it is no longer possible to connect several chips (unless data are transfered serially which makes the net useless). Even worse, it will be very difficult to connect the lattice sites on the chip in the necessary way!

CONCLUSIONS: NEED FOR A NEW TECHNOLOGY

It should be emphasized that we do not advocate to construct a net which does nothing else but solve the diffusion equation. We rather used the diffusion equation as a simple model case. We conclude:

1. One can only accommodate a rather limited number of lattice sites on a simple chip even if one uses the simplest algorithm and the simplest organizational structure.

2. In the case of more than 1 space dimension it is very difficult to provide the necessary couplings on the chip and it is impossible to couple several chips together in a parallel way.

Other problems one would like to have nets for, e.g., deterministic and stochastic differential equations with space dependend potential; population dynamics with a large number of species ($\sim$ 1000); Monte Carlo simulations; etc. These would still require more elements and more connections.

The same applies to programmable or self-programming (i.e., intelligent) nets.

Thus, with conventional technologies it is extremely difficult to make useful nets.

Can one possibly improve conventional technology to meet our needs for making more complex nets?

One might think, for instance, of increasing the chip area. In the extreme case one might have a single net, say, on a 3" wafer which would allow for at least 150 times as many elements as a single chip. However, because of material defects such a net would probably never work. (At present, 10-20 % of the manufactured chips have to be thrown away because of these defects!)

Another possibility would be to use I^2L technology which permits much smaller memory cells. (In this technology several transistors share some of their doped areas; e.g., a pnp transistor could share the n and p regions which a neighbouring npn transistor; cf.[8].) Dynamic memories which use charge instead of voltage or current to code data might also save some space.

However, all improvements of conventional technology will not be able to solve the main problem: the number of connections. (Even in the double Si technology the number of layers of connections is restricted to three due to the "mountains" at the surface of MOS structures.)

We conclude that planar technology cannot really cope with the requirements of neural nets.

To make the necessary connections between the neurons we must leave the surface and dive into the third dimension. A first step would be to leave the elements at the surface and to have various layers underneath which contain the connections. At a later stage one could also think of distributing the elements in the bulk (which would then mean that one could only use bipolar technology because the surface of an MOS structure is amorphous due to the SiO_2 and cannot be used as the substrate of a new layer).

Thus, it will be necessary to use new techniques which are able to produce three dimensional structures as they are needed for nets.

A new technique which will allow for such structures is <u>Molecular Beam Epitaxy</u>, i.e., the growth of epitaxial layers on a substrate in Ultra High Vacuum [6]. A machine has recently been designed which allows for producing very well defined structures [7]. Combined with other methods (like ion implantation or plasma etching) for lateral structures, Molecular Beam Epitaxy can be a powerful technique for making neural nets. Technological details will be published elsewhere [9].

It is our hope that in this way it will be possible to make nets which are not necessarily stupid but which may even be intelligent.

ACKNOWLEDGEMENTS

The authors would like to thank Prof. E. Caianiello who convinced them that parallel processing of data is a problem which calls for a solution, and Prof. B. Bullemer and Mr. P. Nerud for many valuable discussions and contributions to this paper.

REFERENCES

[1] E.R. Caianiello, Outline of a Theory of Thought-processes and Thinking Machines, J. Theor. Biol. $\underline{1}$, 204 (1961).

E.R. Caianiello, G. Simoncelli, Polygonal Inequalities as a Key to Neuronic Equations, Biol. Cybern. $\underline{41}$, 203 (1981).

E.R. Caianiello, Normal Modes in Neural Nets. This volume.

A book by E.R. Caianiello on neural nets is in press.

[2] L. Arnold, R. Lefever, Stochastic Nonlinear Systems, Springer (1981).

[3] F. Szidarovsky, S. Yakowitz, Principles and Procedures of Numerical Analysis, Plenum (1978).

[4] U. Knödel, H.J. Schneider (Ed.), Parallel Processes and Related Automata, Springer (1981).

[5] U. Tietze, Ch. Schenk, Halbleiter-Schaltungstechnik, Springer (1980).

[6] I. Eisele, Molekularstrahlepitaxie und Halbleiterübergitter, Hauptvortrag Frühjahrstagung DPG, Bielefeld (1980).

[7] A. Beck, J. Becker, B. Bullemer, I. Eisele, A New Cell Arrangement for Fast Control of Evaporation Rates, European Workshop on MBE, Stuttgart (1981).

[8] H.H. Berger, S.K. Wiedmann, The Bipolar LSI Breakthrough, part 2, Electronics, Oct 2, (1975), p. 99.

[9] J. Becker, I. Eisele, to be published.

NORMAL MODES IN NEURAL NETS

E.R. Caianiello and G. Simoncelli[+]

Università di Salerno
(+) Accademia Aeronautica Napoli

ABSTRACT

It is shown that the neural equations, which describe a network of binary elements (neurons), admit normal modes that can be exactly computed

1. The set of equations described in Sect. 3 were introduced by the author (neuronic eq.'s) as part of a model of neural activity (Caianiello, 1961), which extends and algebrizes the McCulloch-Pitts neural nets. Clearly such nets may describe as well a variety of situations, e.g. in physics, economics or parallel computing. We recall their exact solution obtained in compact matricial notation (Caianiello, 1973; Caianiello et al., 1975); the "synthesis" of a net, i.e. the evaluation of the F_h's describing a network which performs any a priori fixed sequence of states, is solved with a similar technique. Such networks have normal modes, and constants of motion. The continuous (the arbitrary real parameters entering the F_h) and the discontinuous (jump-like behavior) aspects of a net are strictly connected, with interesting geometrical and group-theoretical implications.

2. Denote with
$$x \equiv \vec{x} \equiv \{x^1, x^2, \ldots, x^N\} \qquad x^h = 0,1$$
$$\xi \equiv \vec{\xi} \equiv \{\xi^1, \xi^2, \ldots, \xi^N\} \qquad \xi^h = \pm 1 \qquad \left[x = \tfrac{1}{2}(1+\xi)\right]$$
variables, vectors, or one-row matrices, whose components have values as specified. Let $F(\xi)$, $\Phi(x)$ be any real functions subject only to the condition
$$F(\xi) \neq 0; \quad \Phi(x) \neq 0$$
for any choice of variables ξ^h, x^h. Call

25

$$1[\Phi] = \{ \begin{matrix} 1 \text{ for } \Phi > 0 \\ 0 \text{ for } \Phi < 0 \end{matrix} \qquad \text{(Heaviside step function)}$$

$$\sigma[F] \equiv \text{sgn}[F] = \{ \begin{matrix} 1 \text{ for } F > 0 \\ -1 \text{ for } F < 0 \end{matrix} \qquad \text{(signum)}$$

Define

$$<F(\xi)> = \frac{1}{2^N} \sum_{(\xi^1 = \pm 1, \ldots, \xi^N = \pm 1)} F(\xi^1, \xi^2, \ldots, \xi^N) \qquad \text{(trace)}$$

The tensor powers of ξ have 2^N components:

$$\eta^\alpha = \begin{cases} 1 \equiv \xi^0 \\ \vdots \\ \xi^h \\ \vdots \\ \xi^{h_1 h_2 \ldots h_r} \\ \vdots \\ \xi^{1 \, 2 \ldots N} \end{cases} \qquad \begin{matrix} h = 1, 2, \ldots, N \text{ (linear terms)} \\ \\ \alpha \equiv h_1 h_2 \ldots h_r \text{ (non linear terms)} \end{matrix}$$

$\eta \equiv \vec{\eta} \equiv \{\eta^\alpha\}$ is thus a vector in 2^N dimensions, $\eta^\alpha = \pm 1$; the α-ordering of the indices $0, 1, \ldots, 2^N - 1$ may be arranged to suit particular needs; here:

$$\vec{\eta} = \binom{1}{\xi^N} \times \binom{1}{\xi^{N-1}} \times \ldots \times \binom{1}{\xi^1} = \begin{pmatrix} 1 \\ \xi^1 \\ \xi^2 \\ \xi^1 \xi^2 \\ \xi^3 \\ \vdots \\ \xi^1 \ldots \xi^N \end{pmatrix}$$

Then, for any $F(\xi) \neq 0$:

$$\sigma[F(\xi)] = \sum_{\alpha=0}^{2^N - 1} f_\alpha \eta^\alpha \equiv f^T \eta$$

where

$$f_\alpha = <\eta^\alpha \sigma[F(\xi)]> = <\sigma[\eta^\alpha F(\xi)]>$$

A similar expansion is easily derived for Heaviside functions.

3. Cosider first the case of <u>linear</u> functions $\Phi(x)$ or $F(\xi)$, hence l.s. boolean functions $1[\Phi(x)]$ and $\sigma[f(\xi)]$. The N.E. of our model, $(u_h \equiv x_h)$, are:

(1) $\quad u_h(t+\tau) = 1\left[\sum\limits_{\substack{h=1\ldots N \\ r=1\ldots L}} a_{hk}^{(r)} u_k(t-r\tau) - s_h\right]$ $\quad$ (I Form: state eq.'s)

They can be equivalently written as

(2) $\quad w_h(t+\tau) = \Sigma a_{hk}^{(r)} 1\left[w_k(t-r\tau)\right] - s_h$ $\quad$ (II Form: excitation eq.'s)

They can be written as well, by enlarging the number of neurons from N to N·L, as if without delays ($a_{hk}^{(r)} \to a_{hk}^{(0)} \equiv a_{hk}$). In matricial notation, setting (NL→N)

$$u_h(m\tau) = u_{h,m}; \quad \vec{u}_m \equiv \begin{pmatrix} u_{1,m} \\ u_{2,m} \\ \vdots \\ u_{N,m} \end{pmatrix}; \quad \Lambda \equiv \{a_{hk}\}$$

we find

(3) $\quad \vec{u}_{m+1} = 1\left[A\vec{u}_m - \vec{s}\right]$ $\quad\quad$ (I Form)

(4) $\quad \vec{w}_{m+1} = A1\left[\vec{w}_m\right] - \vec{s}$ $\quad\quad$ (II Form)

4. Let $\vec{\gamma}_r$ be vectors, and form from (4) the scalar products

$$\vec{\gamma}_r \cdot \vec{w}_{m+1} = \vec{\gamma}_r \cdot A1\left[\vec{w}_m\right] - \vec{\gamma}_r \cdot \vec{s}$$

If

(5) $\quad A^T \vec{\gamma} = 0$

we find

(6) $\quad \vec{\gamma}_r \cdot \vec{w}(t) = -\vec{\gamma}_r \cdot \vec{s} = $ constant

If A is of order N and rank R, there are N-R vectors satisfying (5) and as many linear constants of motion in the net. They can be utilized e.g. as failure detectors; nets may be computed so as to have prescribed constants of motion and no limitation on couplings within rank R. It is also possible, of course, to obtain quadratic constants, etc. (Caianiello et al.,1967,1970)

5. We pass now to the signum representation. A particular condition appears then to simplify remarkably the form of (3) and (4):

$$A\vec{1} = 2\vec{s}$$

this means <u>self duality</u>, and if it holds (3) and (4) become $(A \to \frac{1}{2} A)$:

(7) $\quad \vec{\xi}_{m+1} = \sigma\left[A\vec{\xi}_m\right]$

(8) $\quad \vec{w}_{m+1} = A\sigma\left[\vec{w}_m\right]$

(7), (8) reduce immediately in turn to the form (3), (4) by keeping fixed the state of some given neuron (N-1 neurons are then free). This form simplifies many computations.

Consider now nets of general boolean functions. It is convenient to work directly with the tensorial signum expansions; we can write the NE for a general net as

(9) $\quad \xi_{m+1}^h = \sigma\left[f^h(\xi_m^1, .., \xi_m^N)\right] = \sum_\alpha f^h_\alpha \eta_m^\alpha = f^{hT} \eta_m$

We consider now the normalized ξ-state matrix of the net $\Phi_{(N)}$; with $N = 3$, e.g., it is

$$\Phi_{(3)} = 2^{-3/2} \begin{pmatrix} 1 & -1 & 1 & 1 & -1 & -1 & 1 & -1 \\ 1 & 1 & -1 & 1 & -1 & 1 & -1 & -1 \\ 1 & 1 & 1 & -1 & 1 & -1 & -1 & -1 \end{pmatrix}$$

We can augment the $N \times 2^N$ ξ-matrix $\Phi_{(N)}$ to the $2^N \times 2^N$ η-state matrix, from

$$\eta = \begin{pmatrix} 1 \\ \xi_N \end{pmatrix} x \ldots x \begin{pmatrix} 1 \\ \xi_1 \end{pmatrix}$$

as follows

$$\Phi_{(N)} = \begin{pmatrix} \frac{1}{2} & \frac{1}{2} \\ \frac{1}{2} & -\frac{1}{2} \end{pmatrix} x \ldots x \begin{pmatrix} \frac{1}{2} & \frac{1}{2} \\ \frac{1}{2} & -\frac{1}{2} \end{pmatrix}$$
$$\text{(N times)}$$

$\Phi_{(N)} \equiv \Phi$ is an Hermite matrix such that

$$\Phi = \Phi^T \ ; \ \Phi^2 = 1 \ ; \ \Phi = \Phi^{-1} \ ; \ \det(\Phi_N) = (-1)^N$$

We can thus also augment the N ξ-state NE to the 2^N η-state form

(10) $\quad \vec{\eta}_{m+1} = F\vec{\eta}_m$,

in which F is a $2^N \times 2^N$ matrix whose first row has all elements = 1 , the N "linear" rows have the coefficients at r.h.s. of (9) , and the remaining ones are given by tensor multiplication. Passage from ξ- to η-space linearizes the NE :

$$\vec{\eta}_m = F\vec{\eta}_{m-1} = \ldots = F^m \vec{\eta}_0$$

The augmented (10) give for each state $\vec{\eta}$ of the net at time t its successor at time t+τ. Aside from the normalization coefficient, introduced to simplify the formalism, note now that the columns of the matrix Φ contain all, and only, the possible 2^N states of the net. We can write (10) as a matricial equation:

(11) $\Phi_{m+1} = F\Phi_m$, with $\Phi_0 \equiv \Phi$

The effect of F on Φ_m is to permute its columns, or to suppress some column and bring one of the remaining ones to its place (degeneration) That is

(12) $F\Phi = \Phi P$

where P is a 2^N x 2^N permutation matrix, which may be degenerate. F and Φ have the same eigenvalues (P is always diagonalizable). If P is degenerate, i.e. det(P) = 0, P is a projection and the net exhibits, correspondingly, transient states.

6. We show next that NE exhibit normal modes, which intertwine into the "reverberations" of our model and stem from linearity in 2^N-space. Let the matrix Δ, det(Δ) $\neq$ 0, diagonalize F:

$F\Delta = \Delta\Lambda$, Λ diagonal

Then:

$P\Phi\Delta = \Phi\Delta\Lambda$

i.e. $\Phi\Delta$ digonalizes P. Since P is permutation matrix, its characteristic polynomial (same as of F) is necessarily of type:

$\lambda^a \prod_b (\lambda^b - 1)^{c_b} = 0$,

with

$a + \sum_b b c_b = 2^N$, $c_b \geq 0$

Thus:

b = 1 implies c_1 invariant states

λ = 0 implies transients

b > 1 implies c_b cycles of period b, corresponding to $\lambda_h = e^{\frac{2\pi h i}{b}}$

(b = 1 can of course be regarded as a cycle of period 1). If we set

$\vec{\eta}_m = \Delta \vec{\chi}_m$

then:

$\vec{\chi}_{m+1} = \Lambda \vec{\chi}_m$ or $\chi_{a,m+1} = \lambda_a \chi_{a,m}$

express the wanted normal modes.

7. We are now interested in the synthesis of a net which, starting from a given state, goes in time through a prescribed sequence of states:

$$\vec{\eta}_1 = \vec{x}_1 \quad ; \quad \vec{\eta}_2 = \vec{x}_2 \quad ; \quad \ldots; \quad \vec{\eta}_{2^N} = \vec{x}_{2^N}$$

Define $\mathcal{F}$ such that

$$\mathcal{F}(\vec{x}_1 \ \vec{x}_2 \ldots \vec{x}_{2^N}) = (\vec{x}_2 \ \vec{x}_3 \ldots \vec{x}_{2^N} \vec{x}_1)$$

that is

$$\mathcal{F} X = X\Theta$$

where the $2^N \times 2^N$ permutation matrix shifts the first column to the last place. Then

$$\mathcal{F} = X\Theta X_R^{-1}$$

solves the problem. X_R^{-1} means right-inverse, and pseudoinverse matrices will have to be considered whenever necessary (transients) ; the states $\vec{x}_\alpha$ need not be distinct, they will actually reproduce the behavior described by the characteristic equation if $\mathcal{F}$, X are brought into F , Φ by an appropriate permutation. Note that X is <u>not</u> normalized (unlike Φ), and that our synthesis problem requires only the knowledge of the "linear" rows of $\mathcal{F}$, which is the product of two <u>known</u> matrices (which, brought into the (0-1)-notation,are <u>sparse</u>)

8. Working with this matricial notation, i.e. with η-expansions , does not bring into light the close relation between the continuous and discontinuous aspects of the theory of NE .We can here only quote briefly results that show exactly how the connection comes about (Caianiello et al. ,1981). Consider, as simplest example :

$$f(\xi) = \sigma(\ a\xi^1 + b\xi^2 + c\xi^3\ ) \quad ; \quad (\ a \geqslant b \geqslant c > 0\ , \ a \pm b \pm c \neq 0\ )$$

Then :

$$f(\xi) = \frac{1}{2} (\xi^1 + \xi^2 + \xi^3 - \xi^1\xi^2\xi^3)$$

for any a,b,c which can be <u>sides of a triangle</u> ; or else

$$f(\xi) = \xi^1 .$$

In the cited reference it is shown that the whole coefficient space of the argument splits into sectors, determined by "polygonal inequalities" which generalize the example just given. Each point of a sector yields the same η-expansion; the latter jumps to a different form as soon as one crosses the frontier between two sectors. Since it is

possible to reduce any boolean function or net to a larger linear net.
The consideration of boolean nets cannot yields behaviours that one
cannot also obtain from larger linear nets. Finally, we note that
the analysis of the behaviour and synthesis of a net reduces thus to
the study of permutation matrices P , i.e. to the study of finite
groups generated by the primitive roots of 1, plus degeneracies due
to 0's .

REFERENCES

E.R.Caianiello (1961). Outline of a theory of thought processes
        and thinking machines. J. Theor. Biol. 1 , 204-235
E.R.Caianiello (1973). Some remarks on tensorial linearization of
        general and l.s. boolean functions. Kybernetik 12, 90-93
E.R.Caianiello,W.E.L.Grimson (1975). Synthesis of boolean nets
        and time behaviour of a general mathematical neuron. Biol.
        Cybern. 18 , 111-117
        (this formalism is connected to the classic results of S.W.
        Golomb, the so-called Rademacher-Walsh expansion, etc.)
E.R.Caianiello, A.De Luca,L.M.Ricciardi(1967) . Neural networks:
        reverberations,constants of motion,general behaviour.   In
        Neural Networks (Ed. E.R.Caianiello) p.92-99,Springer-Verlag,
        Berlin.
A.Aiello,E.Burattini,E.R.Caianiello (1970). Synthesis of reverbe-
        rating neural networks. Kybernetik 7 , 191-195
E.R.Caianiello,G.Simoncelli (1981). Polygonal inequalities as a
        key to neuronic equations. Biol.Cybern. 41 , 203-209

A COMMUNICATIVE NEURON MODEL AND ITS COMPUTER SIMULATION

N. Paritsis and C. Meletis

Institute of Childs Health, Athens, 617, Greece; and
Ministry to the Presidency, 2 Evagelistrias, Athens,Greece.

ABSTRACT

A model of a neuron is presented in terms of a number of threshold
elements. Emphasis is given in the communication aspects of the
model which is discussed in relation to the physiological properties
of real neurons. A computer simulation is then carried out. The
program is quite flexible to enable the parameters of the model to
be modified thus it can be used in the simulation of neural networks.

INTRODUCTION

We consider real neurons as bearing similarities with the basic
components of controller and communicator agents. The model of
neuron we are dealing with in the present work is also presented in
(Paritsis and Stewart, 1982).

In this paper we are discussing this model with particular emphasis
given to its neurophysiological aspects. A computer simulation of
the model was carried out (Ioannides, 1982) to study its behavioural
characteristics and to examine the feasibility of its future use for
the simulation of neural networks realizing hyman cognitive faculties.

A MODEL OF A NEURON IN THRESHOLD LOGIC TERMS

In the present work the notion of Threshold Element (TE), in the
sense of (Dertouzos, 1965) and (Muroga, 1971), has been used to describe the proposed neuron's model. TEs are thought of as generaliza-
tions of (McCulloch and Pitts, 1943) logical neurons. TEs have been
appropriately modified, as shown in FIG.1., such that their relations
can be represented in a 2-dimensional figure.

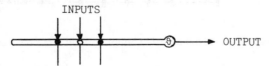

INPUTS

OUTPUT

FIG. 1. A threshold element (TE).

● = excitatory input. o=inhibitory input. ϑ=threshold value.

34

OUTPUT

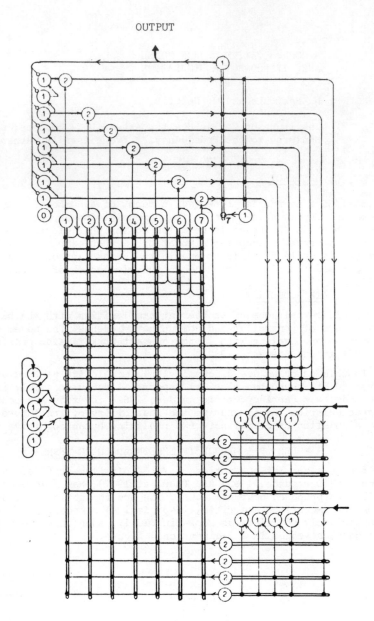

FIG. 2.   Diagram of the proposed neuron model

The language of TEs is used to describe a neuron's model for the following reasons: A) the encoding and decoding processes of neurons are considered as important features of real neurons. Furthermore TEs is a powerful tool and can be used to realize any encoding and decoding processes. B) TEs facilitate the description of operations such as integration, summation etc.

Through the above descriptive mechanism a neuron is represented as a network of threshold elements as in FIG. 2., (Paritsis, 1979). Its structure can be divided in three main TEs subnetworks:
A.   The synaptic decoding transformation net, which decodes the inter-spike interval time code of the input signal and transforms it into a post synaptic strength. This transformation characterizes each type of neuron and can also be related to the learning property, exhibited be neurons, which is not discussed here.
B.   The integration net, which realizes the algebraic summation and integration.
C.   The output encoding transformation net, which receives the output of the integration net, transforms it and encodes it in an inter-spike interval time code.

PHYSIOLOGICAL ASPECTS

We are going to consider next some physiological characteristics of real neurons such as: passive membrane transmission, spontaneous activity, threshold, absolute and relative refractory periods, and also how these characteristics are realized as parts of the proposed model.

Synapses: The synaptic net realizes both the decoding of the synapse's input signal and the passive membrane thransmission of a Post Synaptic Potential (PSP). In the example model, shown in FIG. 2., these are realized as follows: the transformation functions of the excitatory and inhibitory synapses-which are parabolic and linear resp. - realize the special decoding each synapse performs to its input sequence. These functions indicate also that the excitatory synapse is located at a longer distance from the neuron's initiation point than the inhibitory one does. Therefore the resulting PSP from the excitatory transformation (parabolic) is weaker, so to speak, than the PSP from the excitatory one (linear). This is the result of the stronger decay which the excitatory PSP is subject to, during its passive transmission through the membrane, due to the longer distance it travels.

Another characteristic of real neurons, which is realized by the decreasing character of the synaptic transformation functions, is the decay with time of single PSPs due to the decomposition of the chemical transmitters by the existing enzymes.

Spontaneous activity: In this model it is realized as a self excited subnet with output contributing to the increase of neuron's excitability.

Spatial summation: The model uses the spatial summation of PSPs and in general there is no limitations in the number of input synapses.

Temporal summation: Due to the time interval after the last Action Potential (Spike) is created, the neuron's threshold value is at a certain level. More precisely, the threshold value after each spike decays exponentially from an infinite value during the neuron's Absolute Refractory Period, to its resting value i.e. the value of threshold corresponding to the level where the neuron exhibits its spontaneous activity. When the PSP's sum is under the threshold value, held at a time, their influence from the trheshold value is reduced after a time unit by a value equal to this sum. This is known in real neurons, as Temporal Summation and is realized in the model by the positive feedback of the output of each integration element (i.e. the TEs of integration net) to all of them.

The action of the previous subthreshold PSP's sum decays exponentially with time. In the model it may be thought of that this action remains stable. This is not so because this decay with time is incorporated in the model's synaptic transformations.

Threshold, Refractory periods: The neuron's threshold is realized in the present model by a series of TEs of successively reducing thresholds. The time interval during which the neuron's threshold decays exponentially with time to its resting value, after the infinite value it has during the absolute refractory period, is called Relative Refractory Period. The behaviour of neuron's threshold H, as function of time during this interval, can be expressed by:

$$H(t) = H_\infty + (H_0 - H_\infty).\exp(-\lambda(t-t_0)), \text{ FIG. 3.}$$

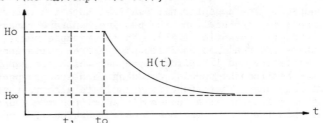

FIG. 3. The threshold H of a real neuron as a function of time t.

Where, t_1 : time when an Action Potential (Spike) happens

$t_0 - t_1$: Absolute Refractory Period

H_0 : resetting threshold

H_∞ : resting threshold

The realization of the threshold in the model is an approximation of a function H(t) of the form shown in FIG. 3. This approximation, shown in FIG. 4., is restricted by the discrete time and by the integer value of the threshold of integration elements. Note that the time unit is equal to threshold elements' response time.

A comparison of FIG. 4 and the encoding (sub)net of FIG. 2. shows that output gates of the model of FIG. 2., (i.e. the elements near the output with threshold value 2), are located in positions corresponding to the approximation points of the exponential function (FIG. 3.). In our example model this approximation is linear but in other cases, where a longer output clock with TEs having a much shorter response time would have been considered, a more accurate approximation of the exponential function H(t) could have been obtained.

The absolute refractory period (t_0-t_1), is realized in the model by both the use of a TE whith inhibion of a strength equal to the sum of excitations which the output elements accepts (in our example 7), and the output's clock resetting. The above happens just after every spike occurrence.

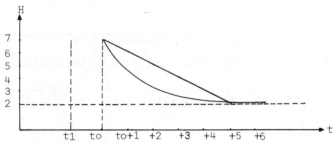

FIG. 4. Approximation of the function H(t) of FIG. 3.

THE COMPUTER SIMULATION

Each functional subnet of threshold elements in the neuron is simulated by an independent subroutine, i.e. the various activities observed in the model, which are briefly described in the Physiological Aspects Section, have been regarded as corresponding to different subroutines called appropriately by the main program.

The simulation gave a better insight of the model's behaviour, esp. its encoding and decoding processes, which led us to further improvements of the model.

The simulation's logic is shown in a flowchart, FIG. 5. The present model was implemented in Fortran language using a PRIME computer at the National Technical University of Athens, details in (Ioannides, 1982).

38

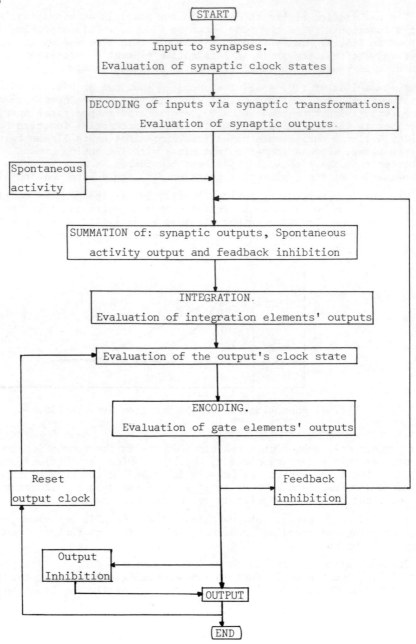

FIG. 5. Simmulation's logic for the neuron's model

CONCLUDING REMARKS

The model exhibits mainly those properties of a real neuron which are described in the Physiological Aspects Section of the present paper. Such model neurons can be used to build up neural networks to simulate human cognitive faculties.

The simulation have shown that the model neuron exhibite A) exhitatory/inhibitory behaviour, whenever appropriate input signale were given to its input synapses, and B) spontaneity, when no input signals were applied to it.

Any number of synapses and also any type of synaptic transformation function can be incorporated in the model. Finally, although the present model decodes signals only according to interspike interval time code other encoding/decoding schemes can be handled by appropriate design of the encoding/decoding subnets.

REFERENCES

Dertouzos, M., 1965. Threshold logic: A synthesis appoach. Research monograph No 32. MIT Press, Cambridge, Mass.

Ioannides, N., 1982. Computer simulation of an adaptive neural network based on a communicative neuron model. Graduate dissertation, Dept of Electrical Enginnering, National Technical University of Athens, Greece.

McCulloch, W., and Pitts, W., 1943. A logical calculus of the ideas immanent in nervous activity. Bulletin of Math. and Biophys 5,115.

Muroga, S., 1971. Threshold logic and its applications. John Wiley and Sons Inc., New York.

Paritsis, N., 1979. A neural network model of colour vision. Ph.D. thesis, Dept. of Cybernetics, Brunel University, U.K.

Paritsis, N., and Stewart, D., 1982. A cybernetic approach to colour perception. Gordon and Breach, London.

SUPERVISED AND UNSUPERVISED LEARNING
ALGORITHMS IN FORMAL NEURONS

Leon Bobrowski

Bionics Department, Institute of Biocybernetics and
Biomedical Engineering, Polish Academy of Sciences
Warsaw, Poland

ABSTRACT

The paper presents some supervised and unsupervised learning algorithms. The discussion is carried on with regard to stochastic approximation methods. A new rule of imposing of the additional information s
on an unsupervised process is proposed. New types of learning algorithms are also presented and analysed. If these algorithms are applied, then a new state of a formal neuron depends not only on the
current state and input signal but also on past events constituting
the learning process.

INTRODUCTION

Learning processes in primates can be considered as the active
acquirement and transformation of the information in neuronal structures providing the achievment of some goals in a given environment.
Numerous experimental works have been aimed at explaining the basic
neuronal mechanism of learning processes, e.g. (Tsukada et al. 1980).
This problem is also considered in many analytical works, e.g.(Amari, 1977; Caianiello, 1967; Kohonen, 1976). In these works various models of the neuronal cells and networks are presented and analysed.
Formal neuron can be also considered as simple model of the neuronal
cells. A formal neuron is excited if and only if the weighted sum of
the input signals is greater than some threshold value θ. The concept
of a formal neuron was applied for instance in the fundamental work
of Rosenblatt (Rosenblatt, 1961). The stochastic approximation gives
sequential rules of achieving the optimal solution under uncertainty
conditions. For instance this is the case when the probability distributions describing the environment are unknown (Cypkin, 1972; Kushner
et al., 1978). The mathematical tool discussed can be directly used
in the analytical consideration of learning algorithms.

THE DESCRIPTION OF THE LEARNING MODEL

A formal neuron with binary inputs x_i and binary output r is consi-dered. Variables x_i form the input vector x $(x = (x_1,\ldots,x_N))$. The fun-ctionning of a formal neuron is described by its decision rule r. As-sume that the dependence of this decision rule upon the parameter vector w is of the form:

$$(1) \quad r = r_w(x) = \begin{cases} 1 & \text{for } \sum_{i=1}^{N} w_i x_i \geqslant \theta \\[2ex] 0 & \text{for } \sum_{i=1}^{N} w_i x_i < \theta \end{cases}$$

where

$$w = [w_1,\ldots,w_N] \in R^N$$

θ is the threshold $(\theta \in R^1)$

For illustration purposes a two layer neuron-like structure is discus-sed. It is assumed that elements A_i of the lower layer form the input vector of the element B (Fig. 1)

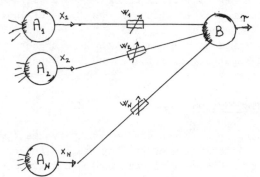

Fig. 1.   A two-layer neuron-like structure

A decision rule of the element B can be obtained as a result of some unsupervised or supervised learning process. Assume the input vectors x(n) appear at the discrete time instants t_n $(t_n = 1,2,3,\ldots)$. In the case of an unsupervised learning process the information on environ-ment of the element B is provided by the input sequence {x(n)} only.

It is assumed that the vectors x(n) appear independently at each step n and their occurrence is described by some unknown stationary probab-ility distribution $p_1(x)$. The distribution $p_1(x)$ describes the envir-onment of the element B. In a supervised learning process each input vector x(n) is accompanied by so-called "teachers decision" s(n) (s = 1 or s = 0). This additional information s determines the pro-

per response of a given neuron-like element to each input vector x.
The occurrence of the pairs (x(n), s(n)) is determined by some unknown probability distribution p(x,s). This stationary distribution
p(x,s) describes the environment of the element B.

During a learning process the parameter vector w is varied in accordance with a selected learning algorithm. It is assumed that
learning algorithms taken into consideration are of stochastic approximation type. Using this approach, the performance measures are
to be taken as follows:

$$(2) \qquad \Psi(w) = \sum_{x} \sum_{s} p(x,s)\, \phi(w,x,s)$$

for a supervised process, and

$$(3) \qquad \Psi(w) = \sum_{x} P_1(x)\, \phi_1(w,x)$$

for an unsupervised process, where $\phi(w,x,s)$ and $\phi_1(w,x)$ are functions
differentiable almost everywhere. Learning algorithms under consideration are iterative search procedures used to determine extremal
points of the regression function $\Psi(w)$. For example, supervised
learning algorithm can be of the following form:

$$(4) \qquad w(n+1) = w(n) + \alpha_n \cdot g(w(n), x(n), s(n))$$

where:

$g(w,x,s) = \nabla_w \phi(w,x,s)$ is the gradient of the function $\phi(w,x,s)$,
α_n are the parameters, for which the following conditions hold

$$(5) \qquad \alpha_n > 0 \;, \quad \sum_{n=1}^{\infty} \alpha_n = \infty \;, \quad \sum_{n=1}^{\infty} (\alpha_n)^2 < \infty$$

If some general conditions are satisfied, then the sequence {w(n)}
generated by algorithms of such type converges to a point w^* with
the probability equal 1.

$$(6) \qquad w(n) = \xrightarrow[n \to \infty]{w \cdot p \cdot 1} w^*$$

The sufficient condition of the convergence with the probability e-
qual 1 to the point w^* is given by the following inequality

$$(7) \qquad \left(\forall \varepsilon > 0\right)\left(\exists \varepsilon_1 > 0\right)\left(\forall w : \rho(w,w^*) > \varepsilon\right) \quad (k(w), w^*-w) > \varepsilon_1$$

where:

$k(w) = \sum_x \sum_s p(x,s)g(w,x,s)$ is the mean value of the correction vector $g(w,x,s)$, $(k(w), w^*-w)$ is the scalar product, $\rho(w,w^*)$ is the
Euclidean distance between the points w and w^*.

The above inequality is associated with unimodality (convexity) of
the function $\Psi(w)$. Due to the specific convergence properties (Ko-

honen, 1976) a resulting decision rule $r_w(x)$ is unique. In other words, final decision rules corresponding a given environment $p(x,s)$ or $p_1(x)$ are always the same.

EXAMPLES OF THE LEARNING ALGORITHMS

Learning algorithms considered in this section are associated with the unimodal performance measure $\Psi(w)$. Firstly, algorithm of error-correction of the perceptron type is discussed. For such an algorithm if $s(n) = 1$, then the increament Δw_i of the i-th parameter is given by

$$(8) \qquad \Delta w_i = \alpha_n x_i \cdot \left(1 - r_w(x)\right)$$

where:
x_i is the i-th component of the input vector $x(n)$ ($x_i = 0$ or $x_i = 1$) if $s(n) = 0$, then the value of this parameter is decreased according to the formula

$$(9) \qquad w_i = -\alpha_n \cdot x_i \cdot r_w(x)$$

It is obvious that if the output r of the element B is equal to a teacher's decision, then there is no change in the value of the parameter w. The presented error-correction procedure constitutes an example of the supervised learning algorithm. Supervised learning algorithms provide the possibility to form optimal decision rules, for which in some cases the probability of error is minimized. For unsupervised algorithms such a possibility does not exist. However in general unsupervised learning algorithms are less complicated and require less information then the supervised algorithms. In the course of an unsupervised process the parameters w_i of the elements A_i being rarely excited are distinguished from those corresponding to elements frequently excited. It is assumed that the parameters w_i associated with elements A_i , which are not excited change their values exponentially.

$$(10) \qquad w_i(n) = w_0 \cdot e^{-\lambda \cdot n} + \widetilde{w}$$

where w_0 is the initial value of the parameter w_i .
The final decision rule of an element whose functioning is based on a unsupervised learning algorithm depends on the frequencies of the input vectors x_α . Two contrary approaches can be applied in an appointment of the unsupervised learning algorithm. The first one consists in the formation of a high-frequency filter. The synthesis of a high-frequency filter is possible under assumption that the parameters decrease is determined by (10), $(\widetilde{w} \leqslant 0)$, and the rule of

parameters increase is given by the following equation (Bobrowski et al. 1980) :

$$(11) \quad \triangle w_i = \alpha_n \cdot c \cdot x_i \left(1 - r_w(x) \right)$$

The construction of low frequency filter (detector of rareness) is possible if except of the parameter increase determined by (10) , ($\tilde{w} \gtrless 0$), we introduce the following rule of the parameters decrease (Bobrowski 1982) :

$$(12) \quad \triangle w_i = -\alpha_n \cdot c \cdot x_i \cdot r_w(x)$$

Let us introduce the so-called decision field $\mathcal{F}(w)$ of the element B:

$$(13) \quad \mathcal{F}(w) = \left\{ x : r_w(x) = 1 \right\}$$

The set $\mathcal{F}(w)$ contains all the input vectors x_α , which excite the element B (parameter vector equal to w) . The final decision field $\mathcal{F}(w^*)$ of the element B with the decision rules (10) and (11) mainly contains vectors x_α , which are the most frequent in a given environment . The set $\mathcal{F}(w^*)$ of the element B with the rules (10) and (12) contains vectors x_α , which rarely appear during the learning process.

SUGGESTIONS FOR NEW LEARNING RULES

The rules (11) and (12) are similar to those used in the supervised learning algorithm. In the described error-correction algorithm, the rule of parameter changes is determined by Eq.(8) or Eq.(9) depending on the value of s. It is small chance that mechanisms generating such complicated changes of correction rules exist in living organisms . For this reason a new way of introducing of the additional information s is to be proposed. In the author's opinion a proposal presented below takes into account the physiological point of view.
The introduction of the information s is possible when the influence of the chosen input vectors x_α on changes of the parameters w is adequately cancel. Let us regard the construction of a high-frequency filter with the rules (10) and (11). We will substitute the rule (11) by the following one:

$$(14) \quad \triangle w_i = \begin{cases} \alpha_n \cdot c \cdot x_i \left(1 - r_w(x) \right) & \text{if } s(n) = 1 \\ 0 & \text{if } s(n) = 0 \end{cases}$$

If s(n) = 0, then there is no parameter increase ($\Delta w_i = 0$) associated with the signal x(n). Due to the information s imposed in such a way some selected high-frequency vectors x_α can be eliminated from the set $\mathcal{F}(w^*)$.

Now, the problem of constructing the detector of rareness based on the rules (10) and (12) will be discussed. Assume that the decision rule (12) is substituted by a new one

$$(15) \qquad w_i = \begin{cases} 0 & \text{if } s(n) = 1 \\ -\alpha_n \cdot c \cdot x_i \, r_w(x) & \text{if } s(n) = 0 \end{cases}$$

If $s(n) = 1$, then there is no parameter decrease associated with the vector $x(n)$. Due to the information s imposed in such way some selected high-frequency vectors x_α can be added to the set $\mathcal{F}(w^x)$ of the rarely occurring vectors. It can be proved that both algorithms satisfy the sufficient condition of convergence (6) . The learning algorithms presented describe a competition of two processes : the process of parameter increase and that of parameter decrease . Final effect of this competition is related not only to the properties of the environment $p_1(x)$ but also the rates of decrease or increase of parameters w_i . These rates are determined by algorithms applied . They depend upon the parameters λ and c occurring in the rules (10) and (11) or (12) . A method of a priori selection of these parameters was presented in ref.'s (Bobrowski et al. 1980 ; Bobrowski 1982) . It relies on the following assumption the environment $p_1(x)$ is such that only one input vector x_α is at high frequency (close to one) and the frequencies of all the remaining vectors are close to zero . The parameters c and λ are so chosen that it is possible to accomplish the synthesis of high- and low-frequency filters for this type of environment. However, for more complex environments generating several input vectors x_α with relatively high frequencies such a synthesis can not be realized . It is due to the fact that there are no frequencies close to one and in such a situation clear differentiation among the frequencies of the input vectors x_α cannot be made. Now, a new adaptive method of adjusting the rates of decrease and increase of the parameters w_i will be presented. Assume that the rule of parameter increase to be used for the synthesis of a high frequency filter (11) is as follows :

$$(16) \qquad \Delta w_i = \alpha_n \cdot c_1 \cdot \Delta t_n \cdot \left(1 - r_w(x)\right) \cdot x_i$$

where : Δt_n is the time interval between the current excitation of the element B and that preceding it (Δt_n is a random variable) , c_1 is a constant.

According to the rule (16) the rate of parameter increase depends upon the frequencies of excitations of the element B . If the element B is rarely excited, then this rate is high. The increase in parameters w_i occurring at the n-th step depends not only on the current values parameter $w(n)$ and input vector $x(n)$ but also on the while train of events constituting the learning process. It is worth noting that the sequence $\{w(n)\}$ of the parameters vectors generated by this algorithm is not a Markowian process.

PROPERTIES OF LEARNING ALGORITHMS WITH "MEMORY"

This Section is concerned with the analysis of learning algorithms with "memory". It is exemplified synthesis of high-frequency filters on the base of the rules (10) and (16) . Algorithms of such type can be described using the following expression:

$$(17) \quad w(n+1) = w(n) + \alpha_n \cdot \left\{ \gamma \cdot (\tilde{w} - w(n) + c_1 \cdot \Delta t_n (1 - r_{w(n)} x(n)) \, x(n) \right\}$$

where $\tilde{w} = (\tilde{w}, \ldots, \tilde{w})$ is the vector whose components are equal to $\tilde{w}$ ($\tilde{w} \leqslant 0$) . Each input vector x_α defines the following hyperplane in the parameter space :

$$(18) \quad h(x_\alpha) = \left\{ w : (x_\alpha, w) = \theta \right\}$$

The vector x_α results in the excitation of the element B ($r_w(x)=1$) if and only if the point w lies above the hyperplane $h(x_\alpha)$ ($(w, x_\alpha) \geqslant \theta$) . The hyperplanes h(x) divide the parameter space into so called decision region D_i (open convex sets). The decision rule of a formal neuron is not changed if the vector w lies in the same region D_i (i.e. $r_{w_1}(x) \equiv r_{w_2}(x)$ if $w_1 \in D_i$ and $w_2 \in D_i$) .

According to the expression (16) the increase in parameters w_i also depends on the time interval Δt_n between successive excitations of the element B ($\Delta t = 1,2,3,\ldots$) . It is assumed that there exist the following conditional probability :
$p_i(w,n)=P\{$the element B was not excited at the i last steps$/w(n)=w\}$, and the mean value of the time intervals Δt_n :

$$(19) \quad T(w,n) = \sum_{i=1}^{\infty} i \, p_i(w,n) < \infty$$

Instead of the algorithm (17) the following one can be used :

$$(20) \quad w(n+1) = w(n) + \alpha_n \left\{ \gamma \cdot (\tilde{w} - w(n)) + c_1 \cdot T(w(n),n)(1 - r_{w(n)} x(n)) \cdot x(n) \right\}$$

In this algorithm the random variable Δt_n is replaced with the mean value T(w,n) being a deterministic function. Asymptotical properties of the algorithm (17) can be deduced from those of the algorithm (20).

Such an approach is justified by the fact that generation of the sequence $\{x(n)\}$ is unaffected by the course of the learning process. It can be proved that for the algorithm (17) the following relation holds :

$$(21) \quad (\forall w \in D_j)(\forall i) \; p_i(w,n) \xrightarrow[n \to \infty]{} (\pi_j)^i$$

where:

$$\Pi_j = P\left\{r_{w(n)} = 0 \ / \ w(n) \in D_j\right\}$$

is the conditional probability connected with the region D_j .
The relation (21) points out, among other things, the asymptotical
independence of the probability $p_i(w,n)$ from the location of the point w within the set D_j . Such an independence follows from the fact
that for the algorithm (17) $\| w(n+1) - w(n) \| \xrightarrow[n \to \infty]{} 0$.

Hence, for each i there exists such value of n that

$$\left(\forall k : n-i \leqslant k \leqslant n\right) \qquad w(k) \in D_j$$

Taking account ot this property, it is possible to restrict consideration to the analysis of events taking place during i steps in one
region D_j only. The relation between the probability π_j and the distribution $p_1(x)$ is of the form:

$$\Pi_j = 1 - \sum_{x \in \mathcal{F}(w} P_1(x)$$

where: $w \in D_j$, $\mathcal{F}(w)$ is given by Eq. (13) .
For the region D_j the asymptotical mean value of time intervals is
given by :

$$(23) \qquad T_j = \sum_{i=1}^{\infty} i \left(\Pi_j\right)^i = \frac{\Pi_j}{(1 - \Pi_j)^2}$$

The following algorithm

$$(24) \quad w(n+1) = w(n) + \alpha_n \left\{\gamma \cdot (\tilde{w} - w(n) + c_1 \cdot T_j \cdot \left(1 - r_{w(n)} \ x(n)\right) x(n)\right\}$$

is also of interest. For this unsupervised algorithm the factor representing the influence of past events has the constant value T_j in
each region D_j . The performance measure associated with this algorithm can be formulated as follows

$$(25) \qquad \Psi_1(w) = \Phi_0(w) + \Phi_1(w) \, \Phi_2(w)$$

where $\Phi_0(w)$ and $\Phi_1(w)$ are convex functions corresponding to the
rules (10) and (11) respectively (Bobrowski et al. 1980) , $\Phi_2(w)$ is
a step function ($\Phi_2(w) = T_j$ for $w \in D_j$).
The function $\Psi_1(w)$ has a local minimum at point w^* . If this point
lies inside some region D_j , then the relation (7) can be given in
the form

$$(26) \quad \left(\exists \varepsilon_2 > 0\right)\left(\forall \varepsilon : \varepsilon_2 > \varepsilon > 0\right)\left(\exists \varepsilon_1 > 0\right)\left(\forall w_A : \varepsilon_2 > \varsigma(w_A, w^*) > \varepsilon\right)$$
$$\left(K_1(w_A), w^* - w_A\right) > \varepsilon_1$$

where ε_2 is the sphere radius such that the sphere $K(w^*, \varepsilon_2)$ belongs to the region D_j :

$$K_\perp(w) = \gamma \cdot (\tilde{w} - w) + c_j \, T_j \sum_x p_\perp(x) \left(1 - r_w(x)\right) x$$

Now the condition (7) will be examined under assumption that $w^* \in D_j$ and $w_A \in D_i$ ($i \neq j$). From Eq.(26) the following equation results:

$$(27) \quad \left(K_\perp(w_A), w^* - w_A\right) = \left(\gamma \cdot (\tilde{w} - w_A) + c_i \, T_i \, h_i, \; w^* - w_A\right)$$

where:

$$(28) \quad h_i = \sum_x p_\perp(x) \left(1 - r_{w_A}(x)\right) x$$

Let w_k be a point belonging to the sphere $K(w^*, \varepsilon_2)$ and the segment (w^*, w_A). Hence we have

$$(29) \quad \gamma \cdot (\tilde{w} - w_A) = \gamma(\tilde{w} - w_k) + \gamma(w_k - w_A)$$

and $h_i = h_j + \Delta h(j, i)$

where:

$$\Delta h(j, i) = \sum_{x \in F^+(w_A, w_k)} p_\perp(x) x - \sum_{x \in F^-(w_A, w_k)} p_\perp(x) x$$

$$\bar{F}(w_A, w_k) = \left\{ x : (w_A, x) > \theta \quad \text{and} \quad (w_k, x) < \theta \right\}$$

$$\bar{F}^+(w_A, w_k) = \left\{ x : (w_A, x) < \theta \quad \text{and} \quad (w_k, x) > \theta \right\}$$

Moreover

$$K_\perp(w_A) = K_\perp(w_k) + c_i \cdot (T_i - T_j) \cdot h_j + c_i T_i \, \Delta h(j, i) + \gamma \cdot (w_k - w_A)$$

and

$$\left(K_\perp(w_A), w^* - w_A\right) = \left(K_\perp(w_k), w^* - w_A\right) + c_i T_i \cdot \left(\Delta h(j, i), w^* - w_A\right) +$$

$$+ c_i (T_i - T_j) \cdot \left(h_j, w^* - w_A\right) + \gamma \cdot \left(w_k - w_A, w^* - w_A\right)$$

It is assumed that the relation (26) holds. Hence:

$$(k_1(w_k), \; w^* - w_k) > 0$$

The inequality :

$$(k_1(w_A), \; w^* - w_A) > 0$$

results from the condition (30) under assumption that :

$$c_1 \cdot (T_i - T_j) \cdot (h_j, w_k - w_A) + \gamma \cdot (w_k - w_A)^2 \quad 0$$

or

$$c_1 \cdot (T_i - T_j) \cdot (h_j , \overset{*}{w} - w_A) + \gamma \cdot (\overset{*}{w} - w_A)^2 > 0$$

where:

$\overset{*}{w} \in D_j$ and $w_A \in D_i$

Using these inequalities it is possible to deduce whether the convergence condition (26) holds in the whole parameter space . To make the analysis of the dependence of the process $\{w(n)\}$ on past events more general rule (16) can be substituted by a new one

$$(34) \quad \Delta w_i = \alpha_n \cdot c_1 \cdot f(\Delta t_n) \cdot (1 - r_w(x)) \cdot x_i$$

where $f(\cdot)$ is a monotonic function.

The greater the increase rate of the function $f(\Delta t)$ is greater the differences $T_i - T_j$ are. It follows from the inequality (32) that high rate of the increase of the function $f(\Delta t)$ can cause the function $\Psi_1(w)$ (25) to lose the unimodality property. Too large values of the time T_i ($T_i = \infty$) can be avoided by introducing the function $f(\Delta t)$ with "saturation". For example:

$$(35) f(\Delta t_n) = \begin{cases} \Delta t_n & \text{for } \Delta t_n \leqslant A \\ A & \text{for } \Delta t_n > A \end{cases}$$

where A is a large constant.

The aim of the next example is to present a model of determining the parameters c_1 and λ occurring in algorithms with "memory" .

An example: Given the element B with M different input vectors x ($M = 2^N - 1$ is a large number). It is assumed that the vectors x appear with the same probability

$$(36) \quad P_1(x) = P\{x(n) = x\} = \frac{1}{M}$$

and the final decision field $F(\overset{*}{w})$ contains almost one half ($\approx \frac{1}{2}M$) of all the input vectors x . In this case $\pi = \frac{1}{2}$ for $w \in D_j$. It follows from Eq. (23) then $T_j = 2$. According to Eq. (28)

$$h_{max} \overset{def}{=} \max_i \{h_i\} = \sum_x P_1(x) \cdot x = 2^{N-1} \cdot \overline{1}$$

where : $\overline{1} = [1, 1, \ldots, 1]'$

Morover it is assumed that

$$h_j \simeq \frac{1}{2} h_{max} = 2^{N-2} \cdot \overline{1}$$

If the point $\overset{*}{w}$ lies in the region D_j ($\forall x : w \notin h(x)$), then

$$\nabla \Psi_1(\overset{*}{w}) = 0$$

Hence
$$\gamma \cdot (\tilde{w} - w^*) = c_1 T_j h_j$$

or
$$\gamma \cdot \| \tilde{w} - w^* \| = c_1 2^{N-1} \sqrt{N}$$

and
$$(37) \qquad \gamma = \frac{c_1 2^{N-1} \sqrt{N}}{\| \tilde{w} - w^* \|}$$

If it is assumed that the point w^* lies in the centre of the cube with one of the vertices lying the origin of coordinates and its edge is equal to $|\theta|$ then :

$$\| \tilde{w} - w^* \| \simeq \frac{1}{2} |\theta| \cdot \sqrt{N}$$

Under these assumptions the relation among parameters of the unsupervised learning algorithm is as follows

$$(38) \qquad \gamma = c_1 \frac{2^N}{|\theta|}$$

Similar relations can also be obtained for distributions $p_1(x)$ different from (36) . In more general case one can introduce the requirement that the sum of the probabilities $p_1(x)$ associated with the vectors x belonging to the set $F(W^*)$ is equal to a given constant.

$$(39) \qquad \sum_{x \in F(w^*)} p_1(x) = \alpha$$

It follows from this equality that $T_j = \frac{1-\alpha}{\alpha^2}$ for $w^* \in D_j$.

CONCLUDING REMARKS

The presented unsupervised learning algorithms with "memory" provide a means for synthesis of high- or low-frequency filters to be used in relatively complex environments $p_1(x)$. To accomplish such a synthesis in full one hase to impose an additional condition. Namely the set C_1 of input vectors having higher probabilities and the set C_o of those with lower probabilities are to be linearly separable. The discussed adaptive method of adjusting the rates of decrease and increase of the parameters w_i offers the possibility to satisfy the condition (39). Due to this condition the decision fields $F(w^*)$ cannot be too large or too small. Hence the influence of distribution $p_1(x)$ on the size of the decision field $F(w^*)$ is significantly reduced. Finally, the synthesis of the frequency filters with imposition of the additional information s is considered. We will take into consideration the rule (10) and the following one:

$$(40) \quad \Delta w_i = \begin{cases} c_1 \Delta t_n \left(1 - r_w(x)\right) x_i & \text{for } s(n) = 1 \\ 0 & \text{for } s(n) = 0 \end{cases}$$

where Δt_n is the same random variable as in Eq.(16) . According to this rule the influence of the information s on the increase or decrease in parameters w_i also depends on past events constituting a learning process. Due to the imposition of the information s some high frequency input vectors x can be eliminated from the final decision field $F(w^*)$. Conditions similar to (39) imply that other vectors x_* should be also added to the field $F(w^*)$. Such an approach makes it possible to obtain better controlability properties of a learning process than those corresponding to the rule (14). The consideration presented deals with the formation of high-frequency filters. Similar conclusions can be obtained for the detectors of rareness. Howewer , there are non-solved problems related to learning algorithms with "memory" . For instance problems associated with the convergence and the rate of convergence of such processes require more rigorous analysis. The influence of past events constituting a learning process on these factors is also of interest.

REFERENCES

Amari, S. (1977). Neural theory of association and concept-formation Biol. Cybern. 26 , 175-185

Bobrowski,L. , Caianiello,E.R. (1980). Comparison of two unsupervised learning algorithms. Biol. Cybern.37 , 1-7

Bobrowski,L. (1982). Rules of forming receptive fields of formal neurons during unsupervised learning processes. Biol.Cybern. 43 , 23-28

Caianiello,E.R. (1967). Outline of a theory of thought processes and thinking machines. J.Theoret.Biol. 2 , 204-235

Cypkin,J.Z. (1972) Foundationsof the theory of learning systems Nauka, Moscow (in Russian)

Kohonen,T. ,Oja,E. (1976) Fast adaptive formation of orthogonalizing filters and associative memory in recurrent networks of neuron-like elements. Biol.Cybern. 21 , 85-95

Kushner, H.J. ,Clark,D.S. (1978) Stochastic approximation methods for constrained and unconstrained systems.Springer-Verlag New York

Tsukada,Y. ,Agranoff,B.W. (Ed.) (1980). Neurobiological basis of learning and memory.John Wiley , New York

Rosenblatt,F. (1961) Principles of neurodynamics: Perceptrons and the theory of brain mechanisms.Spartan Books, Washinton,D.C.

Speech Recognition

NEW ASPECTS ON THE SUBSPACE METHODS OF
PATTERN RECOGNITION

Erkki Oja

University of Kuopio
Department of Applied Mathematics
P.O. Box 138, 70101 Kuopio 10
Finland

ABSTRACT

Subspace methods are decision-theoretic vector space methods in which
each pattern class is represented by a relatively low-dimensional
subspace. Classification is usually based on projections, which
computationally involves only inner products between a test vector
and a set of basis vectors and is therefore very fast. Several attempts
at constructing the classification subspaces in an optimal way have
been reported, most of them based on class correlation matrices computed from samples. A promising way to compute subspaces with high
discriminatory power, recently introduced by Kohonen, is to use decision-directed learning. Variants of the basic method have been developed. They are analyzed mathematically and results are reviewed
on their application to phonemic recognition of speech.

1. ORTHOGONAL EXPANSIONS AND SUBSPACES IN PATTERN VECTOR SPACES

Statistical pattern recognition techniques in general rely on dividing
the vector space of objects to be classified into disjoint regions.
The regions are defined by their boundaries which in the basic paradigm are defined in terms of discriminant functions. In contrast, the
subspace methods, first suggested by Watanabe (1965, 1967), are based
on linear representations of vectors of each class. The basic idea is
to classify a new object to the class whose representation gives the
best fit.

The natural mathematical framework for the linear representation
approach is the use of orthogonal expansions and projections. If the
pattern space is the n-dimensional Euclidean space R^n or its subset, let $x \in R^n$ denote a pattern vector and $(u_1, u_2, \ldots, u_n)$
an arbitrary orthonormal basis of R^n. Then

$$x = \sum_{i=1}^{n} (x^T u_i) u_i = (\sum_{i=1}^{n} u_i u_i^T) x = Ix. \tag{1}$$

If only a subset of $(u_1, \ldots, u_n)$ is used in the expansion, say, $(u_1, \ldots, u_s)$ with $s < n$, then

$$\hat{x} = \sum_{i=1}^{s} (x^T u_i) u_i = (\sum_{i=1}^{s} u_i u_i^T) x = Px \tag{2}$$

with P an idempotent symmetric projection matrix. Now $\hat{x}$ is an approximation of x, with approximation error

$$\| x - \hat{x} \|^2 = x^T x - x^T P x . \tag{3}$$

If x is random with $E(xx^T) = R$ finite, then

$$\begin{aligned} E(\| x - \hat{x} \|^2) &= E(x^T x) - E(x^T P x) \\ &= \text{trace}(R) - \sum_{i=1}^{s} E(u_i^T x x^T u_i) \\ &= \text{trace}(R) - \sum_{i=1}^{s} u_i^T R u_i . \end{aligned} \tag{4}$$

This is minimized with respect to $u_1, \ldots, u_s$ if the u_i are the orthonormal eigenvectors of R corresponding to the largest eigenvalues. This solution is related to the Karhunen-Loève expansion applied to pattern recognition (Watanabe, 1965, Chien and Fu, 1967). It has been an underlying factor for most of the work in subspace classifiers.

Instead of applying one and the same transformation (2) for all pattern vectors as in conventional linear feature extraction and data compression, the subspace methods use a different transformation for each class separately. If there are K classes $\omega^{(1)}, \ldots, \omega^{(K)}$, then K separate vector sets are used:

$$(u_1^{(1)}, u_2^{(1)}, \ldots, u_{s^{(1)}}^{(1)}) \quad \text{to} \quad (u_1^{(K)}, u_2^{(K)}, \ldots, u_{s^{(K)}}^{(K)}) .$$

These sets have the property that within each set, the vectors are orthonormal - or can be made such by Gram-Schmidt orthonormalization - but the individual sets may be quite independent of each other. The numbers $s^{(i)}$ are generally different for each class, and each substantially smaller than the overall dimensionality n.

Each of the K vector sets defines a subspace corresponding to class $\omega^{(r)}$, $L^{(r)} = L(u_1^{(r)}, u_2^{(r)}, \ldots, u_{s^{(r)}}^{(r)})$ with $\dim(L^{(r)}) = s^{(r)}$. Geometrically, these are linear manifolds passing through the origin of the pattern space R^n. They determine directions in R^n but no magnitudes. For class $\omega^{(r)}$, the vector

$$\hat{x}^{(r)} = \sum_{i=1}^{s^{(r)}} u_i^{(r)} u_i^{(r)T} x \tag{5}$$

is the orthogonal projection of x on $L^{(r)}$, and (3) gives the squared length of the orthogonal residual. It is reasonable to base classification on the discriminant functions

$$\| \hat{x}^{(r)} \|^2 = \sum_{i=1}^{s^{(r)}} (x^T u_i^{(r)})^2 \tag{6}$$

with classification rule

Classify x in $\omega^{(k)}$ if $\| \hat{x}^{(k)} \|^2 > \| \hat{x}^{(r)} \|^2$, $r \neq k$. (7)

All this is easily visualized geometrically.

Rule (7) is independent of the norm of x. This rule cannot discriminate between objects whose vector representations have roughly the same directions in the pattern space while the magnitude is the primary discriminating factor, unless some prior transformation is applied. However, there are situations in which this independency of magnitude is exactly what is desired; notably, in case of spectra and other signals whose overall intensity is not important compared to the mutual ratios of signal elements. The subspace methods have been applied to other kinds of data, too (Kulikowski, 1970, Watanabe and Pakvasa, 1973, Therrien, 1975, Noguchi, 1976).

Rule (7) is very easy to compute since only inner products between x and the basis vectors of the classes are needed. If very high speed in classification is desired as in real-time applications, this operation can be accomplished by special processors. The crucial question which remains is the determination of the subspaces or the vector sets $(u_1^{(r)}, \ldots, u_{s^{(r)}}^{(r)})$ in the first place.

2. SOME EXPLICIT STATISTICAL CRITERIA

The classical subspace method CLAFIC (CLAss-Featuring Information Compression) presented by Watanabe (1965, 1967) is based on eigenvector expansions of class correlation matrices $E(xx^T \mid x \in \omega^{(k)})$, $k = 1,\ldots,K$. Later, Watanabe and Pakvasa (1973) presented an orthogonalized version, MOSS. That, too, starts from CLAFIC basis vectors.

For the two-class case, Fukunaga and Koontz (1970) presented a related method of dimensionality reduction in which a linear transformation is applied such that the two transformed class correlation matrices have exactly the same eigenvectors. This has been generalized by Kittler (1977, 1978) to a multiclass case. Wold in a series of papers (see Wold, 1976) has introduced an approach based on statistical linear models, which is related to subspace methods.

Another approach to the problem is is to use explicit optimization with statistical objective functions and constraints. Denote the orthogonal projection matrix of class $\omega^{(i)}$ by

$$P^{(i)} = \sum_{k=1}^{s^{(i)}} u_k^{(i)} u_k^{(i)T} .$$ (8)

This is useful for briefness of notation, although the matrices themselves should not be used in actual computations. Some pertinent objective function extremizing criteria are (Kuusela, 1981)

$$\max_{P^{(i)}} [E(x^T P^{(i)} x \mid \omega^{(i)}) - \sum_{j \neq i} \theta^{(i,j)} E(x^T P^{(i)} x \mid \omega^{(j)})] ,$$ (9)

$$\min_{P^{(i)} j \neq i} \sum \theta^{(i,j)} E(x^T P^{(i)} x \mid \omega^{(j)})$$

under constraint $E(x^T P^{(i)} x \mid \omega^{(i)}) = $ constant, (10)

$$\max_{P^{(1)},\dots,P^{(K)}} \min_{i} [E(x^T P^{(i)} x \mid \omega^{(i)}) - \max_{j \neq i} E(x^T P^{(j)} x \mid \omega^{(i)})].$$ (11)

All of these can be solved numerically in terms of basis vectors $u_i^{(k)}$ $(k = 1,\dots,K \; ; \quad i = 1,\dots,s^{(k)})$. In fact, all involve class correlation matrices since

$$E(x^T P^{(i)} x \mid \omega^{(j)}) = E(\sum_{k=1}^{s^{(i)}} (u_k^{(i)T} x)^2 \mid \omega^{(j)})$$

$$= \sum_{k=1}^{s^{(i)}} u_k^{(i)T} E(x x^T \mid \omega^{(j)}) u_k^{(i)} .$$ (12)

The solutions of (9), (10) and (11) will be functions of these correlation matrices.

The explicit or implicit dependency of solutions (basis vectors) on first and second order moments of data only is shared by practically all suggested non-learning subspace methods. The validity of this statistics on class discrimination may be questioned. In practice, even relatively elaborate statistical criteria based on correlation matrices, like (11) above, do not yield appreciable improvement over CLAFIC which may be considered the simplest version of this approach (Kuusela, 1981).

One of the reasons is that the first and second order moments, especially for non-Gaussian data, do not carry enough information for placing the class boundaries optimally. The central regions close to the actual subspaces are represented accurately enough, but these are not the regions where classification errors tend to happen.

A solution to this problem was offered by Kohonen (1979) who combined decision-directed learning with the subspace model. Kohonen's algorithm is reviewed and analyzed in the following.

3. KOHONEN´S LEARNING SUBSPACE METHOD

The method is based on supervised, decision-directed learning. A set of prototypes of known classification are used by the algorithm one at a time, and the subspaces are suitably 'rotated' at each step. To explain the learning rule, the following notation is introduced.

1. Let $L^{(i)}(m)$ and $L^{(i)}(m+1)$ denote the subspaces corresponding to i-th class at the m-th step and the (m+1)-th step of the algorithm, respectively. Let $x(m)$ be the m-th prototype vector.

2. Let multiplication of the subspace $L^{(i)}(m)$ by an elementary matrix $I + \mu x(m)x(m)^T$, with μ a scalar, mean

$$(I + \mu x(m)x(m)^T)L^{(i)}(m) = \{z \mid z = (I + \mu x(m)x(m)^T)u, \ u \in L^{(i)}(m)\}.$$

$$(13)$$

The set thus obtained is also a linear subspace. Note that positive μ tends to increase in magnitude the inner products between $x(m)$ and the vectors of $L^{(i)}(m)$, thus bringing $L^{(i)}(m)$ closer to $x(m)$, while a negative μ tends to push $L^{(i)}(m)$ away from $x(m)$.

3. Let $A_{i,i}(m)$ denote the event 'at step m, the prototype vector $x(m)$ is actually of class i but is classified according to rule (7), using the basis vectors of $L^{(1)}(m),\ldots, L^{(K)}(m)$, to class j'.

With this notation, the learning rule of Kohonen´s algorithm is essentially as follows (Kohonen et al, 1979, 1980):

1.   If $A_{i,i}(m)$, then

$$L^{(i)}(m+1) = (I + \mu(m)x(m)x(m)^T)L^{(i)}(m),$$

$$L^{(k)}(m+1) = L^{(k)}(m), \quad k \neq i \quad ;$$

$$(14)$$

2.   If $A_{i,j}(m)$, $j \neq i$, then

$$L^{(i)}(m+1) = (I + \alpha(m)x(m)x(m)^T)L^{(i)}(m),$$

$$L^{(j)}(m+1) = (I - \beta(m)x(m)x(m)^T)L^{(j)}(m),$$

$$L^{(k)}(m+1) = L^{(k)}(m), \quad k \neq i, \quad k \neq j .$$

$$(15)$$

There $\mu(m)$, $\alpha(m)$, and $\beta(m)$ are positive scalars which may depend on the amount of misclassification measured in terms of the values of discriminant functions (Kohonen et al, 1979, Riittinen, 1981).

To analyze learning rule (14), (15) mathematically, let

$U^{(i)}(m) = (u_1^{(i)}(m), u_2^{(i)}(m),..., u_{(i)s}^{(i)}(m))$ be the matrix whose columns are the orthonormal basis vectors of subspace $L^{(i)}(m)$. Then the basic 'rotation' in (14), (15) can be written as

$$V^{(i)}(m+1) = (I + \mu(m)x(m)x(m)^T)U^{(i)}(m),$$

$$U^{(i)}(m+1) = V^{(i)}(m+1)R^{(i)}(m+1) \tag{16}$$

in which each basis vector $u_j^{(i)}(m)$ is first multiplied by the matrix $I + \mu(m)x(m)x(m)^T$ (in fact, no matrix-vector product is needed due to the elementary form of the multiplier matrix) and then the columns of the ensuing matrix $V^{(i)}(m+1)$, which in general are not orthonormal any more, are orthonormalized. Matrix $R^{(i)}(m+1)$ is introduced in (16) for mathematical notation only; in practice, the Gram-Schmidt method should be used (see Oja and Karhunen, 1981).

Assume now that the $x(m)$ sequence is statistically independent. Also, let the parameters $\mu(m)$, $\alpha(m)$, and $\beta(m)$ be non-random in (14), (15). Then the algorithm yields for an arbitrary class i:

$$E(V^{(i)}(m+1) \mid U^{(i)}(m))$$

$$= (I + \mu(m)E(x(m)x(m)^T \mid A_{i,i}(m)))P(A_{i,i}(m))U^{(i)}(m)$$

$$+ \sum_{i \neq j}(I + \alpha(m)E(x(m)x(m)^T \mid A_{i,j}(m)))P(A_{i,j}(m))U^{(i)}(m)$$

$$+ \sum_{i \neq j}(I - \beta(m)E(x(m)x(m)^T \mid A_{j,i}(m)))P(A_{j,i}(m))U^{(i)}(m)$$

$$+ \sum_{\substack{k \neq i \\ r \neq i}} P(A_{k,r}(m))U^{(i)}(m)$$

$$= \sum_{k,r} P(A_{k,r}(m))U^{(i)}(m) + (\mu(m)P(A_{i,i}(m))E(x(m)x(m)^T \mid A_{i,i}(m))$$

$$+ \alpha(m)\sum_{i \neq j} P(A_{i,j}(m))E(x(m)x(m)^T \mid A_{i,j}(m))$$

$$- \beta(m)\sum_{i \neq j} P(A_{j,i}(m))E(x(m)x(m)^T \mid A_{j,i}(m)))U^{(i)}(m). \tag{17}$$

The first coefficient $\sum P(A_{k,r}(m))$ is in fact equal to one. The coefficient matrix in (17) is now a weighted sum of *conditional correlation matrices* of the $x(m)$ sequence, conditioned on the correct and false classifications. When the class boundaries are determined by Kohonen´s algorithm, the misclassifications in the prototype set have an influence on them. The method tends to optimize the classification accuracy instead of the least squares representation ability of the subspaces.

Equation (17) suggests the following new 'averaged' algorithm for computing the matrices $U^{(i)}(m)$ and their limits, if they converge. This algorithm makes explicit use of the conditional correlation matrices $E(x(m)x(m)^T \mid A_{i,j}(m))$ appearing in (17).

1.   At step 0, compute initial matrices

$$S^{(i)}(0) = \sum_{x(m)\in\,\omega^{(i)}} x(m)x(m)^T .$$

Choose matrices $U^{(1)}(0),\ldots,U^{(K)}(0)$, each having orthonormal columns which are the basis vectors of a set of initial subspaces $L^{(1)}(0),\ldots,L^{(K)}(0)$. In accordance to CLAFIC, the columns of $U^{(i)}(0)$ can be chosen as the eigenvectors of $S^{(i)}(0)$ corresponding to largest eigenvalues. Fix initial dimensions $s^{(i)} = \dim(L^{(i)})$ which are the numbers of columns of matrices $U^{(i)}(0)$.

2.   At step k, perform classifications for all prototypes using rule (7) and subspaces $L^{(i)}(k-1)$, which remain constant during the classification. Compute estimates for $E(x(m)x(m)^T \mid A_{i,j}(m))$ in the form

$$S_{i,j}(k) = \sum_{\substack{x(m)\in\,\omega^{(i)} \\ x(m)\to\,\omega^{(j)}}} x(m)x(m)^T \qquad (18)$$

where the sum is taken over those prototype vectors only which actually are in class i but are classified into class j.

3.   Compute matrices

$$S^{(i)}(k) = S^{(i)}(k-1) + \sum_{j\neq i}\alpha_{i,j}S_{i,j}(k) - \sum_{j\neq i}\beta_{i,j}S_{j,i}(k)$$

with parameters $\alpha_{i,j}$ and $\beta_{i,j}$ chosen suitably.

4.   Compute the eigenvectors of each $S^{(i)}(k)$ corresponding to the $s^{(i)}$ largest eigenvalues and set these as columns of $U^{(i)}(k)$. The dimensions $s^{(i)}$ may be changed at this step.

5.   Increment index k by one and go to step 2.

The algorithm above has been termed by the present author the
'Averaged Learning Subspace Method' (ALSM) due to its close relation
with Kohonen´s original learning subspace method. A more detailed
explanation of the algorithm and its performance is given by Oja and
Kuusela, 1982.

A number of tests have been performed on the ALSM algorithm using
speech data (Kuusela, 1981). Section 4 and the references therein
give a detailed account of the data acquisition system. The pattern
vectors were spectral phonemes. In an experiment with K=18 classes
and pattern space dimension n=30, and the size of the training set
equal to 3861 and that of the test set equal to 3851, the percentage
of correct classifications for CLAFIC were 83.3 % (test set), 84.3 %
(training set). The corresponding percentages for the ALSM were
90.8 % (test set), 93.6 % (training set). Results on the performance
of the learning subspace method compared to some standard methods like
the nearest neighbour classifier are given by Jalanko and Riittinen,
1981.

The training algorithms for the learning subspace methods are relatively complicated, and the data has to be recycled. Once convergence
has been obtained, the resulting classification rule (7) is very
fast. Computing the basis vectors of the subspaces by learning subspace methods produces a marked increase in classification accuracy
over the nonlearning subspace methods. In real-time signal analysis,
the speed and accuracy of classification is essential, while the
design of the classifier may often be accomplished off-line.

4. APPLICATION IN SPEECH RECOGNITION

The subspace methods discussed above have been applied to the classification of phonemes in a project for recognizing Finnish speech at
Helsinki University of Technology.

The Otaniemi speech recognition system used at HUT and the results obtained have been described in detail in several reports (Kohonen et
al, 1980, 1981, Haltsonen, 1981, Jalanko, 1980, Reuhkala et al,
1982, Riittinen et al, 1981). The phoneme data consists of a
large number of samples, which are DFT-computed 30-component spectra
of the speech signal. The classes of stationary phonemes are represented by linear vector subspaces, computed from training samples
using Kohonen´s learning subspace method.

Kohonen´s algorithm, due to its iterative nature, yields an extra
advantage in speech recognition. It is possible to use essentially
the same algorithm for both segmenting the continuous speech waveform and labeling (Jalanko et al, 1978). Segmentation is based on
the distances of the spectral vectors to the phoneme subspaces. Those
instants can be found at which the speech waveform is closest to
some stationary region. Then labeling is performed by classification
rule (7). The resulting phonemic transcription can then be classified
in isolated word recognition by comparing them with reference strings

stored in a dictionary (Reuhkala et al, 1979, Kohonen et al, 1980).

REFERENCES

Chien, Y. T., and Fu, K. S., 1967. On the generalized Karhunen-Loève expansion. IEEE Transactions on Information Theory, 13, 3, 518 - 520.

Fukunaga, K., and Koontz, W. L. G., 1970. Application of the Karhunen-Loève expansion in feature selection and ordering. IEEE Transactions on Computers, 19, 4, 311 - 318.

Haltsonen, S., 1981. Studies on automatic phonemic segmentation of speech and automatic recognition of isolated words. Dr. Tech. Thesis, Helsinki University of Technology, Department of Technical Physics.

Jalanko, M., Haltsonen, S., Bry, K.-J., and Kohonen, T., 1978. Application of the orthogonal projection principles to simultaneous phonemic segmentation and labeling of continuous speech. Proc. 4th Int. J. Conf. on Pattern Recognition, Kyoto, 1006 - 1008.

Jalanko, M., 1980. Studies of learning projective methods in automatic speech recognition. Dr. Tech. Thesis, Helsinki University of Technology, Department of Technical Physics.

Jalanko, M., and Riittinen, H., 1981. A comparison of several speech preprocessing and classification methods. Proc. 2nd Scand. Conf. on Image Analysis, Espoo, Finland, 235 - 240.

Kittler, J., 1977. Feature selection methods based on the Karhunen-Loève expansion, in Pattern Recognition - Theory and Application (Eds. Fu and Whinston), pp. 61 - 74. Noordhoff, Leyden.

Kittler, J., 1978. The subspace approach to pattern recognition, in Progress in Cybernetics and Systems Research, vol. III (Eds. Trapp, Klir, and Ricciardi), pp. 92 - 97. Hemisphere Publ. Co., Washington.

Kohonen, T., Németh, G., Bry, K.-J., Jalanko, M., and Riittinen, H., 1979. Spectral classification of phonemes by learning subspaces. Proc. 1979 IEEE Int. Conf. on Acoustics, Speech, and Signal Processing, Washington, DC, 97 - 100.

Kohonen, T., Riittinen, H., Jalanko, M., Reuhkala, E., and Haltsonen, S., 1980. A thousand-word recognition system based on the learning subspace method and redundant hash addressing. Proc. 5th Int. Conf. on Pattern Recognition, Miami Beach, FL, 158 - 165.

Kohonen, T., Haltsonen, S., Jalanko, M., Reuhkala, E., and Riittinen, H., 1981. An overview of the Otaniemi speech recognition system. Proc. 2nd Scand. Conf. on Image Analysis, Espoo, Finland, 227 - 234.

Kulikowski, C. A., 1970. Pattern recognition approach to medical diagnosis. IEEE Transactions on Systems Science and Cybernetics, 6, 3, 173 - 178.

Kuusela, M., 1981. Statistical optimization methods for constructing the subspace classifier (in Finnish). Dipl. Eng. Thesis, Helsinki University of Technology, Department of Technical Physics.

Noguchi, Y., 1976. Subspace method of feature extraction and non-symmetric projection operators. Bull. Electrotechnical Laboratory 40, 7, 11 - 27.

64

Oja, E., and Karhunen, J., 1981. An analysis of convergence for a
    learning version of the subspace method. To appear in Journal of
    Math. Anal. Appl.
Oja, E., and Kuusela, M., 1981. The ALSM algorithm – an improved sub-
    space method of classification. Submitted for publication.
Reuhkala, E., Jalanko, M., and Kohonen, T., 1979. A redundant hash
    addressing method adapted for the postprocessing and error –
    correction of computer-recognized speech. Proc. 1979 IEEE Int.
    Conf. on Acoustics, Speech, and Signal Processing, Washington, DC,
    591 – 594.
Reuhkala, E., Riittinen, H., Haltsonen, S., Ventä, O., Mäkisara, K.,
    and Kohonen, T., 1982. The on-line version of the Otaniemi speech
    recognition system. Proc. 1982 IEEE Int. Conf. on Acoustics,
    Speech, and Signal Processing, Paris.
Riittinen, H., Haltsonen, S., Reuhkala, E., and Jalanko, M., 1981.
    Experiments on an isolated-word recognition system for multiple
    speakers. Proc. 1981 IEEE Int. Conf. on Acoustics, Speech, and
    Signal Processing, Atlanta, GA, 975 – 978.
Riittinen, H., 1981. Development and generalization of the learning
    subspace method (in Finnish). Lic. Tech. Thesis, Helsinki Uni-
    versity of Technology, Department of Technical Physics.
Therrien, C. W., 1975. Eigenvalue properties of projection operators
    and their application to the subspace method of feature extract-
    ion. IEEE Transactions on Computers, 24, 9, 944 – 948.
Watanabe, S., 1965. Karhunen-Loève expansion and factor analysis –
    theoretical remarks and applications. Trans. 4th Prague Conf. on
    Information Theory, Statist. Decision Functions, and Random Pro-
    cesses, Prague, 675 – 660.
Watanabe, S., Lambert, P. F., Kulikowski, C. A., Buxton, J. L., and
    Walker, R., 1967. Evaluation and selection of variables in
    pattern recognition, in Computer and Information Sciences, vol. 2
    (Ed. Tou), pp. 91 – 122. Acad. Press, New York.
Watanabe, S., and Pakvasa, N., 1973. Subspace method in pattern re-
    cognition. Proc. 1st J. Conf. on Pattern Recognition, Washington,
    DC, 25 – 32.
Wold, S., 1976. Pattern recognition by means of disjoint principal
    components models. Pattern Recognition, 8, 127 – 139.

SPEECH SEGMENTATION AND INTERPRETATION USING A SEMANTIC SYNTAX-DIRECTED TRANSLATION

R.De Mori*, Attilio Giordana** and Pietro Laface***

    *Department of Computer Science
    Concordia University
    Montreal H3G 1M8
    Quebec, Canada

    **Istituto di Scienze dell'Informazione
    Universitá di Torino
    Corso Massimo D'Azeglio 42
    10125 Torino, Italy

    ***CENS - Istituto di Elettrotecnica Generale
    Politecnico di Torino
    Corso Duca degli Abruzzi 24
    10129 Torino, Italy

ABSTRACT

A Semantic Syntax-Directed Translation is presented. Its rules are used to segment continuous speech and, at the same time, to give them phonetic interpretations.

1. INTRODUCTION

Semantic Syntax-Directed Translation (SSDT) has been recently used for pictorial pattern recognition (1). This paper proposes another version of an SSDT suitable to be used for segmenting continuous speech into Pseudo-Syllabic Segments (PSS) and for assigning phonetic interpretations to them.

The speech signal is transformed into the frequency domain by a Fast Fourier Transformation from which some acoustic cues are extracted. These cues are unambiguously described by a language L1. An SSDT transforms these descriptions into a lattice of phonetic interpretations and delimits the bounds of PSS, as described in (2). Such a translation is controlled by rules inferred by the designers, based on a large number of experiments and their knowledge about acoustic phonetics.

2. THE SEMANTIC SYNTAX DIRECTED TRANSLATION SCHEME

Definition 1.
According to (1), an SSDT is a 5-tuple:
$$<N,\Sigma,\Delta,S,P>$$
where:
N is a set of nonterminal symbols;
Σ is a set of input symbols;
Δ is a set of output symbols;
$S \in N$ is the start symbol;
P is the set of rules;

The set Σ of input symbols is given in Table I. Every symbol is associated with a vector of attributes. The meaning of the attributes is given in Table II. The set Δ of output symbols is given in Table III. The start symbol S is denoted PSS (Pseudo-Syllabic Segment).

The rewriting rules in P have the following general form:

$$P_k: X \rightarrow YB \; ; \; YG \; ; \; Alg(k).$$

where $X \in N$ is a nonterminal symbol; $Y \in N^*$ is a possibly empty string of nonterminal symbols; $B \in \Sigma^*$ is a (possibly empty) string of input symbols; $G \in \Delta^*$ is a set of strings of output symbols.

The sequences YB, YG can appear in the reverse order, i.e. BY, GY. In any case, Y is in the same position in both expressions.

Alg(k) is an algorithm that may contain a condition made of a logical expression of predicates defined by semantic attachments; the rule can be applied only if the condition is verified.

Each symbol is associated with a vector of attributes. The attributes associated with X belong to the vector A(X). In a similar way, the attributes associated with the symbols of B are grouped into A(B).

The algorithm Alg(k) may contain a semantic rule fk(A(Y),A(B)) which allows one to compute the attributes of A(X) of X given the attributes of A(Y) and A(B). Another semantic rule f'k(A(B)) allows one to compute the attributes of the output hypotheses G, given the attributes of the symbols in B which have been translated into G. The portion of the rule corresponding to the generation of hypotheses may not appear in some rules.

A parser analyses a description of acoustic cues. Whenever a string of the input description appears to be generated by a rule pk, the second part of pk is used for generating phonetic hypotheses. Every time a complete derivation of the symbol PSS, of the type:

$$PSS =^* \Rightarrow \text{description of acoustic cues}$$

is performed, a PSS is delimited. PSSs are described by the set of phonetic features produced by the translation. Each PSS, with its phonetic description, is then used for generating hypotheses about more detailed acoustic cues using context-dependent rules. Context-dependent rules will not be described in this paper.

The segmentation grammar is a context-free grammar. The use of conditions considerably reduces the nondeterminism allowing a fast parsing. Parsing is seen as a problem solving activity and for the sake of brevity is not described here.

3. THE RULES OF THE SEGMENTATION GRAMMAR

The rules of the segmentation grammar are introduced in this section with comments that will help to a better understanding of them.

p1   PSS := ab ; ab ; Alg(1) .

p2   := aV ; aV ; Alg(2) .

Rules p1 and p2 establish that a PSS generates ab if the predicate P1, contained in Alg(1), is true, otherwise it generates aV. As will be seen later b and V always generate one vocalic segment. The predicate P1 is true if between the vocalic segment in b or V and the next vocalic segment there are no strings generated by the nonterminal symbol UN, that will be introduced later.

Rules p1 and p2 do not have associated semantic or translation parts. a, b and V are rewritten as follows:

p3   a:= X1   ;   SON   ; Alg(3) .
p4   a:= X2   ;   SINIL   ; Alg(4) .
p5   a:= X3   ;   SNCL   ; Alg(5) .
p6   a:= UN   ;   UN   ; Alg(6) .
p7   a:= UN X4 ;   UN PREVS ; Alg(7) .
p8   b:= V   ;   V   ; Alg(8) .
p9   b:= V X4   ;   V POSTVS ; Alg(9) .
p10 V:= VOCPK ;   VOCALIC ; Alg(10) .
p11 V:= VOC   ;   VOCALIC ; Alg(11) .
p12 V:= UPK   ;   VOCALIC ; Alg(12) .

For the sake of brevity, the semantic rules for attributes composition in algorithms (Alg(3) - Alg(12)) are not explained. SINIL means Single Intervocalic Nonsonorant Interrupted Lax consonant while PREVS and POSTVS stand respectively for PREVocalic and POSTVocalic Sonorant consonant in a cluster with nonsonorant consonant.

Alg(4) contains a predicate P2 which is true if X2 is rewritten with a simple symbol of the alphabet; Alg(5) contains a predicate P3 which is true if the duration of the consonantal part is higher than a threshold.

Alg(12) contains a predicate P4 which is true if UPK does not follow a V. P5 in Alg(9) is true if X4 precedes a UN.

The remaining rules are given in the following. For the sake of brevity, rules for attribute composition have been omitted.

```
p13   UN := X5 ;                        NC
p14      := X5 Y1 ;                     NC
p15      := X6 ;                        NI
p16      := X6 Y1 ;                     NI
p17      := X6 X5;                      NA
p18      := X6 X5 Y1;                   NA
p19   X1 := (HIGH-DIP + LONG-MIDDLE-DIP + SNPK +
                                   k > 0
            + SHORT-MIDDLE-DIP + TRNS)
p20   X2 := (SHORT-DEEP-DIP + SHORT-MIDDLE-DIP +
                                   o          o
            + BUZZDIP)(BRSTPK + SNPK) (TRNS)
p21   X3 := ((BUZZDIP +SHORT-MIDDLE-DIP + HIGH-DIP +
            + LONG-MIDDLE-DIP)(SNPK +
                         * k > 0        o
            + BRSTPK) )          (TRNS)
p22   X4 := SNPK    HIGH-DIP
                         k > 0
p23   X5 := (NS + NSDP + NSPK)
p24   Y1 := (HIGH-DIP + SHORT-MIDDLE-DIP + TRNS)
p25   X6 := (LONG-DEEP-DIP +SHORT-DEEP-DIP + BUZZDIP
            + SHORTMIDDLE-DIP)
```

'o' means that the expression of which it is the exponent can be present only once or absent.

A special parser has been designed for using the translation rules. The specific knowledge about the type of rules and the predicates has made the parser design particularly effective, avoiding backtracking. As the parser is an 'ad hoc' tool for a specific application, it will not be described.

4. EXAMPLE

The following acoustic description was obtained for the Italian word "prenotazione" (reservation). For the sake of brevity parameters and parameters composition are omitted in this example.

```
LONG-DEEP-DIP(t1,t2)
SNPK(t2,t3)
HIGH-DIP(t3,t4)
VOCPK(t4,t5)
LONG-MIDDLE-DIP(t5,t6)
UPK(t6,t7)
SHORT-DIP(t7,t8)
TRNS(t8,t9)
VOC(t9,t10)
LONG-DEEP-DIP(t10,t11)
NSPK(t11,t12)
VOCPK(t12,t13)
SHORT-MIDDLE-DIP(t13,14)
UPK(t14,t15)
```

As there is no UN between t4 and t7, and UPK(t6,t7) does
not follow a V, P4 is true on UPK(t6,t7) and Pl is true on
VOCPK(t4,t5); thus Alg(l) assigns t5 as the ending time of
the PSS and pl is applied.

As Pl is true, P5 is false and p9 cannot be applied; p8
and pl0 are applied and VOCPK(t4,t5) is translated into
VOCALIC(t4,t5).

P2 is false, p3, p4, p5 cannot be applied because the
first symbol that must be generated by a is LONG-DEEP-DIP.
Based on the above considerations the following chain of
rules can be applied for generating the acoustic description between tl and t5:

```
          pl         p7              pl5            p25
   PSS ---->ab ---> UN X4 b---> X6 X4 b--->

                      p22
       LONG-DEEP-DIP X4 b--->

                                    p8
       LONG-DEEP-DIP SNPK HIGH-DIP b--->

                                    pl0
       LONG-DEEP-DIP SNPK HIGH-DIP V --->

       LONG-DEEP-DIP SNPK HIGH-DIP VOCPK .
```

The translation rules and the corresponding semantic
rules associated with p7, pl5, p22, and pl0 generate the
following phonetic transcription:

   NI(tl,t2) PREVS(t2,t4) VOCALIC(t4,t5) .

The parser now starts from the description corresponding
to the PSS ending symbol and attempts to delimit the second
PSS and to generate phonetic features about it. The
results of this operation are given in the following.

```
   PSS2:
         SON(t5,t6) , SNCL(t5,t6)
         VOCALIC(t6,t7)
   PSS3:
         NI(t7,t9)
         VOCALIC(t9,tl0)
   PSS4:
         NA(tl0,tl2)
         VOCALIC(tl2,tl3)
   PSS5:
         SON(tl3,tl4) , SINIL(tl3,tl4)
         VOCALIC(tl4,tl5)
```

5. RESULTS

The Translation System has been extensively tested using
unconstrained sentences of the spoken Italian language.

Segmentation errors were less than 1% on the average, two phonetic hypotheses were generated on a set of 9 phonetic classes. The right hypothesis was not generated in less than 1% of the cases.

TABLE I

Symbol	Attributes	Description
VOCPK	tb, te,ml, m2, rmin, rmax	vocalic peak of Total Energy (TE).
SNPK		peak of TE for a sonorant consonant.
BRSTPK		burst peak.
NSPK		frication peak.
UPK		uncertain peak.
LONG MIDDLE SHORT DEEP DIP HIGH	tb, te, emin	dips of TE.
BUZZDIP		dip with buzz-bar.
NSDP		dip with frication.
TRNS	tb, te, rmin	prevocalic conso-nantal transition.
SN	tb, te	sonorant tract in a peak.
NS	tb, te	nonsonorant tract in a peak.
VOC	tb, te	vocalic tract in a peak.

* LONG and MIDDLE are linguistic attributes concerning the duration, while MIDDLE, DEEP, and HIGH indicate the level of depth.

TABLE II

Attribute	Description
tb	time of beginning
te	time of end
ml	maximum signal energy in the peak
m2	maximum energy in the 3 - 5 kHz band
rmin	minimum ratio between low (200 - 900 Hz) and high (5 - 10 kHz) frequency energies
rmax	maximum ratio between low and high frequency energies
emin	minimum energy in a peak

TABLE III

Symbol	Primary Phonetic Feature
VOCALIC	Vowel
NI	Nonsonorant Interrupted Consonant
NA	Nonsonorant Affricate Consonant
NC	Nonsonorant Continuant Consonant
SON	Sonorant Consonant
SNCL	Cluster of Sonorant Consonants
VC	The "v" consonant
SINIL	Single Intervocalic Nonsonorant Interrupted Lax Consonant

6. REFERENCES

(1) - K.C.You and K.S.Fu,'A Syntactic Approach to Shape Recognition Using Attributed Grammars', IEEE Transactions on System, Man and Cybernetics, vol.SMC-9, 334-345.

(2) - R.De Mori, 'Computer Model of Speech Using Fuzzy Algorithms', Plenum Press, New York, 1982.

A CONTINUOUS SPEECH RECOGNITION SYSTEM BASED ON A DIPHONE
SPOTTING APPROACH

C. Scagliola and L. Marmi

Elettronica San Giorgio - ELSAG S.p.A.
Via Hermada, 6 - 16154 Genova - Italy

ABSTRACT

A continuous speech recognition system is described, whose organization is based around the concept of diphone spotting. This consists of continuously measuring the similarity of the current portion of signal pattern with a complete set of selected phonetic events, called diphones because the most significant of them are transitions between pairs of phonemes.

The entire set of measures feeds a linguistic decoder that operates on a state space representation of the language, whose states are the diphones that compose the words of the lexicon. Durational constraints and optional phonological rules are included in the language representation. The linguistic decoder recognizes the sentence as that path through the network which attains the highest cumulative similarity score. Additionally, the decoder has the task of detecting the end of the sentence.

A preliminary test on 50 sequences of 3 to 7 connected digits gave recognition rates as high as 99.6% on digits, or 98% on sequences, thus confirming the validity of this approach.

1   INTRODUCTION

Continuous speech recognition systems, by the very nature of the problem, cannot reasonably attempt at recognizing a spoken message as a whole but rather have to represent and reconstruct it in terms of some elementary acoustic units. In fact it is easy to see that, even with a very small vocabulary, a very large number of different messages can be produced when a few words are connected together. For instance, if the vocabulary is composed of the ten digits, we get one million different six-digit sequences! Most commonly such systems make use of the classical paradigm of syntactic pattern recognition (cf. Fu, 1974): after preprocessing, the pattern is segmented into

73

pattern primitives, which are then identified, usually by template matching procedures; subsequently the pattern, which is represented now as a string of primitives, is classified (or rejected) by a syntax analyzer, which produces also a structural description of it. In the case of speech recognition, the primitives are usually phonemes (e.g. Schwartz and Makhoul, 1975), or phones (e.g. Lowerre and Reddy, 1980). More recently other phonetic entities of the transitional type have also been considered as basic speech units, like demisyllables (e.g. Ruske and Schotola, 1981) or even entire syllables (e.g. Hunt,1980).

In all the systems of this kind, the main source of recognition errors appears to be the segmentation operation itself (cf. Ruske and Schotola, 1981; Hunt et al. 1980; Klatt, 1980 a and 1980 b), essentially because of its being based on incomplete acoustic information on the speech wave, like amplitude, spectral derivative, zero crossings etc.

In the presence of segmentation errors, the system can sometimes recover the correct sentence interpretation, by adopting sophisticated error correcting parsers. However, especially in the case of omitted segments, most of the times the designer of the syntax analyzer has to compensate for the deficiencies of the segmenter by manually including the most frequent errors as alternative word descriptions in the language representation (cf. Lowerre and Reddy, 1980).

The system to be described in the present paper tries to overcome the above mentioned difficulties by avoiding segmentation and delaying every decision to the full message level. The general philosophy of the system, based on the concept of diphone spotting (Scagliola, 1981; cf. also Knipper 1981),is introduced in the next section, while sections 3 and 4 give details of its major components, viz. the acoustic-phonetic processor and the linguistic decoder. The results of a preliminary evaluation of the system in the recognition of arbitrary -length sequences of connected italian digits are presented in section 5, and finally, in section 6, the main characteristics of the system are summarized and discussed.

2   GENERAL SYSTEM PHILOSOPHY

In the proposed approach the usual segmentation and labelling block is replaced with one that continuously measures the similarity of a portion of the incoming speech pattern, centered around the present time interval, with a complete set of basic phonetic events, the diphones, as illustrated in fig. 1. Each of these measures, which are numbers in the range (0,1), can be interpreted as an evaluation of the possibility that the present time interval is contained within the relevant phonetic event.

This set of measures is the input of the linguistic decoder which operates on a state space representation of the language, whose states are the diphones that constitute the words of the lexicon. The linguistic decoder recognizes the spoken sentence as the one which attains the highest cumulative similarity score among all the possible ones.

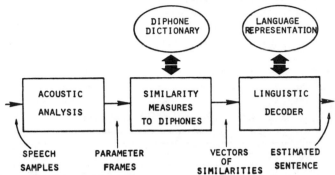

Fig. 1   Continuous Speech Recognition via diphone spotting

The main thrust of this approach is that any decision is taken only at the full message level, where all the pieces of information, from acoustic-phonetic to lexical and syntactic, and possibly semantic, are available. Delaying decisions to the highest levels reduce errors and more than that, avoids the complications needed to recover from errors.

3   THE ACOUSTIC-PHONETIC PROCESSOR

3.1 THE DIPHONE DICTIONARY

In building a dictionary of elementary phonetic events, we wanted to make use of the smallest units that took into account coarticulation effects. This led us to adopt the diphones as basic units (Scagliola, 1981), in conformity also with previous experiences in speech synthesis (cf. Vivalda et al. 1979). However, as an engineering compromise, a diphone was defined as approximately spanning only the transition between adjacent phonemes, rather than the interval between their centers, as in the most common definition (cf. Paul and Rabinowitz, 1974; Klatt, 1980 a). So, also steady-state units were included in the diphone dictionary. Moreover, longer transitional events, spanning three phonemes, were also considered in some special case.

At present, only the diphones involved in the recognition of connected digits have been actually selected. They include mostly CV (Consonant-Vowel), CC an VV transitions (but not VC ones), besides the steady-state vowels, some steady-state consonants and a few triphones.

Fig. 2 shows the waveform and the associated sequence of LPC spectra,   derived from the stored parametric representation (see section 3.2 below) of the diphone /CI/ (as in cheese), as plotted for documentation purposes by the interactive program used to select the diphones.

Two different diphone dictionaries were built for the connected digit recognition task: in the first one, collected quickly from a small one-speaker training set, just to get some idea of system's performance, all the diphones were assigned the same length of 50 msec (5 frames) and a single template was extracted for each of the 36 diphone labels, by simply playing back the original 50 ms waveform and verifying that it sounded as expected. In the second dictionary extracted from the same training set, the diphones were more carefully selected, assigning each one the most appropriate length and allowing multiple templates for some of them (typically the vowels), leading to a total of 38 diphone labels and 51 templates.

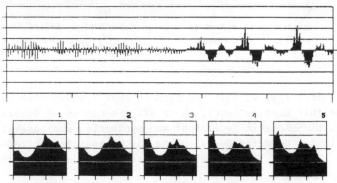

Fig. 2 Waveform with associated sequence
of LPC spectra of the diphone /CI/

3.2   PARAMETRIC REPRESENTATION AND SIMILARITY MEASURE

In a preliminary implementation the popular LPC analysis was used, although recent results showed that FFT based spectral representations may yield a better distance measure with smaller computation and storage requirements (cf Davis and Mermelstein, 1980; Billi et al, 1982). The speech signal, collected with a close-talking microphone,is low-pass filtered at 3.4 KHz and sampled at 8 KHz. Every 10 ms a 20 ms Hamming window is applied to the signal, and a set of 10 autocorrelation and 10 linear prediction coefficients, derived by the autocorrelation method (Makhoul, 1975) is stored for further processing. When a diphone is selected, the autocorrelation coefficients associated with the inverse filter of the all-pole model (Itakura, 1975) are computed from the linear prediction coefficients and stored in the diphone dictionary.

To measure the similarity between a portion of speech and a diphone template, the log-likelihood ratio (Itakura, 1975) is computed between pairs of corresponding frames and then averaged over the number of frames of the template. This distance measure is then transformed into a number in the range (0,1) through a smooth function between two predetermined distance thresholds. Finally, for each diphone,

the maximum among all the measures in which a given frame was involved is taken as the similarity value assigned to that frame. In this
way a good similarity measure obtained by a diphone in a given position, is assigned not only to the center frame of the portion of speech
compared, but rather to all the frames involved. This explains why the
similarity score may also be seen as the possibility that a frame belongs to a given phonetic event.

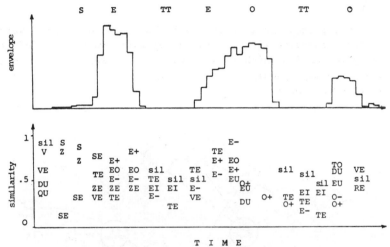

Fig. 3   Output of the acoustic-phonetic processor, with superimposed signal envelope, relative to the words SETTE-
OTTO(7-8) spoken continuously

A way of looking at the output of the acoustic-phonetic processor
is like the one shown in Fig. 3, where for each frame the diphone labels are ordered according to their decreasing similarities (actually
only one every five frames is depicted for simplicity). This sequence
of labels and associated similarities is the input of the linguistic
decoder, whose task is that of finding the sequence of labels that ob-
taines the maximum cumulative similarity score among all the sequences
that satisfy the language constraints.

4   THE LINGUISTIC DECODER

4.1 THE LANGUAGE REPRESENTATION

In the first implementation we chose a simple language representation in the form of a directed graph, whose nodes represent phonetic
states and are labelled with the corresponding diphones. The language
is finite-state, but can produce sentences with an infinite number of
symbols. Fig. 4 shows the subnetwork for digits 6 (SEI) and 7 (SETTE)
used in the connected digit recognition task. Two characteristics are
worth noticing here:

1) lower and upper bounds were imposed to the time (number of frames) a path could remain in each state. These limits, which depend on the particular diphone, on the position in the word and on the stress value, are very important to avoid the erroneous recognition of abnormally short or long phonetic events. Different contexts, i.e. different arrival times in a given phonetic state, are expanded as separate nodes at decoding time by associating a counter to each state.

2) Optional phonological rules are included, both within a word and at the connection with the following word. In the case of italian connected digits which always end with a vowel, this means that a diphthong may appear between two digits when the latter begins with a different vowel.

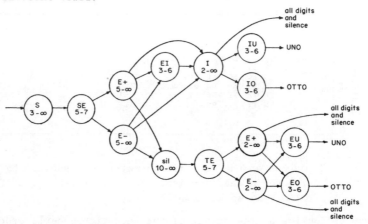

Fig. 4   Subnetwork for digits 6 (SEI) and 7 (SETTE)

4.2 THE DECODING ALGORITHM

The main feature we required for the algorithm was that of being oriented toward real-time operation. This means that decoding should not begin only once the end of the sentence has been detected, but rather it should proceed along with acoustic analysis and similarity measurement (cf. Vicenzi and Scagliola, 1982), so that, once the sentence ends, the interpretation may be already done. Two important implications derive from this requirement. First the algorithm cannot make use of such pieces of information on the sentence like its total length, or the minimum cost to reach the end (cf. Nilsson, 1971). Second, we can delegate the linguistic decoder itself to determine the end of the sentence, making use of linguistic as well as acoustic information. In the recognition of sequences of connected digits however, where the length of the sequence is unknown, the end of the sentence is detected by the linguistic decoder when the best scoring path is in a state of silence whose duration is longer than a predefined value.

The adopted algorithm, that we will not describe in detail here, makes use of a best-few search strategy without backtracking, similar to the one adopted in the Harpy system to search a graph of phones (Lo werre and Reddy, 1980). At each step, unlikely candidate paths are pru ned out from further search, by dropping those paths whose cumulative similarity score is lower than the locally best one by more than a se- lected threshold.

The amount of computation required is thus approximately linear with the length of the sentence, or, in other terms, approximately constant in the unit time (within a random variation due to the larger or smaller phonetic evidence in the input and to the number of alterna tive paths that can be followed at a given point), while the amount of memory is kept to a minimum by an explicit cleanup procedure that eli minates dead paths.

Moreover, differently from the Harpy System, the decision on the phonetic states traversed is not delayed until the end of the sentence (Lowerre and Reddy, 1980). Rather, as soon as an only interpretation remains possible for some interval, the relevant portion of immediate memory (list of old states) is released and a compact description of the phonetic states and of the words already recognized (their name, duration and average similarity) is written in two separate lists. This has two important implications that make the proposed system's behavior agree closely with recent models of speech perception (cf. Cole and Jakimik, 1980; Newell, 1980):1) phonetic units and words are recognized in the forward direction; 2) the decision delay is kept short (in actual experiments this was usually around a quarter of a second, only occasionally exceeding half second).

When the end of a sentence is detected, only the best scoring path which satisfies the requisite of ending in a state of non-phone- tic silence (i.e. a silence which is not the occlusion part of a plosi ve consonant) lasting more than a given time is retained and the inter pretation of the sentence completed.

As an example Fig. 5 shows the original waveform of a three-digit sequence and the segmentation implicitely performed by the linguistic decoder while recognizing the basic phonetic units. In Fig. 5 some things are worth noticing, like the accurate localization of CV transi tions, the early detection of the initial/S/, when its level is about the same as the silence, the correct placement of the diphthong /IO/ between the digits SEI and OTTO, and the end-of-sentence decision ta- ken after .4 sec. of silence.

5   RESULTS ON CONNECTED DIGIT RECOGNITION

The system described was tested on the connected digit recognition task, where the digit sequence length was unknown. 50 three to seven digit long sequences, for a total of 250 digits, were uttered by the same speaker who had provided, more than 8 months before, the speech

80

material from which the diphone templates had been selected.

Two series of tests were performed with the two diphone dictionaries mentioned in section 3.1. In both series, different values of the
threshold used to prune unlikely candidate paths were used, and only
the results obtained with the best thresholds (i.e. those that most
restricted the number of retained paths, without degrading performance) are reported here.

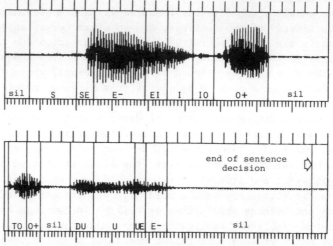

Fig. 5 Waveform of the sequence SEI-OTTO-DUE (6-8-2)
with diphone boundaries detected by the linguistic decoder

With the first diphone dictionary, there was only one digit misclas-
sified and one digit was omitted; the accuracy therefore can be expres
sed either as 96% recognition rate on digit sequences or as 99.2% on
digits. With the second, more carefully selected, dictionary, only the
digit omission remained, and the above figures become 98% and 99.6%
respectively. Of course these results have a poor statistical validity
(for instance, the limits of the 95% confidence interval of the first
percentage given above are 90% and 100%), but nevertheless they indicate that quite high performances can be obtained. This is also confir
med by a few other tens of tests performed afterwards, in which no error occurred.

6   DISCUSSION AND CONCLUSIONS

We have described a continuous speech recognition system based on
a novel approach which consists of continuously evaluating the presence in the speech flow of elementary phonetic events, like the transiti
ons between pairs of phonemes. In this way acoustic and phonetic knowledge sources are more completely integrated than in the classical ap
proaches, and the whole acoustic-phonetic processing has been greatly

simplified. Besides the segmentation operation is avoided, thus elimi-
nating a possible and probable source of errors, while the decision
on the right number of phonemes is passed on to the linguistic decoder, where all the necessary pieces of information are available.

The linguistic decoder operates on a simple state space representation of the language, which includes optional phonological rules and
constraints on minimum and maximum duration of each phonetic state.
The main feature of the decoding algorithm is its being realtime oriented. In fact decoding proceeds along with acoustic analysis and
similarity measurements, with a best-few search strategy, and the decoder is also given the responsibility of deciding when the sentence
is terminated, making use of acoustic-phonetic as well as syntactic-
semantic information.

The method as a whole appears to be a robust one, requiring no
particular care in the way sentences are uttered. In fact additional
tests demonstrated that the system recognizes correctly utterances in
which the words are separated by short or long pauses (or no pause
at all, as usual), or in which the duration of a same repeated word
may differ by a very large ratio, say 5:1. In this respect the proposed method compares favourably with those based on complete word templates, which instead search for the string of "concatenated" templates
that best fit the input pattern and which perform time normalization
with the usual 2:1 limit in the duration ratio (cf. Sakoe, 1979; Myers
and Rabiner, 1981).

Maybe the proposed approach is more computation intensive than
those based on some form of phone or syllable segmentation, but, on
the other hand, it involves simpler and more ripetitive algorithms
and a simpler control strategy. The implication of the latter quality
is that the problems encountered in coordinating the various knowledge
sources (see for instance Goodman and Reddy, 1980) are much allevia-
ted, while the implication of the former one is that it makes the method more amenable to a custom hardware implementation. However, an
approximate evaluation of the computation power necessary even for lar
ge vocabularies (that should require only a few hundred diphones), indicates that this is well within the capability of present multiproces
sor hardware (Manara and Stringa 1981), especially if a spectral distance measure simpler than the log-likelihood ratio is adopted.

Many problems are still to be solved, like the automatic adaptation of the phonetic knowledge to a new speaker, or the use of a better similarity measure that took into account also the signal intensity and that, in general, better reflected perceptual evidence. However the results obtained with the preliminary implementation are rather encouraging and we believe that the proposed approach is sound
and promising.

AKNOWLEDGEMENT - We wish to thank A.M. Colla who derived the second
diphone dictionary and helped us with part of the experiments.

REFERENCES

Billi R., Oreglia, M., Pieraccini, R., Scagliola, C. and Vicenzi C. (1982). Performance analysis of speaker-trained isolated word recognition systems. Proc. Int. Zürich Seminar on Dig. Comm., Zurich

Cole, R.A. and Jakimik J. (1980). A model of speech perception, in Perception and Production of Fluent Speech (Ed. R.A. Cole) pp 133-164, Lawrence Erlbaum Associates, Hillsdale.

Davis, S.B. and Mermelstein, P. (1980). Comparison of parametric re presentations for monosyllabic word recognition in continuously spo ken sentences IEEE Trans. on ASSP, ASSP-28,pp 357-366.

Fu, K.S. (1974). Syntactic Methods in Pattern Recognition. Academic Press, New York.

Goodman, G. and Reddy, R. (1980). Alternative control structures for speech understanding systems, in Trends in Speech Recognition (Ed. W.A. Lea), pp 234-246, Prentice-Hall, Englewood Cliffs.

Hunt, M.J. Lennig, M. and Mermelstein, P. (1980). Experiments in syl lable-based recognition of continuous speech. Proc. Int. Conf. ASSP, Denver.

Itakura, F. (1975). Minimum prediction residual principle applied to speech recognition. IEEE Trans. on ASSP, ASSP-23, pp 67-72.

Klatt, D.H. (1980 a). SCRIBER and LAFS: two new approaches to speech analysis, in Trends in Speech Recognition (Ed. W.A. Lea), pp 529-555, Prentice-Hall, Englewood Cliffs.

Klatt, D.H. (1980b). Speech perception: a model of acoustic-phonetic and lexical access, in Perception and Production of Fluent Speech (Ed. R.A. Cole), pp. 243-288, Lawrence Erlbaum Associates, Hillsdale.

Knipper, A. (1981). Acoustic events in CV syllables with liquid and nasal sounds. Signal Processing, 3, pp 389-396.

Lowerre B. and Reddy, R. (1980). The HARPY speech understanding systems, in Trends in Speech Recognition (Ed. W.A. Lea), pp. 340-360, Prentice-Hall. Englewood Cliffs.

Makhoul, J. (1975). Linear prediction: a tutorial rewiew. Proc. of the IEEE, 63, pp 561-580.

Manara, R. and Stringa, L. (1981). The EMMA system: an industrial experience on a multiprocessor, in Languages and Architectures for Image Processing (Eds. M.J.B. Duff and S. Levialdi), pp 215-227, Academic Press, London.

Myers, C.S. and Rabiner, L.R. (1981). A level building dynamic time warping algorithm for connected word recognition. IEEE Trans. on ASSP, ASSP-29, pp 284-297.

Newell, A. (1980). Harpy, production systems and human cognition, in Perception and Production of Fluent Speech (Ed. R.A. Cole), pp. 289-380, Lawrence Erlbaum Associates, Hillsdale.

Nilsson, N. (1971). Problem-Solving Methods in Artificial Intelligence (Chapt. 3), McGraw-Hill, New York.

Paul, J.E. and Rabinowitz, A.S. (1975). An acoustically based continuous speech recognition system. Proc. IEEE Symp. on Speech Recognition, Carnegie-Mellon University, Pittsburgh.

Ruske, G. and Schotola, T. (1981). The efficiency of demisyllable segmentation in the recognition of spoken words. Proc. Int. Conf. ASSP, Atlanta.

Sakoe, H. (1979). Two level DP-matching, a dynamic programming-based pattern matching algorithm for connected word recognition, IEEE Trans. on ASSP, ASSP-27, pp 588-595.

Scagliola, C. (1981). The use of diphones as basic units in speech recognition. Proc. 4th FASE Symp. on Acoustic and Speech, Venice.

Schwartz, R. and Makhoul, J. (1975). Where the phonemes are: dealing with ambiguity in acoustic-phonetic recognition. IEEE Trans. on ASSP, ASSP-23, pp 50-53.

Vicenzi, C. and Scagliola, C. (1982). Multiprocessor architecture for real-time speech recognition system. Proc. Int. Conf. ASSP, Paris.

Vivalda, E. Sandri, S., Miotti, C. and Scagliola, C. (1979). Unlimited vocabulary voice response system for Italian. Proc. Int. Conf. Comm. Boston.

Image Recognition

RECENT TRENDS IN IMAGE ANALYSIS

Azriel Rosenfeld

Computer Vision Laboratory, Computer Science
Center, University of Maryland, College Park, MD   20742

ABSTRACT

This paper surveys recent trends in image analysis techniques, with
emphasis on the types of models on which these techniques are based.
Some researchers are developing approaches based on models for human
visual performance, while many others are using models for the data
being analyzed. The latter class of models have become increasingly
global and increasingly structured, and are also beginning to handle
higher-dimensional types of data. References are given to recent
work that illustrates these trends.

1. INTRODUCTION

The field of image analysis, one of the largest branches of
pattern recognition, is over 25 years old. It has numerous practical applications in areas such as document processing (character
recognition), medicine, industrial automation, reconnaissance and
remote sensing, to name only the largest branches. In addition to
these applications, there is extensive ongoing work on the theoretical foundations of the subject and on the development of new techniques. General-purpose image analysis or "computer vision" systems
are also a major goal of artificial intelligence research.

This paper surveys recent trends in image analysis techniques,
with emphasis on the types of models on which these techniques are
based. Some researchers are developing approaches based on models
for human visual performance, while many others are using models

The support of the National Science Foundation under Grant MCS-79-
23422 is gratefully acknowledged, as is the help of Janet Salzman
in preparing this paper. A different version of this paper was presented at the Golden Jubilee Celebration International Conference on
Information Science and Technology, Indian Statistical Institute,
Calcutta, India in January 1982.

for the data being analyzed. The latter class of models have become increasingly global and increasingly structured, and are also beginning to handle higher–dimensional types of data. References are given to recent work that illustrates these trends.

2. MODELS FOR THE PERCEIVER

In recent years, there has been considerable development in our understanding of how to design image analysis techniques, whether for general purposes or for specific applications. Today's techniques are quite likely to be model-based, rather than heuristic. In this connection, we can distinguish between two classes of models: models for the perceiver of the data, and models for the data that are to be perceived.

Researchers in artificial intelligence are interested in developing general-purpose computer vision systems. One criterion for the success of such a system is that it be able to emulate human visual performance on a variety of tasks. Thus many of these researchers are concerned with computer models of human vision - in other words, with models of the perceiver. They share this concern with perception psychologists, many of whom have begun to make use of computational models.

Excellent examples of computer vision research motivated by the desire to model human vision are provided by the work of the late David Marr and his colleagues and students (Marr, 1976, 1978, 1979, 1980). This work includes studies of edge detection (Marr and Hildreth, 1980), stereopsis (Marr and Poggio, 1979), and motion perception (Ullman, 1979). There is an increasing degree of communication and collaboration between perception psychologists and computer vision specialists (Beck and Rosenfeld, in press), and this can be expected to result in benefits to both fields.

3. MODELS FOR THE DATA

Image analysis techniques should always be based, at least implicitly, on models for the data to be analyzed - e.g., models for (particular types of) reflectivity characteristics, textures, shapes, etc. Computer vision systems designed for a specific pattern recognition task can employ highly specific models, while those intended to be general-purpose should make use of models that are as general as possible. A wide variety of models have been proposed for the statistical characterization of images (Rosenfeld, 1981). On the importance of using models in image analysis see (Rosenfeld and Davis, 1979).

Several general trends can be observed as regards the types of models that are currently being used or proposed. There is a tendency to use models that are more global in nature, i.e., that characterize larger pieces of the data - regions rather than pixels, or large neighborhoods rather than smaller ones. At the same time, models are becoming more structured; they are making greater use of context or convergent evidence, of hierarchical representations, and of structured inference schemes. Even more important, there is increased interest in models that represent the underlying three-dimensional scenes, rather than merely the two-dimensional images obtained from these scenes, as well as in models for higher-dimensional data (three spatial dimensions, time-varying data, or both). These trends will be briefly discussed in the following sections.

4. GLOBALNESS

The traditional approach to image analysis often begins at the pixel level, treating the image as a mixture of pixel populations and segmenting it by pixel classification. A more global approach regards the image as composed of homogeneous regions, and segments it by constructing a partition into such regions, e.g., by region growing, merging, or splitting. An extensive treatment of region-based methods of image analysis can be found in the book by Pavlidis (1977). An analogous development in texture analysis (Maleson et al., 1977) regards textures as composed of homogeneous microregions, and characterizes them in terms of statistical properties of these regions.

When an image is regarded as composed of homogeneous regions, the most common assumption is that these regions are each statistically stationary, so that the image can be approximated by a step function that is constant on each region. Haralick (1979, 1981) has developed a more general "facet model" based on piecewise linear (or higher-order), rather than piecewise constant, approximation, and has shown that this model yields improved results in many situations.

Higher-order facet models relate the value of each pixel to the values of a relatively large set of its neighbors. Even if one does not use such models, one can still make use of large neighborhoods in analyzing an image. There has been considerable interest in "pyramid" image representations using successively reduced resolutions, so that local operations at high levels of the pyramid correspond to large-scale operations on the original image; see (Rosenfeld, 1980) for a review of this work. A more interesting possibility is to permit interactions bewteen levels of the pyramid; this allows the higher-resolution information at low levels, and the less noisy information at high levels, both to contribute to the results.

5. STRUCTURE

The classical pattern recognition paradigm was that of statistical classification, but it was long realized that this paradigm was not adequate for the analysis of structured data. One approach to structural pattern recognition is the syntactic paradigm, which has been extensively developed by Fu and his students. A recent treatment of this approach can be found in (Fu, 1981); see also Pavlidis' overview in (Pavlidis, 1979).

There has been an increased use of structural approaches at many levels of the image analysis process. In segmentation or classification at the pixel level, more use is being made of context in the classification decisions. For a recent review of compound decision techniques see Fu and Yu (1980). "Relaxation" techniques, in which classification probabilities (or degrees of class membership) are iteratively adjusted, provide an alternative approach, which is reviewed in (Rosenfeld and Davis, 1981). For some recent work on the foundations of relaxation processes, including approaches based on Bayesian inference and on optimization, see (Peleg, 1980; Hummel and Zucker, 1980; Faugeras and Berthod, 1981). Relaxation processes are also being used in image matching and in relational structure matching (Ranade and Rosenfeld, 1980; Kitchen, 1980; Faugeras and Price, 1981). Another type of contextual support is used in segmentation schemes based on convergent evidence (Nakagawa and Rosenfeld, 1978; Milgram, 1979; Milgram et al., 1979; Danker and Rosenfeld, 1981).

Another important trend is toward the use of structured decision processes (decision trees, inference nets, etc.) in image analysis. Two recent approaches based on production systems are described in (Ohta et al., 1979; Nagao and Matsuyama, 1980). This approach is expected to become increasingly important in the development of "expert systems" for analyzing images.

6. DIMENSIONALITY

A final group of trends in modeling relates to the dimensionality of the data being modelled. There has been a rapid growth of interest in the analysis of real-time image sequences, which can be regarded as three-dimensional data in which two of the dimensions are spatial and one is temporal; for a review of research in this area see (Nagel, 1978), and for two recent collections of papers see (Badler and Aggarwal, 1979; Aggarwal and Badler, 1980). Research is also being done on the extension of image analysis techniques to three-dimensional spatial data arrays, as might be obtained, e.g., by "stacking" slices of a specimen or by tomographic reconstruction; see (Liu, 1977; Zucker and Hummel, 1981; Morgenthaler and Rosenfeld, 1981) on 3D "edge detection" (i.e., surface detection), (Artzy et al., 1981) on surface following, and (Lobregt et al., 1980; Tsao and Fu, 1981) on thinning. There is considerable interest in analyzing two-dimensional arrays that contain three-dimensional information about a scene in the form of range data; for some examples see (Oshima and Shirai, 1979; Duda et al., 1979; Sugihara, 1979; Milgram and Bjorklund, 1980).

Another very important problem is that of extracting scene information (including illumination, reflectivity, surface slant, and range) from one or more intensity images. This subject, which has received considerable recent attention (Barrow and Tenenbaum, 1978, 1981; Tenenbaum et al., 1981; Brady, 1981), is also closely related to the modeling of human vision.

7. CONCLUDING REMARKS

Image analysis has matured considerably over the past decade. Many techniques originally introduced on heuristic grounds are now much better understood, and there is increasing use of methods derived on the basis of models. Approaches to image analysis are becoming more global and more structured, and are being applied to higher-dimensional data. As the subject enters its second quarter-century, it is developing firmer scientific foundations, and is providing a growing repertoire of increasingly powerful techniques for a widening range of applications.

REFERENCES

Aggarwal, J. K., and Badler, N. I., 1980. Special issue on motion and time-varying imagery. IEEE Trans. Pattern Analysis Machine Intelligence 2, 493-588.

Artzy, E., Frieder, G., and Herman, G. T., 1981. The theory, design, implementation and evaluation of a three-dimensional surface detection algorithm. Computer Graphics Image Processing 15, 1-24.

Badler, N. I., and Aggarwal, J. K., 1979. Abstracts of the workshop on computer analysis of time-varying imagery.

Barrow, H. G., and Tenenbaum, J. M., 1978. Recovering intrinsic scene characteristics from images, in Computer Vision Systems (Eds. Hanson and Riseman), pp. 3-26. Academic Press, NY.

Barrow, H. G., and Tenenbaum, J. M., 1981. Computational vision. Proc. IEEE 69, 1981, 572-595.

Beck, J., and Rosenfeld, A., eds., in press. Human and Machine Vision. Academic Press, NY.

Brady, M., guest ed., 1981. Special Volume on Computer Vision. Artificial Intelligence 17, 1-508.

Danker, A., and Rosenfeld, A., 1981. Blob extraction using relaxation. IEEE Trans. Pattern Analysis Machine Intelligence 3, 79-92.

Duda, R. O., Nitzan, D., and Barrett, P., 1979. Use of range and reflectance data to find planar surface regions. IEEE Trans. Pattern Analysis Machine Intelligence 1, 259-271.

Faugeras, O. D., and Berthod, M., 1981. Improving consistency and reducing ambiguity in stochastic labeling: an optimization approach. IEEE Trans. Pattern Analysis Machine Intelligence 3, 412-424.

Faugeras, O. D., and Price, K. E., 1981. Semantic description of aerial images using stochastic labeling. IEEE Trans. Pattern Analysis Machine Intelligence 3, 633-642.

Fu, K. S., 1981. Syntactic Pattern Recognition and Applications. Wiley, NY.

Fu, K. S., and Yu, T. S., 1980. Statistical Pattern Classification Using Contextual Information. Wiley, NY.

Haralick, R. M., 1980. Edge and region analysis for digital image data. Computer Graphics Image Processing 12, 60-73.

Haralick, R. M., and Watson, L., 1981. A facet model for image data. Computer Graphics Image Processing 15, 113-129.

Hummel, R. A., and Zucker, S. W., 1980. On the foundations of relaxation labeling processes. Proc. 5th Intl. Joint Conf. on Pattern Recognition, 50-53.

Hwang, J. J., Lee, C. C., and Hall, E. L., 1979. Segmentation of solid objects using global and local edge coincidence. Proc. Conf. on Pattern Recognition and Image Processing, 114-121.

Kitchen, L., 1980. Relaxation applied to matching quantitative relational structures. IEEE Trans. Systems, Man, Cybernetics 20, 96-101.

Liu, H. K., 1977. Two- and three-dimensional boundary detection. Computer Graphics Image Processing 6, 123-124.

Lobregt, S., Verbeek, P. W., and Groen, F. C. A., 1980. Three-dimensional skeletonization: principle and algorithm. IEEE Trans. Pattern Analysis Machine Intelligence 2, 75-77.

Maleson, J. T., Brown, C. M., and Feldman, J. A., 1977. Understanding natural texture. Proc. DARPA Image Understanding Workshop, 19-27.

Marr, D., 1976. Early processing of visual information. Philos. Trans. Royal Soc. London B 275, 483-524.

Marr, D., 1978. Representing visual information - a computational approach, in Computer Vision Systems (Eds. Hanson and Riseman), pp. 61-81. Academic Press, NY.

Marr, D., 1979. Representing and computing visual information, in Artificial Intelligence: An MIT Perspective (Ed. Winston), pp. 15-80. MIT Press, Cambridge, MA.

Marr, D., 1980. Visual information processing: the structure and creation of visual representations. Philos. Trans. Royal Soc. London B 290, 199-218.

Marr, D., and Hildreth, E., 1980. Theory of edge detection. Proc. Royal Soc. London B 207, 187-217.

Marr, D., and Poggio, T., 1979. A computational theory of human stereo vision. Proc. Royal Soc. London B 204, 301-328.

Milgram, D. L., 1979. Region extraction using convergent evidence. Computer Graphics Image Processing 11, 1-12.

Milgram, D. L., and Bjorklund, C. M., 1980. Range image processing: planar surface extraction. Proc. 5th Intl. Joint Conf. on Pattern Recognition, 912-919.

Morgenthaler, D. L., and Rosenfeld, A., 1981. Multidimensional edge detection by hypersurface fitting. IEEE Trans. Pattern Analysis Machine Intelligence 3, 482-486.

Nagao, M., and Matsuyama, T., 1980. A Structural Analysis of Complex Aerial Photographs. Plenum, NY.

Nagel, H. H., 1978. Analysis techniques for image sequences. Proc. 4th Intl. Joint Conf. on Pattern Recognition, 186-211.

Nakagawa, Y., and Rosenfeld, A., 1978. Edge/border coincidence as an aid in edge extraction. IEEE Trans. Systems, Man, Cybernetics 8, 899-901.

Ohta, Y. I., Kanade, T., and Sakai, T., 1979. A production system for region analysis. Proc. 6th Intl. Joint Conf. on Artificial Intelligence, 684-686.

Oshima, M., and Shirai, Y., 1979. A scene description method using three-dimensional information. Pattern Recognition 11, 9-17.

Pavlidis, T., 1977. Structural Pattern Recognition. Springer, NY.

Pavlidis, T., 1979. Hierarchies in structural pattern recognition. Proc. IEEE 67, 737-744.

Peleg, S., 1980. A new probabilistic relaxation scheme. IEEE Trans. Pattern Analysis Machine Intelligence 2, 362-369.

Ranade, S., and Rosenfeld, A., 1980. Point pattern matching by relaxation. Pattern Recognition 12, 268-275.

Rosenfeld, A., 1980. Quadtrees and pyramids for pattern recognition and image processing. Proc. 5th Intl. Conf. on Pattern Recognition, 802-811.

Rosenfeld, A., ed., 1981. Image Modeling. Academic Press, NY.

Rosenfeld, A., and Davis, L. S., 1979. Image segmentation and image models. Proc. IEEE 67, 764-772.

Rosenfeld, A., and Davis, L. S., 1981. Cooperating processes for low-level vision: a survey. Artificial Intelligence 17, 245-263.

Sugihara, K., 1979. Range data analysis guided by a junction dictionary. Artificial Intelligence 12, 41-69.

Tenenbaum, J. M., Fischler, M. A., and Barrow, H. G., 1981. Scene modeling: a structural basis for image description, in Image Modeling (Ed. Rosenfeld), pp. 371-389. Academic Press, NY.

Tsao, Y. F., and Fu, K. S., 1981. A parallel thinning algorithm for 3D pictures. Computer Graphics Image Processing 17, 315-331.

Ullman, S., 1979. The Interpretation of Visual Motion. MIT Press, Cambridge, MA.

Zucker, S. W., and Hummel, R. A., 1981. A three-dimensional edge operator. IEEE Trans. Pattern Analysis Machine Intelligence 3, 324-331.

A NOTE ON THE ESTIMATION OF A-PRIORI PROBABILITIES IN PATTERN RECOGNITION

Silvano Di Zenzo

IBM Scientific Center, Rome, Italy

ABSTRACT

Pattern classification of collections of individual objects exhibits peculiar aspects. It should be context dependent even when there is no stochastic dependence among the members of the collection. If these are to be classified into, say, m classes $C(1),..,C(m)$, the first step must be the estimation of the fractions $p(1),..,p(m)$ of individuals in each class. One should manage to get estimates of the most probable value of the compound random variable $(p(1),..,p(m))$. A LS method is proposed. The estimates of the $p(i)$'s are to be entered as a-priori probabilities in the individual classifications. As an individual may be classified differently if considered alone or as a member of a collection, one has apparent paradoxes (which would find their rather obvious explanation in a more lengthy analytical treatment).

INTRODUCTORY REMARK

There is increasing interest in context-dependent classification of collections, probably as a by-product of multispectral image classification problems. There is, of course, an abundance of previous research to list just a few.

The role of a-priori probabilities in this connection seems to have been somewhat underestimated, and only few papers can be quoted (ref. 1, 2, 3). Besides being a prerequisite for correct classification of individual objects, the estimation of the a-priori probabilities is sometimes the main task of classification. E. g. in crop inventory with Landsat data they represent areal proportions; the same applies, e. g., in stars vs. galaxies discrimination.

A MATHEMATICAL FORMULATION OF THE RECOGNITION PROBLEM

A *recognizer* T can be modeled as a set of sensing devices $T_1, .., T_n$ together with a capability of processing sensed data. Each T_i can measure a certain magnitude X_i. $X_1, .., X_n$ will be called *test variables*. By no means are the test variables confined to be physical magnitudes; for example, they could be questions in a questionnaire.

By an *observation* of an object S made by T it is meant the measurement of the values that $X_1, .., X_n$ take at S.

It is intended that S is a value-bearing individual for the compound variable $X=(X_1, .., X_n)$. In other words, $X_1, .., X_n$ are some of the variables which characterize the state of S as a *system*. As a system, S will be a value-bearing individual for other magnitudes Y, Z, .. not directly observable by T. If X were a complete state variable for S, then Y, Z, .. would depend functionally on X. In the general case X is not complete, and only a stochastic dependance can be assumed between Y, Z, .. and X (as a limit case, there might be no dependence at all).

In any case one assumes that the measurement of $X_1, .., X_n$ conveys some information about the values actually taken by Y, Z, .. at S. That leads to the problem of getting estimates of Y, Z, .. based on the observed values of $X_1, .., X_n$, which in turn leads to the problem of getting estimates of such conditional probabilities as

(1) $\qquad p(y \mid x) = p(Y=y \mid X=x)$

Here x and y are elements in the ranges R(X) and R(Y) of X and Y respectively. Without loss of generality let X take values in $\mathbb{R}^n$ so that x is an n-tuple $x=(x_1, .., x_n)$ of reals. The right-hand side of (1) is a short for the second: the notation is made non-ambiguos letting random variables be denoted by uppercase letters and their values by same lowercase letters with or without affixes.

If estimates of (1) could be obtained directly, the problem of estimating Y would be solved: given X=x' , a good estimate of Y would be that y which maximizes $p(y \mid x')$.

Estimates of (1) cannot be obtained directly.

Usually X can take a great number of technically distinguishable values: for each, a conditional probability density (1) should be estimated. On the other side, what is usually done to acquire knowledge about the dependence between X and Y is to measure X on a *training sample* of objects of known Y. To allow direct estimation of (1) the sample should be *large* for every possible pair of values of X and Y. In practical situations, only a limited number of sample objects is available.

Bayes theorem, and the fact that the inferred variable always takes few values, overcome the difficulty (in the applications the inferred variable is indeed a *class-index*, and the task is to classify objects into a set of possible classes C(1),..,C(m) :

(2) $p(i \mid x) = p(x \mid i)p(i)/\Sigma_{i'}p(x \mid i')p(i')$

Due to its nature of a class-index, the variable to be estimated will henceforth be denoted I. $R(I) = \{1,..,m\}$.

By (2) , the estimation of $p(i \mid x)$ is reduced to those of $p(x \mid i)$ and $p(i)$. These are less difficult. If, e.g., m=2, it is only necessary to obtain two estimates $f_1(x)$ and $f_2(x)$ of the objective densities $p(x \mid I=1)$ and $p(x \mid I=2)$: two training samples are needed, one made of objects almost surely belonging to C(1), and a similar one for C(2).

Probabilities $p(i) = p(I=i)$ will be given special attention in this article. The object of the article is indeed to derive a method for getting estimates for these probabilities. This shall be done in the next paragraph.

In the rest of this paragraph, how the actual classification is carried out in most cases will be briefly examined.

The *training of the recognizer* will provide (a) estimates $f_i(x)$ of the objective conditional probability densities $p(x \mid i)$, (b) estimates p_i of the objective probabilities $p(i)$.

When the training is completed, the actual classification can be carried out as follows: an object whose observed value of X is x is classified as belonging to class C(h) whenever, for i=1,..,m, i≠h, one has

(3) $p_i f_i(x) < p_h f_h(x).$

This classification rule follows from (2): for fixed x, p(i|x) is maximum when p(x|i)p(i) is maximum.

In the above formulation, *perception* fits a question-and-answer scheme in which the questions are built into the *sensors* of the recognizer. The recognizer T tests the object S by $T_1, .., T_n$, and receives information in the form of values of the test variables.

The object S is in general a complex object, made up of an assembly of subobjects S(k), k=1,..,N. A digital image is a typical example: it may be regarded as an assembly of picture elements.

There exists interdependence among the S(k), at least in general. More precisely, let $\xi(k)$ be a complete state variable for S(k), then some sort of stochastic dependence is to be expected among the $\xi(k)$. For example, there is stochastic dependence between the gray levels of two spatially near pixels in a picture.

A further aspect of the perception process is found in the fact that $T_1, .., T_n$ are often applied more than once to S, that is, T *scans* S.

As a consequence, that of classifying each S(k) separately is generally not a good strategy: the classification of each S(k) should be *context-dependent*, the *context* being the whole of S.

That is obvious when there is dependence among the S(k). That holds true also when there is *objective* independence among the S(k) (in the sense of the Theory of Probability) provided they are classified as members of a fixed set S. This less obvious result is a corollary of the treatment in the next paragraph.

A METHOD FOR THE ESTIMATION OF A-PRIORI PROBABILITIES

Let S={ S(1),..,S(N)} be a fixed set of value-bearing objects for both X and I. The observation of these objects by T has provided values x(1),..,x(N) for the compound test variable X, where x(k) is in turn an n-tuple $x(k)=(x_1(k), .., x_n(k))$.

It is assumed that the recognizer has already been trained, hence estimates $f_i(x)$ of the probabilities p(x|i) are available for each i. The task is that of classifying S as a whole, which includes the estimation of the fraction of its members belonging to each class C(i), i=1,..,m, and, after, a maximum-likelihood assignment of each

object S(k) to a particular class C(i) (in general, to classify
S as a whole will include more than that, the final goal being to
assign S, as an individual by itself, to one of another set of
possible categories @(1),..,@(M): this higher level step of the
classification process is outside the present scope).

 The key point is to interpret correctly the a-priori probabilities
$p(i)=p(I=i)$. For i=1,..,m, $p(i)$ represents the fraction of objects
of class C(i) within the fixed set S. It must be emphasized that
$p(i)$ has nothing to do with any abstract probability of encountering
an object of class C(i) outside S.

 In a pattern recognition context, $p(i)$ is to be treated as a random variable to be estimated: probability-theoretic arguments suggest
to get estimates of the most probable value, not of the expected
value. Based on the above interpretation, methods for the obtention
of such estimates can be derived rather simply.

 First, the usual iterative procedure for the estimation of proportions in mixtures of known density functions can be derived as
follows. For i=1,..,m, let p_i be an estimate of $p(i)$. Then

(4)
$$p_{ik} = \frac{f_i(x(k))p_i}{\sum_{h=1}^{m} f_h(x(k))p_h}$$

is an estimate of $p(i \mid x(k))$, that is, of the probability that S(k)
will belong to C(i). From the above interpretation of $p(i)$ one has

(5)
$$p_i = \frac{1}{N} \sum_{k=1}^{N} p_{ik}$$

Indeed, p_i has to be the average of the individual probabilities
of belonging to class C(i). From (4),(5) the iterative scheme
follows immediately. Usually that scheme is derived in a different
way: $\{x(1),..,x(N)\}$ is treated as an independent sample drawn from a
mixture, and the scheme follows from likelihood equations. These
have many solutions, and the scheme may converge to meaningless
limits (ref. 4) .

 It has been shown that the scheme is locally convergent, i.e.
converges for an initial estimate sufficiently near a maximum
likelihood estimate (ref. 1) . Refined iterative procedures have
been experimented (ref. 5) , (ref. 6) .

Difficulty to attain the global maximum by iterative schemes, and their increasing computational complexity, suggest to explore other methods of estimation.

Least squares will be explored in what follows.

Let A be the set of the distinct values of X observed at the objects in S.

A remark on the expected cardinality of A seems convenient. In practice, the X_i are either discrete in principle or quantized, so $R(X)$ is a finite set. Besides, most of the combinations of values for $X_1,..,X_n$ are usually unlikely to appear. For large samples, an order of 10^2 for the ratio between the cardinality of S and that of A is to be expected in most applications.

For every a$\in$A, let $N(a)$ be the number of the objects that gave the *answer* a to the *test* T.

For large $N(a)$, the difference between the two sides of the following *consistence equation*

(6) $\sum_{i=1}^{m} Nf_i(a)p_i = N(a)$

can be expected to be small. Indeed, for any given $\epsilon>0$, the probability that the absolute value of that difference will be less than ϵ approaches 1 for increasing $N(a)$.

There are as many equations (6) as there are elements in A. They form a linear system in the unknown $p_1,..,p_m$. LS estimates of these might be found based on that system, however better results are obtained on minimizing

(7) $\sum_{a\in A} N(a)\{N(a) - \sum_{i=1}^{m} Nf_i(a)p_i\}^2$

The results of the experimentation of the method shall be given in a moment.

It is easy to show that (6) are stronger than ML equations.

Indeed, as $R(X)$ is a discrete set, the linear system of consistency equations is equivalent to

(8) $\sum_{i=1}^{m} p_i f_i(x) = N(x)$

where, for every x$\in$R(X), $N(x)$ is the number of objects in S that gave the answer x to the test T. (8) is a system of as many equations as there are elements in $R(X)$. The likelihood function is

(9) $\qquad L = \sum_{k=1}^{N} \log \{ \sum_{i=1}^{m} p_i f_i(x(k)) \}$

An unconstrained maximum problem over the p_i's is obtained on substituting $1 - \sum_{i=1}^{m-1} p_i$ for p_m.

The likelihood equations are

(10) $\qquad \dfrac{\partial L}{\partial p_i} = \sum_{k=1}^{N} \dfrac{f_i(x(k)) - f_m(x(k))}{f_m(x(k)) + \sum_{j=1}^{m-1} p_j (f_j(x(k)) - f_m(x(k)))} = 0$

where $i = 1, .., m-1$. These can be rewritten

(11) $\qquad \dfrac{\partial L}{\partial p_i} = \sum_{x \in R(X)} \dfrac{N(x)(f_i(x) - f_m(x))}{f_m(x) + \sum_{j=1}^{m-1} p_j (f_j(x) - f_m(x))} = 0$

Now assume that (8) hold. Then

(12) $\qquad \dfrac{\partial L}{\partial p_i} = \sum_{x \in R(X)} (f_i(x) - f_m(x)) N = N - N = 0$

Hence also (11) hold.

Under the constraints $p_i \geq 0$, (7) is a quadratic programming problem which can be solved by relaxation and projection.

SIMULATION RESULTS

Simulation has been carried out for $n=1$ (only one test variable), $m=2$ (only two classes $C(1)$ and $C(2)$), $N=100\,000$ (samples of $100\,000$ individual objects $S(1)$, $S(2),..,S(100\,000)$). The range $R(X) = \{1, 2, .. , 10\}$ has been assumed for the test variable X. The probability distributions $p(x|1)$ and $p(x|2)$ of the test variable for the two populations have been taken as follows:

$p(x|1)$	$\frac{1}{30}$	$\frac{2}{30}$	$\frac{3}{30}$	$\frac{4}{30}$	$\frac{5}{30}$	$\frac{5}{30}$	$\frac{4}{30}$	$\frac{3}{30}$	$\frac{2}{30}$	$\frac{1}{30}$
$p(x|2)$	$\frac{1}{30}$	$\frac{1}{30}$	$\frac{2}{30}$	$\frac{2}{30}$	$\frac{3}{30}$	$\frac{3}{30}$	$\frac{3}{30}$	$\frac{6}{30}$	$\frac{5}{30}$	$\frac{4}{30}$
x	1	2	3	4	5	6	7	8	9	10

This is a case of very bad separation. Notice that the two densities have the same support (i. e. are non-zero in the same points). The simulation experiment consists in drawing $p_1 N$ samples from the first distribution and $p_2N = (1-p_1)N$ from the second, and, after, in estimating p_1 and p_2. As a result of the experimentation done up to now, values of p_1, p_2 in the range $(0.05, 0.95)$ are estimated with an expected error of 0.015.

REFERENCES

(1) Peters, B. C., and Coberly, W. H., 1975. The numerical evaluation of ML estimate of mixture proportions. Univ. Houston, Dept. Math. Report 43, NAS-9-12777.

(2) Di Zenzo S., 1980. Pattern Recognition Problems in the Classification of Multi-images. In *Map Data Processing* (Ed. Freeman, H.), pp 247-264. Academic Press, New York.

(3) Strahler, A. H., 1980. The Use of Prior Probabilities in ML Classification of Remotely Sensed Data. *Remote Sensing* 10, 135-163.

(4) Duda, R. O., and Hart, P. E., 1973. Pattern Classification and Scene Analysis. Wiley, New York.

(5) Peters, B. C.,and Walker, H. F., 1975. An Iterative Procedure for ML Estimates of the Parameters for a Mixture of Normal Densities. Univ. Houston, Dept. Math., Report 43, NAS-9-12777.

(6) Walker, H. F., 1976. Evaluation of ML Estimates of the Parameters for a Mixture of Normal Distributions from Partially Identified Samples. Univ. Houston, Dept. Math., Report 54, NAS-9-15000.

3-D PATTERN RECOGNITION TECHNIQUES

G.Garibotto - R.Tosini

CSELT - Centro Studi e Laboratori Telecomunicazioni S.p.A.
Via G.Reiss Romoli, 274 - 10148 TORINO (Italy)

ABSTRACT

The problem of 3-D object description is considered with reference to an application of computer-assisted neurosurgery. In order to achieve a satisfactory description of the spatial evolution of the sample object a method for obtaining 3-D skeletons, using a quasi-euclidean distance, is described. Examples of 3-D reconstruction are used to compare some different feature selection strategies.

3-D OBJECT REPRESENTATION

Recognition and classification of three-dimensional objects is a fundamental problem in artificial vision and in most biomedical and industrial applications of Tomography. In the following this problem in considered. With reference to an application of computer-assisted stereotactic neurosurgery (Garibotto et alii, 1981). Starting from a set of photographs of suitably prepared and stained brain slices (Schaltenbrand, Wahren, 1977), some cerebral structures, primarily involved in functional neurosurgery, have been reconstructed in the 3-D space. Unfortunately these 3-D prototypes can be used just as a reference guide to the surgeon, during his intervention, since significant variability in size and shape has been proved among different human brains. Moreover the functional properties of these cerebral structures have not been fully investigated so far.

Hence an improvement in the neurosurgical practice depends on the possibility to adapt the 3-D atlas prototypes to the actual measurements (such as in high resolution tomography).

An efficient coding of this 3-D information is necessary to achieve strong data compression without loosing the most significant features of the object.

Local informations on the existence of branches, their relative distance and extension, is particularly important when the objects are to be classified against a set of stored prototypes.

This problem can be solved by using a suitable transformation from the 3-D reference space to a feature space, to perform a symbolic description of the object. This operation has to satisfy some contraints:

a) the transformation has to be invertible in order to guarantee a reliable correspondence between the symbolic representation of the object and the original data

b) this description has to be invariant to rotations, so that the recognition task comes to be independent with respect to the object position in the reference system;

c) invariance to scale factors is also requested, for normalization purposes.

Recently this problem has been addressed by using a generalized cylinder description (Marr, 1980). In the paper we propose a new representation technique which is based on a 3-D skeleton of the sample object, according to a quasi-euclidean distance.

3-D SKELETON

Following a generalization of the medial axis transformation [3] the skeleton of a 3-D object is defined as the locus of points, inside the object, having minimum distance from at least two elements on the external surface.

If the skeleton elements are expanded into spheres with a radius equal to this distance, the original object can always be recovered without distortion.

Computation of the minimum distance. In the digital case the first step, towards the evaluation of the skeleton points, is the computation of the minimum distance from the outer surface for each sample of the 3-D binary object. A new volume of data is obtained in which the samples of the object are replaced by their distance from the surface. Due to the large amount of computation involved, this distance estimation is usually performed in a local neighbourhood of the actual sample point, with an approximation to the Euclidean distance.

Many different solutions have been proposed in the 2-D case (Blum, 1967) (Montanari, 1968). In the paper the analysis is carried out within a cube of 3x3x3 elements centered on the current sample, and the approximated unitary distances along axes and diagonals are chosen (3, 4, 5) as depicted in Fig. 1.

In this case the approximation error with respect to the Euclidean distance is always below 6% . For the examples of section 5 the maximum absolute error ϵ_{max} of reconstruction is $|\epsilon_{max}| < 2$ volume elements, which is quite satisfactory for our purposes.

These approximated unitary distances are added to the estimates of the adjacent samples and the minimum of these values is selected as the minimum distance of the current sample from the surface of the object. This minimum distance is called the energy E of the current sample P and it represents the radius of the sphere, centered on P, which is internally tangent to the external surface of the object. This operation is performed recursively on the previously computed distances both in the forward and backward direction, in order to achieve zero phase. Because of the sequential scanning of the input volume of data the past computed samples are included into the local neighbourhood depicted in Fig. 2.

Evaluation of the skeleton elements.   A criterion of dominance between the volume elements has to be defined in order to isolate the skeleton samples.

Definition: A sample point P is covered by another point Q, PcQ, if their distance (in the chosen metric) is less than the difference of the associated minimum distances, Ep, Eq respectively, i.e.:

$$d\,(P, Q) \leqslant Eq - Ep \qquad \text{and} \qquad Ep < Eq \qquad (1)$$

According to this definition the point P is irrelevant in the reconstruction of the original object.

Definition: The skeleton elements are selected as the sample points which are not completely covered by any other point in the volume. The transitivity property of this operation allows us to carry out the analysis just in a (3x3x3) neighbourhood of the current sample. Unfortunately that stringent condition of dominance introduces some redundancy which can be significantly reduced with a more selective choice.

FEATURE SELECTION

The list of skeleton elements which satisfy the previous criterion is still too large for pattern recognition purposes. In the example of Fig. 3 the original object was made of $\approx$ 61 000 points and the associated skeleton has 7 000 elements approximately. A strong reduction is obtained by keeping only those elements which are responsible for significant variations in the reconstruction. This operation is performed according to some different strategies which are briefly summarized in the following.

In any case it is necessary to establish a distortion measure in order to correctly evaluate the performance of each technique. The proposed error measure ϵ is the sum of the discarded elements of the skeleton, weighted by their energy (minimum distance from the surface of the object)

$$\epsilon = \sum_{i \,\epsilon\, S_d} E_i \qquad (2)$$

S_d being the set of N_d discarded elements and E_i the associated energy.

Threshold selection. In this case the dominance test is performed with different thresholds so that the relation 1) comes to

$$d\,(P, Q) - (E_q - E_p) \leqslant T \qquad \text{for} \qquad E_q > E_p \qquad (3)$$

and the threshold value T depends on the direction in the 3-D space. Since this analysis is carried out in a local neighbourhood of the sample, three values are selected, $T = (T_1, T_2, T_3)$, according to the local direction of the main axes and diagonals, as in Fig. 1. Fig. 3 shows the perspective views of the reconstructed objects with different thresholds. By using $T = (0, 0, 0)$ the original object is correctly recovered and the corresponding skeleton is comprised of $\approx 7\,000$ elements. With a choice $T = (1, 1, 1)$ approximately 1600 elements of the skeleton are selected (Fig. 3c), the reconstruction error is $\epsilon = 5\,468$ and the number n_d discarded elements in the subset S_d of 2) is $N_d = 1\,754$. Thresholds $T = (2, 2, 2)$ determine significant distortions in the reconstruction (Fig. 3b and Table 1) but the major characteristics of the object are still preserved.

In this case only the elements which have local maximum energy are retained so that the reconstruction is smoother than the original and sharp edges are definitely lost.

Energy analysis (minimum gradient). It is possible to take advantage of additional constraints in the selection of the skeleton elements.

In fact the energy associated with each skeleton point (value of the minimum radius) decreases from the local maxima up to the surface of the object. If the slope (energy gradient) is constant, the associated sphere will be tangent to the surface in that direction. Otherwise an additional point has to be inserted to cover the missing volume elements outside that sphere. This situation is shown in Fig. 4.

Fig. 3d) shows an example of reconstruction, according to this selection criterion. This solution seems a reasonable compromise between accuracy in the reconstruction and significant reduction of elements in the description of the object.

Iterative selection of sample points. In this case the skeleton elements are selected in different steps. At first just the local maxima are retained, and the volume elements, inside the spheres associated to these points, are deleted. A new set of local maxima is then selected with the additional constraint for their local neighbourhood to be fulfilled by at least 50% of the samples. Otherwise they give no contribution to the object description.

In this case a strong reduction of data is achieved (Table 1), without losing the most relevant features of the object.

With reference to the previous example a result quite similar to that of Fig. 3 a) has been obtained just keeping 113 skeleton elements.

CONCLUSIONS

In the paper we progress a 3-D object representation in terms of its skeleton elements. In order to minimize the influence of small perturbances on the surface of the object some different selection criteria have been considered. A further step towards the development of efficient 3-D pattern recognition techniques is a tree-like representation of the skeleton elements. This operation can be accomplished by using a cluster analysis according to some reference structures (cylinders, ellipsoides, spheres) which are then connected together.

The preliminary results presented here are referred to an application of computer assisted neurosurgery. The final goal of this research will be a 3-D matching between the atlas prototypes and the current noisy tomographic estimates in order to take advantage of the accurate 3-D atlas information in the neurosurgical practice.

SELECTION TECHNIQUE	ERROR ϵ	N_d DISCARDED ELEMENTS	SKELETON SAMPLES
A) Thresholds			
T = (0, 0, 0)	0	0	7000
T = (1, 1, 1)	5 468	1754	1893
T = (2, 2, 2)	52 341	11388	202
B) Minimum gradient	10 224	3174	793
C) Iterative selection	56 884	12387	113

Table 1 -A comparison between different techniques for the selection of 3-D skeleton elements. ϵ is the reconstruction error and N_d is the number of discarded elements with respect to the original object.

REFERENCES

G.Garibotto, S.Garozzo, C.Giorgi, G.Micca, G.Piretta.   Three-Dimensional Digital Signal Processing in Neurosurgical Applications. Proceed. of the Int. Conf. on Digital Signal Proc., pp. 434 444, Firenze, 1981.

G.Schaltenbrand, W.Wahren. Atlas for Stereotaxy of the Human Brain. 1977 Georg. Thienne Publish., Stuttgart.

D. Marr. Representing and Computing Visual Information. Artificial Intelligence, vol. 2, pp. 17-80, 1980, MIT Press.

H. Blum. A transformation for extracting new descriptions of shape. Model for the Perception of Speech and Visual Form., pp. 362-380 (MIT Press, Cambridge, Mass. 1967).

U. Montanari. A method for obtaining skeletons using a quasi-euclidean distance. Journal of ACM 15, pp. 279-290 (1968).

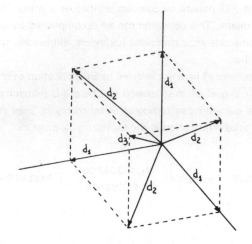

Fig. 1 - Selection of unitary distances D = (d₁, d₂, d₃) = (3, 4, 5)

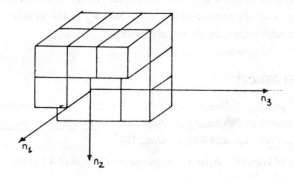

Fig. 2 - 3-D mask for the recursive estimation

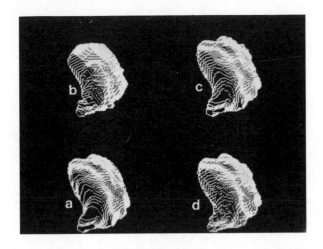

Fig. 3 - 3-D reconstruction of cerebral structure (thalamus) from the skeleton elements: a) original; b) threshold T = (2, 2, 2); c) T = (1, 1, 1); d) minimum gradient

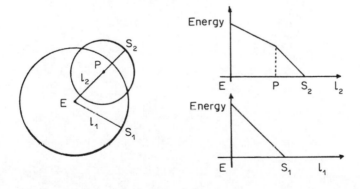

Fig. 4 - Example of the minimum-gradient selection criterion: a) ideal object comprised of two circles; b) energy distribution along the direction l_1 and l_2

A DIGITAL PROCESSING TECHNIQUE FOR RECOGNITION OF MOVING OBJECTS

P. Borghesi, V. Cappellini and A. Del Bimbo

Istituto di Elettronica, University of Florence and IROE-CNR, Florence, Italy

ABSTRACT

The digital processing of a sequence of image frames is presented for the detection and classification of moving objects. A tracking algorithm is also described. No a priori knowledge is assumed about size, shape, texture and stationary or non-stationary components of analyzed images. The classification method is essentially based on edge detection and Fourier transform evaluation of the object boundary. Some experimental results are presented.

INTRODUCTION

Systematic displacements of some image components from frame to frame can be taken as a strong hint to look for moving object detection. Object silhouettes from a sequence of frames can be extracted without any detailed a priori knowledge about size, shape and texture of the stationary part of the scene.

There have been several studies which deal with moving pictures, e.g. measuring gray level differences between consecutive frames and separating non stationary from stationary components (Potter, 1975), or finding and tracking prominent gray level features from the moving pictures (Chien and Jones, 1975). Although these methods are efficient in simple scene analysis, it seems difficult to apply them for more complex scenes which are common in real applications. Furthermore this problem was studied under the assumption that objects show high contrast against background, so there was a little problem in detecting boundaries of objects (Chow and Aggarwal, 1977). An approach has been recently proposed which seems to overcome some of the above mentioned difficulties (Yachida, Asada and Tsuji, 1978).

A useful aspect of analysis of moving images compared with static images is that interframe information can be utilized in addition to spatial difference of the gray level. This key idea is the starting point to solve various problems in analysis of moving pictures: an efficient system was recently proposed on this line (Lev, Zucker and Rosenfeld, 1977). In the system described in this paper the above idea is further developed to eliminate or reduce some unpleasant effects, e.g. produced by light reflections on metal surfaces. To increase object detection efficiency, a non linear smoothing of original image frames is performed before edge extraction. After the separation of non stationary components, each object is isolated and the Fourier transform of boundary points is evaluated to get a shape description for recognition purpose. In the tracking step a model of the first fra me is generated and used in a matching process to identify the same object in the subsequent frames.

HARDWARE CONFIGURATION

Fig. 1 shows a block diagram of the used hardware system. The computer is a PDP 11-34, a 16 bits machine with 128 Kbytes of memory, two disks (5 + 5 Mbytes), a magnetic tape (800-1600 bpi) and a printer terminal. A TESAK interfacing unit is provided, containing an external memory of 64 Kbytes to store the pictures acquired by a black and white TV camera. The same unit performs an 8 bits analog-to-digital conversion at 30 Mbytes/s rate.

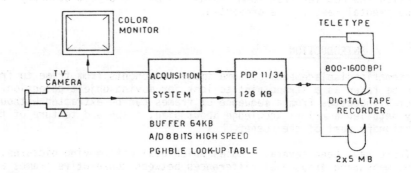

FIG. 1.   Block diagram of the used hardware processing
           system.

Programmable look up tables are available to obtain display of color pictures. Once a frame has been sampled, a digitized picture stored in the external memory is sent to the system and recorded in the magnetic tape or in a disk. Any sequence of picture data, stored in the magnetic tape or in a disk, can be displayed as a dynamic picture on the co lor display, which is very useful to examine and evaluate the interme diate processing results.

SOFTWARE DESCRIPTION

The processing sequence of image frames contains the following steps.

1- Learning phase, including the acquisition and the modelling of the objects which the system has to recognize (off-line processing).

2- Tracking of moving objects, which requires the following sub-steps:

    2.1- preprocessing of input sequence by a non linear smoothing algorithm;

    2.2- edge detection of each frame by the gradient method;

    2.3- moving object detection: non stationary components of the input sequence are separated from stationary ones (which constitute the background of the image);

    2.4- post-processing;

    2.5- segmentation of the single frame (with silhouettes of the moving objects in a two level code) to get single object separation;

    2.6- object modelling, taking into consideration only the shape of the silhouettes of the detected objects (interior part is ignored), by using the FFT algorithm applied to the boundary.

3- Object recognition, by performing a matching of the spectra to evaluate the "distance" between the shape of the object to be detected and the model shape stored in the computer memory during the learning phase.

DETAILED DESCRIPTION OF EACH STEP

In the following, a more detailed description of each processing step is given.

1- In this phase spectra are obtained and then stored in a disk.

2- The tracking requires the evaluation of a model which describes the kinetic state and some features of the shape for each object. The inertial invariants of the boundary curve and its length were chosen as the descriptors of the geometrical characteristics. Kinetic state includes the centroid position and rate. These data are used to predict the position of the objects in the next frame. A matching algorithm is used for coupling the detected objects in the subsequent frames with those ones detected before. This matching is based on the comparison of the geometrical features above described, which are updated in each frame as well as the kinetic state of each tracked object. If the differences of the shape description are in absolute value less than a fixed threshold and if the estimated centroid position has a distance from real position less than a fixed tolerance, the object is considered matched and the model is updated. No occlusion is supposed to occur during the tracking with small variations of the object rate. This processing is useful also to get a sequential estimate of the spectrum module of each object. The following sub-steps are performed in each frame:

    2.1- The processing here performed is a variation of the smoothing described already (Lev, Zucker and Rosenfeld, 1977), to reduce the noise in the image. The intensity value at each point is replaced by the average of itself and its neighbourhood, except those which have gray level differences greater than a fixed threshold in absolute value. For the point P_0 (Fig. 2), its updated value is given by

$$P_0' = \frac{1}{n} \sum_{P_i \in S} P_i \qquad (1)$$

where $S = \{ P_i : |P_i - P_0| \leq k \}$ and $i = 0,1,\ldots,8.$

P_{15}	P_{14}	P_{13}	P_{12}	P_{11}
P_{16}	P_4	P_3	P_2	P_{10}
P_{17}	P_5	P_0	P_1	P_9
P_{18}	P_6	P_7	P_8	P_{24}
P_{19}	P_{20}	P_{21}	P_{22}	P_{23}

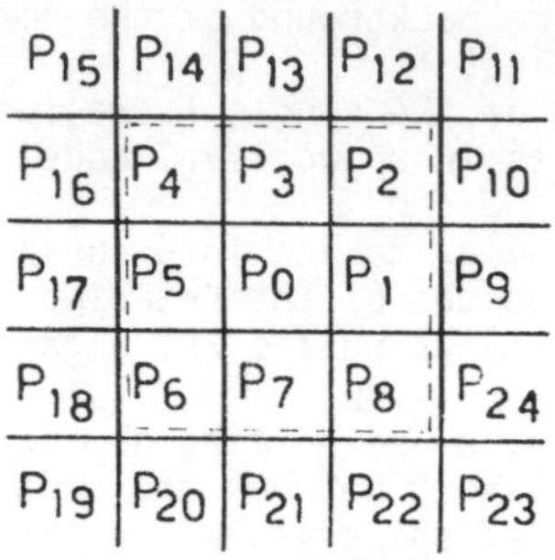

FIG. 2.   Position of the points P_i (P_i denotes also the gray level value) in the image to be processed.

This procedure has the following advantages:
a) Near a boundary whose contrast is greater than k it does not include in the average evaluation any point around the edge. This allows a smoothing of the points on either side of the boundary without any damage for the boundary, as a linear smoothing usually would do.
b) In a homogeneous region, noise components, such that their differences are less than k, are smoothed.
c) A textured region, whose elements have differences in intensity less than k, will be smoothed into a homogeneous region.
Further, by appropriately choosing the threshold value, the noise in the image can be reduced without any loss of significant information and this processing can be iterated to obtain better results. It is sometimes useful to apply masks larger than 3·3 and reduce the numebr of iteration (two iterations of a 9·9 operator produce similar results to eight iterations of a 3·3 operator with the same threshold). After several experimental tests, it was concluded that two iterations of a 3·3 operator are sufficient to obtain good results.
2.2- An approximate Sobel gradient operator is used for detecting edges between regions with different gray level. The edge magnitude is obtained by applying gradient method at every pixel of a frame sequence:

$$\underline{G}(x,y) = \nabla I(x,y) \tag{2}$$

$$G_x(x,y)_{P=P_0} = \left(\frac{\partial I}{\partial x}\right)_{P=P_0} = P_4 + 2P_5 + P_6 - P_8 - 2P_1 - P_2 \tag{3}$$

$$G_y(x,y)_{P=P_0} = \left(\frac{\partial I}{\partial y}\right)_{P=P_0} = P_2 + 2P_3 + P_4 - P_6 - 2P_7 - P_8 \tag{4}$$

The module is approximated as follows:

$$\|\underline{G}(x,y)\| = \left[G_x^2(x,y) + G_y^2(x,y)\right]^{1/2} \cong |G_x(x,y)| + |G_y(x,y)| \tag{5}$$

with reference to Fig. 3.

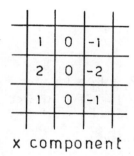

x component

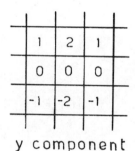

y component

FIG. 3.   Definition of x-y components of the used edge operator.

2.3- Moving object detection is performed by using a point to point subtraction between two pictures of k-th and (k+n)-th frame as

$$D(i,j,k,k+n) = F(i,j,k) - F(i,j,k+n) \tag{6}$$

and a thresholding of $D(i,j,k,k+n)$ is used to get a two level image as follows

$$B(i,j,k,k+n) = 1 \quad \text{if } D(i,j,k,k+n) > T$$
$$B(i,j,k,k+n) = 0 \quad \text{elsewhere} \tag{7}$$

As a final result, the shapes of the objects   are obtained

by the union of previous binary images

$$U(i,j,k) = B(i,j,k,k+n) \qquad k \in N , \; n \in n_{max} \qquad (8)$$

where k is the number of the frame in which the objects are detected and N, n_{max} are two suitable integer numbers.

2.4- Reducing of noise is often necessary to get better re-sults. Small areas are eliminated and small holes are filled while also irregularities of boundary curves are reduced. A simple but efficient processing is performed, by using a 3·3 operator with a statistical decision criterion. For each pi-xel it is to be decided if it would change its level or not, and the decision depends on its originary level and those ones of the pixels which surround it. Larger masks are not advisable due to the related computing difficulties. The al-gorithm is defined as in the following

$$
\begin{array}{ll}
P'_0 = 0 & \text{if } \displaystyle\sum_{i \in S_0} P_i < 5 \qquad S_0 = 1,2,\ldots,8
\end{array}
$$

if $P_0 = 0$ $\qquad\qquad (9)$

$$P'_0 = 1 \qquad \text{otherwise}$$

$$
\begin{array}{ll}
P'_0 = 0 & \text{if } P_i = P_j = 1 \\
 & \text{where } j = i + 1 \quad \text{if } i < 8 \\
 & \text{and } \quad j = 1 \qquad \text{if } i = 8
\end{array}
$$

if $P_0 = 1$ $\qquad\qquad (10)$

$$P'_0 = 1 \qquad \text{otherwise}$$

where P'_0 is the updated value of P_0 and P_i are the pixels surrounding it as illustrated in Fig.2 (dashed line).

2.5- Binary image segmentation was developed using tracking of boundary points. To detect a boundary point, a scanning of the input image is performed. Subsequent points are obtained by using a counter-clockwise boundary tracking according to a 8 points chain coding scheme shown in Fig. 4, starting from the first detected point up to return to the starting one. Thus a closed curve is obtained, enclosing a single ob-ject; this surrounded object can be separated from the other ones and also subtracted from the group. In this way the se-paration of each object detected by iteration of this pro-cess, can be accomplished.

2.6- A model which describes the shape of the object is obtained. A simple and fast method, based on circular scanning of the object boundary, was used. The centroid of the curve, which encloses the object, is evaluated; the intersection points with the boundary of straight lines from the center (with a constant angular increment) are evaluated as shown in Fig. 5.

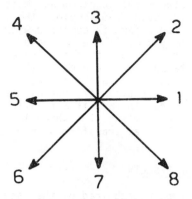

FIG. 4. 8 points chain coding used for counter-clockwise
boundary tracking.

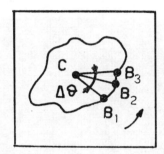

FIG. 5. Circular scanning procedure of the object boundary.

In this step, samples of distance values of boundary points
from the centroid of the curve are also obtained. A common
standard FFT algorithm is used to evaluate the spectrum of
the boundary function.

3- Object recognition is based on the key idea of "distance" in the
frequency domain. Two objects with the same shape but different
size are supposed equivalent. The distance between the object and
the model is defined as follows:

$$\delta = \sum_{k=1}^{M} \left\| |F_o(j\omega_k)| \; / \; |F_o(0)| \; - \; |F_m(j\omega_k)| \; / \; |F_m(0)| \right\| \qquad (11)$$

where $F_o(j\omega_k)$ are the samples of the object spectrum, $F_m(j\omega_k)$

are the ones of the model spectrum and M is a suitable positive integer number (by using 256 samples, the value M = 20 was selected). Each detected object is compared with each model stored in the computer memory and, if the evaluated distance is less than a fixed threshold, the object is considered to be recognized. Only modules of the spectra are used in the matching process, so it is impossible to distinguish differences among the phases of the spectra; this is really very useful because a rotational invariance is obtained. In fact if a rotation occours, it determines a shift of boundary function which implies a linear phase variation in its Fourier transform with no module changement.

EXPERIMENTAL RESULTS

A digitized image frame, as acquired by the used TV-computer system, containing a spanner, a nut and a washer, is shown in Fig. 6. The three objects are moving, each one independently from the other. They are detected and recognized by means of the above digital processing technique.

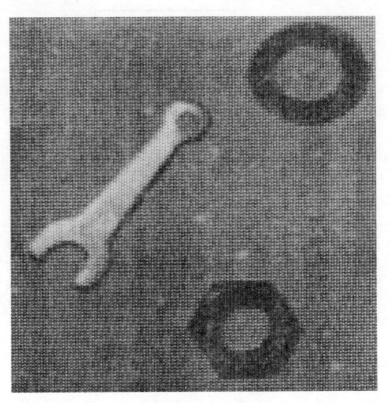

FIG. 6.   Digitized image frame containing a spanner, a nut and a washer.

Fig. 7 shows the object recognition and tracking after three subsequent movements of the spanner and the washer and two movements of the nut (practically the nut was in the same position in two image frame acquisitions). As it is seen, the proposed digital processing technique is perfectly working.

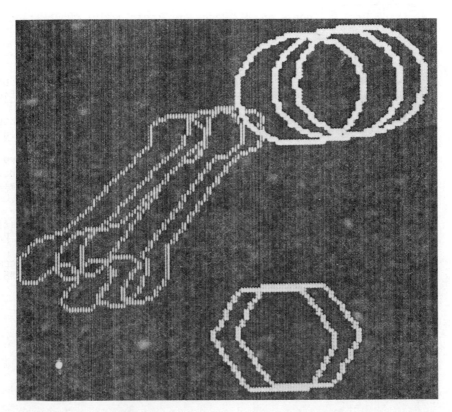

FIG. 7.   Object recognition and tracking after three subsequent movements of the spanner and the washer and two movements of the nut.

CONCLUSIONS

A simple but efficient software system was developed to get moving object recognition and tracking. It takes advantage from previous works on the same topic, getting however a greater simplicity and a higher efficiency. In particular, in comparison with other techniques (Yachida, Asada and Tsuji, 1978), a good independence from the back-ground gray level constraints and from the number of required frames was obtained.

The presented technique can be successfully applied anywhere it is required to analyse sequences of image frames to recognize moving objects and to track their trajectory. In particular it can be applied, by using a suitable fast acquisition-processing system, in robotics and dynamic processing of biomedical images.

Acknowledgements

We thank Drs. C. Conese and M. Poggi for their useful cooperation.

REFERENCES

Potter, J. L., 1975. Scene segmentation by velocity measurement obtained with a cross-shaped template. Proc. of 4th Int. Conf. Artificial Intelligence, 803-810.

Chien, R. T., and Jones, V. C., 1975. Acquisition of moving objects and hand-eye coordination. Proc. of 4th Int. Conf. Artificial Intelligence, 737-741.

Chow, W. K., and Aggarwal, J.,1977. Computer analysis of planar curvilinear moving images. IEEE Trans. on Computers, vol. C-26, 179-185.

Yachida, M., Asada, M., and Tsuji, S., 1978. Automatic motion analysis system of moving objects from the records of natural processes. Proc. of 4th Int. Conf. Pattern Recognition, 726-730.

Thompson, W. B., 1980. Combining motion and contrast for segmentation. IEEE Trans. on Pattern Analysis and Machine Intelligence, vol. PAMI-2, n. 6.

Lev, A., Zucker, S. W., and Rosenfeld, A., 1977. Iterative enhancement of noisy images. IEEE Trans. Syst. Man. Cybern., vol. SMC-7, 435.

SHAPE RECOGNITION USING THE HOUGH TRANSFORM

V.Cantoni - Istituto di Informatica e Sistemistica
            Università di PAVIA

G.Musso - Elettronica San Giorgio, Via Hermada 6,
          GENOVA - ITALY

ABSTRACT

In this work some shape recognition techniques, based on the Hough
Transform method, are examined. Starting from a formal definition of
the Hough Transform and its generalization, to include operations on
non analytical shapes, a shape recognition and location process is described, focusing the attention on the particular properties of this
transformation and on the use we can do of them in implementing such a
procedure in digital systems.

1. INTRODUCTION

The importance of handling efficiently information in form of bidimensional arrays of data, such as images, is continuously increasing in
the application domain. At present, taken into account the actual advances in computer technologies, in both the aspects of architectural
and component possibilities, many industrial applications of image pro
cessing and recognition can be considered as a complex, but not impossible or not cost-effective design task.
In industrial applications of vision systems, the role of shape descrip
tion and recognition is one of the most important, and many generalized methods, scale-rotation invariant, of shape description are continuously studied by several researchers (see references).
Among them, the Hough Transform method, due to its own mathematical
properties that allow to describe analytical and non-analytical shapes,
may be used efficiently in many applications concerning both recognition and data compression. In this work some aspects of application of
the Hough Transform will be examined, with remark concerning its imple
mentation features in multiprocessing architectures, to achieve reason
able speed of operation as regards real time or near-real-time shape
recognition and location processes.
In section two, some formal definitions of Hough Transform and its gene
ralization are given, making reference to shape recognition and location processes.
Section three illustrates the techniques used to implement such a process and the basic idea concerning the use of Hough methods in this

kind of tasks. In addition, some properties of Hough Transform methods
are summarized and their use in implementation in digital systems is
described with an emphasis for its capability to realize recogni
tion processes in multiprocessing environment.

2. THE HOUGH TRANSFORM

The Hough Transform was studied to detect global countours which are
gathered by a mapping between ordinary image space and a parameter
space, in which every analytical curve C, of a family $\mathbb{C}$, is represented in compressed fashion by its parameter values.
Let $\mathbb{C} = \{C_i\}$, $i = 1\div N$, be a set of analytical curves, each of which
may be described by a form $f_i (\{(x,y)\}, \{a_{ik}\}) = 0$, where, $\{a_{ik}\}$ deno
tes the parameter set associated to the function f_i, and $\{(x,y)\}$ the set
of points of bidimensional space that satisfies $f_i(\{(x,y)\},\{a_{ik}\})=0$.
If we indicate with Z the bidimensional point set containing all subsets $Z_i^* = \{(x_i,y_i)\}$ of points belonging to the curve C_i, and with P a
space having $(\max \{k\}+1)$ dimensions as parameter space, we define the
Hough Transform H by:

$$H : Z_i^* \to p_i \in P \quad \text{where} \quad Z_i^* \subset Z \;\; \forall i \tag{1}$$

which assigns to every set $\{(x_i,y_i)\} \equiv Z_i^*$ the corresponding point
$(\{a_{ik}\}, i)$ in P.
In image processing the transform H defines in the parameter space,
for every edge element $e(x',y')$ considered as a curve segment, a locus
$\Gamma(e)$ of points representing the subset $C' \subset \mathbb{C}$ to which this element may
belong. That is, eq. (1) implicitly defines the following mapping from
each edge element $e(x',y')$ to a locus of points in the parameter space
P :

$$H: e \in C_i \to \Gamma(e) \subset P \tag{2}$$

such that

$$\bigcap_{e \in C_i} \Gamma(e) = p_i \in P \tag{3}$$

where p_i is considered the transformation of curve C_i.

Let us consider the following example in which the transform of a family of two analytical curves is computed $(Z \equiv R^2, i = 2, K = 2)$:

$$\begin{cases} y = a_{11}x + \dfrac{a_{12}}{x} \\ i = 1 \end{cases} \qquad \begin{cases} y = a_{21}x^2 + a_{22} \\ i = 2 \end{cases} \tag{4}$$

If in a computation we do not care of directions of the picture edge
elements $e(x',y')$, then the locus of points $\Gamma(e)$ in 3-dimensional parameter space generated by an edge element belonging to curves defined in (4), is represented by two straight lines:

$$\begin{cases} a_{12}^* = y'x' - a_{11}^* \, x'^2 \\ i = 1 \end{cases} \qquad \begin{cases} a_{22}^* = y' - a_{21}^* x'^2 \\ i = 2 \end{cases} \tag{5}$$

in which a_{ij}^* are variables in P .

The cross point of all straight lines computed from the complet set of edge elements belonging to curve C_i is the parameter set (a_{i1}, a_{i2}), defining the curve C_i; that is :

$$\bigcap_{e\,\varepsilon\,C_i} \{(a_{i1}^*, a_{i2}^*)\}_e \equiv (a_{i1}, a_{i2}) \tag{6}$$

If we use edge directional information, then the locus $\Gamma(e)$ is reduced to a couple of points in P :

$$
\begin{cases}
a_{11} = \dfrac{y' + \lambda x'}{2x'} \\[2mm]
a_{12} = \dfrac{(x'y'-\lambda x'^2)}{2} \\[2mm]
i = 1
\end{cases}
\qquad
\begin{cases}
a_{21} = \dfrac{\lambda}{2x'} \\[2mm]
a_{22} = y' - \dfrac{\lambda x'}{2} \\[2mm]
i = 2
\end{cases}
\tag{7}
$$

where λ indicates the line direction in $e(x',y')$.

In order to achieve capability to recognize and locate non analytical shapes, defined by pictorial models represented by a specified subset of points (K.R.Sloan, 1980), the Hough Transform method was generalized.
Let us consider a model C^* and denote with C the set of edge points, which can be obtained by a translation, rotation and uniformly scaling of the model C^*; we assume that C has the same shape as C^* do, that is C belongs to a family of possible representations of the same shape.
The element C is described, with Hough method, by a point in the four-dimensional parameter space P :

$$p = (x_o, y_o, \Theta, S)$$

where x_o, y_o, Θ, S are the parameters of the quoted evolutions of the model C^*: x_o, y_o measure the translation, Θ measures the rotation and S is the scaling factor. This mapping rule is known as Generalized Hough Transform and, in a lot of practical recognition problems, allows a serious reduction in computational complexity.
Let us consider the case of a continuous shape C, given in polar coordinates $\rho(\varphi)$, and assume to know the tangent direction of the model $\beta(\varphi)$. In this case the points of the locus $\Gamma(e)$ in parameter space P, corresponding to the shape C, can be obtained from the values that satisfy the equations for all values of φ :

$$
\begin{cases}
X_{\Gamma(e)} = X_e - S_\Gamma \rho(\varphi) \cos(\Theta_{\Gamma(e)} + \varphi) \\[2mm]
X_{\Gamma(e)} = Y_e - S_\Gamma \rho(\varphi) \sin(\Theta_{\Gamma(e)} + \varphi) \\[2mm]
\Theta_{\Gamma(e)} = \Psi_e - \beta(\varphi)
\end{cases}
\tag{8}
$$

Where (see fig. 1) :

(X_e, Y_e)	are the picture edge element co-ordinates
φ	is the independent variable
$\rho(\varphi)$	is the polar description of the model
$\beta(\varphi)$	is the tangent direction of the model in φ
Ψ_e	is the contour direction relative to the edge element e

S_Γ is the scaling factor

$\Theta_{\Gamma(e)}$ is the rotation parameter

and $p \equiv (x_0, y_0, \Theta, S) = \bigcap_{e \in C} \Gamma(e)$

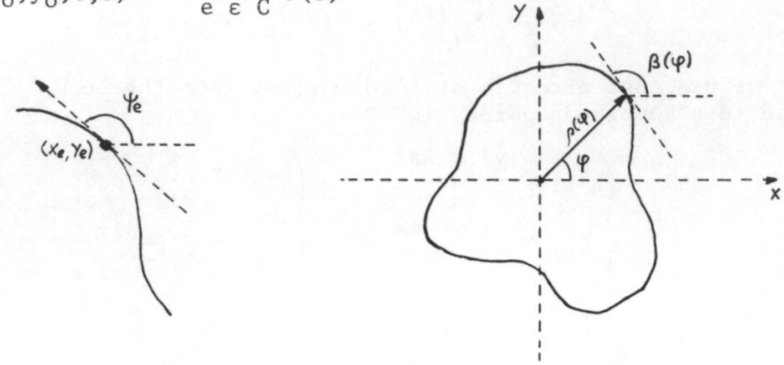

Fig. 1

If we assume that no scaling is present ($S_r=1$) and that we are not interested in rotation detection, but rotations are permitted, the para
meter space P is reduced to the bidimensional image space, and the
points of locus $\Gamma(e)$ can be obtained by :

$$
\begin{cases}
X_{\Gamma(e)} = X_e - \rho(\varphi)\cos\left[\varphi + \Psi_e - \beta(\varphi)\right] \\
Y_{\Gamma(e)} = Y_e - \rho(\varphi)\sin\left[\varphi + \Psi_e - \beta(\varphi)\right]
\end{cases}
\tag{8a}
$$

For recognition purposes the Hough method is used by evaluating the di
stribution of points in parameter space obtained by putting in (8) the
observed values X_e, Y_e, Ψ_e in the image. A recognition takes place when
a peaked distribution is obtained in a point in P, approximating the
Hough Transform of the shape.
In (8) the model is completely described, given $\rho(\varphi)$ and $\beta(\varphi)$, referred to a suitable choice of a polar system origin. In digital computer,
this information can be supplied by a table, normally named R-table,
which gives, for a suitable finite set of values of independent variable φ, the two corresponding values for ρ and $(\varphi - \beta)$.
The R-table defines the mapping of equation (2) through the computations defined in (8); that is, for each tern (X_e, Y_e, Ψ_e), detected in
the image, the set $\{X_{\Gamma(e)}, Y_{\Gamma(e)}\}$ is computed, using the R-table and
equations (8).
In many cases, a convenient selection of the model origin of a polar
co-ordinate system, used to define the model, reduces the number of map
ping operations and, consequently, a saving is obtained in computing
time. Particularly, this is achieved when some geometrical symmetry
is present in the shape. As an example, by selecting the shape bary-
center as origin for the model description, it is easily shown that
the following correspondence between shape and locus $\Gamma(e)$ does exist:

TABLE I	
shape	locus $\Gamma(e)$
Circle	point
regular triangle	
square	side
regular polygon	
rectangle	couple of side
parallelogram	
point symmetric shape	locus of half shape

3. THE HOUGH TECHNIQUE

Some mathematical properties described above present interesting aspects in the application field, due to power with which we can describe shapes in transforming the image space into the parameter space.
This parameter shape representation may be used in the digital image field for data compression (S.Q.Shapiro, 1980) or for shape recognition and location purposes.
We refer here to some works that have been already done, describing in detail Hough Techniques, and we will concentrate our attention on reviewing how mathematical properties can be efficiently applied in pattern recognition and scene analysis tasks (S.D. Shapiro, 1980; H.Nokatami, 1980; D.Guentry, 1980).
A typical Hough's shape recognition process is composed of the following steps:

a) an edge detector operates on the image data and determines whether a pixel belongs to an edge;

b) for each edge pixel, the orientation (Ψ_e) of the edge segment to which it belongs is estimated;

c) for each edge pixel, the points mapped in parameter space through the R-table, describing the shape we are looking for, are computed. This mapping allows all local evidences of curves in the family C to contribute to a global decision about the shape searched;

d) a decision rule is applied to the point distribution in P, to determine whether the searched shape is detected and, if so, what are its particular location and orientation. Let us point out that all this information is contained in the parameter representation.

The implementation of such a process on digital computers implies to solve some problems arising from detection accuracy of edge orientation and from the choice of an origin point, able to optimize the shape sensitivity in the P-mapping distribution.
However, a shape recognition process based on the Hough technique seems to be very effective from the point of view of its parallel implementation capability. Indeed we have to remark that the P-mapping process, consisting in entering the defined R-tables with each edge point in the image, is a point-dependent procedure and not region-dependent.
This feature offers the possibility to segment the image into a set of a priori-defined sub-images, on which we may execute independently

the mapping process, no matter of the possible cuts done on the shapes present, and without requiring higher processing level to supervise the partition done. The only global operation required consists in the collection of points mapped in P space (through the set of R-tables) by all edge elements, and to apply the decisional algorithm to the distribution so obtained. The above capability of parallel computing takes place at pixel level, before any computation on the image is performed; at higher computing level it is furthermore possible to segment the P-mapping process, allocating the R-tables (relative to the shape or sub-shape set to recognize) on distinct processors; each of them executes its "reduced" P-mapping process. Even in this case, after the P-mapping is executed, it is only necessary to collect all mapped points from the processors and to apply to them the decisional criterion.

Of course a mixing of the two kinds of parallelism is always possible, obtaining in this way a considerable increase of the recognition process speed. At the opposite side of the advantages deriving from those parallel processing capabilities, we have to take into account some drawbacks, arising when we operate on digital images and, in general, when we are implementing a Hough's procedure on digital systems.

In these cases we have to introduce approximations both in model description and in the unknown shape description. In particular we have to choose a boundary discretization of model shape which may represent an acceptable trade-off between unambiguous model description and computation complexity. Another problem that must be solved in implementation phases, consists in the optimization of the recognition sensitivity in parameter space, with particular reference to the choice of the model origin. Normally, a general solution does not exist for these problems, but, depending on the particular shape recognition task we are interested, we have to determine the appropriate solution. Considering the case of noiseless images, the higher is the number of points N_m used to describe the model and the number of edge points N_e detected, the higher is the number of points (votes) $N_m \cdot N_e$ obtained in parameter space (N_m of which are expected in the position corresponding to the Hough Transform of the model shape), consequently the higher is the computation cost required by the mapping operations: it depends linearly on the global number of votes obtained.

In the case of degraded images, the vote distribution is usually spreaded around the correct position, for the unreliable estimation of the edge element orientation and for the shape distortion introduced by noise. This can cause errors in detection (falsed or missed); in this case it is often advisable to describe the model using a larger number of points and to introduce some kind of smoothing in the edge orientation algorithm.

When we are considering asymmetric shapes, it is often necessary to detect also information about shape orientation. In order to detect rotation we can operate in two different ways: to consider a three-dimensional parameter space (as in (8)), or, alternatively, to segment the shape in two (or more) sub-parts, and to detect the single sub-parts through the appropriate number of R-tables. In the second case, the presence of the shape is detected by the simultaneous presence of the component sub-parts in a proper positional relation, and the orientation is computed by the space disposition of the various origin points associated with each sub-part.

We are just investigating the last solution that, in terms of the computation cost, seems to be very promising, especially when, by partitio ning the shape, you can simplify the locus Γ as described previously.

4. CONCLUSIONS

As automation develops towards robotics, the importance of designing very flexible sensorial capability becomes a fundamental task. One of the most important processes in the domain of robotics concerns the possibility of handling physical objects with all the implications that an automatic handler often involves: to recognize, to locate, to orient. The Generalized Hough Transform method represents, at least from a theoretical point of view, a possible solution to the above three kinds of problem, including the independence of scale factor.
In practice, on considering the implementation of real systems, we must take into account a set of functional performances imposed by the specific process in which we are interested. In the field of robotics, and more generally in the industrial automation, we have to solve problems concerning speed of operation, flexibility, system simplicity, reliability of operation, etc.
Focusing our attention on speed, and considering the large amount of operations necessary to perform a Hough recognition process on a complex shape, especially when an accurate boundary description is required, we have to solve the problem of identifying the computer architecture that will satisfy our needs. Generally we shall use the intrinsic parallelism of the Hough Transform to implement the algorithm in a mul tiprocessing architecture.
As technology will develop powerful multiprocessors with cost/effectiveness indexes matched with industrial automation or with other fields of application of automation (office, biomedicine, etc.), the Hough Transform Methods, as many others that actually seem to be too complex, will be ready for real applications.

REFERENCES

V.Cantoni, M.Ferretti (1980). A new simple method of detecting edges in digital pictures. Proceedings of Int.Conf. on "Image Analysis and Processing", Pavia, p. 47

R.O.Duda, P.E.Hart (1979). Use of the Hough transform to detect lines and curves in pictures. Comm. Ass. Mach., vol. 15, p. 923-936

S.A.Dudani et al.(1977). Aircraft Identification by Moment Invariants. IEEE Transactions on Computer, vol. C-26, p. 39

D.Guentry, L.Norton Wayne (1980). Automatic Guidance of Vehicles using Visual Data. Proceedings V Intern.Conf. on Pattern Recognition, p. 46

P.V.C. Hough (1962). Methods and Means for recognizing complex Patterns. U.S. Patent 3069654, Dec. 18, 1962

M.K.Hu. Visual Pattern Recognition by Moment Invariant. IRE Transactions on Information Theory, p. 179

128

A.Jannino, S.D.Shapiro (1978). A Survey of the Hough Transform and its extensions for curve detection. Proceedings IEEE Comp. Soc. Conf. on Pattern Recognition and Image Processing, Chicago, p. 32

H.Nokatami et al. (1980). Extraction of vanishing point and its applications to scene analysis based on image sequence. Proceedings V Intern. Conf. on Pattern Recognition, Miami, p. 370

D.P.Reevs, A.Rostanpour (1981). Shape Analysis of Segmented Objects Using Moments. Proceedings of IEEE Comp. Soc. Conf. on Pattern Recognition and Image Processing, August 1981, p. 171

S.D.Shapiro (1980). Use of the Hough Transform for Image Data Compression. Pattern Recognition, vol. 12, n. 5, p. 333

I.Sklansky (1978). On the Hough Transform for Curve detection. IEEE Transactions on Computer, vol. C-27, n. 10, p. 21

K.R.Sloan, D.H. Ballard (1980). Experience with the Generalized Hough Transform. Proceedings V Intern. Conf. on Pattern Recognition, Miami, p. 174

G.Y.Tang, T.S.Huang. Using the Creation Machine to Locate Airplanes on Aerial Photos. Pattern Recognition, vol. 12, p. 431

T.P.Wallace, P.A.Wintz (1980). An Efficient Three-Dimensional Aircraft Recognition Algorithm Using Normalized Fourier Descriptions. Computer Graphics and Image Processing, vol. 13, p. 99

H.Wechsler, I.Sklansky (1977). Finding the rib cage in chest radiographs. Pattern Recognition, vol. 9, n. 1, p. 21

R.Y.Wong, E.L.Hall (1978). Scene Matching with Invariant Moments. Computer Graphics and Image Processing, vol. 8, p. 16.

General Pattern Recognition

C-CALCULUS: AN OVERVIEW

E. R. Caianiello, A.Gisolfi, S.Vitulano

Scuola di Perfezionamento in Scienze Cibernetiche e Fisiche
Istituto di Scienze dell'Informazione
Facoltà di Scienze - Università di Salerno -

A CALCULUS OF PARTITION

1) We propose to present some applications to Pattern Recognition of
a "mathematical game" started some years ago by one us (Caianiello,
1973), which as named "C-calculus" for reasons which will be reminded
in the sequel. We wish to state forthwith that it is simpler in principle than ordinary arithmetics; various fields can be envisaged in
which it might prove of use: e.g. manifold topology, integration
theory, fuzzy sets (where it might provide a natural tool for numerical computation), measure theory in physics, data-base structures,
neural models, etc. This, we hope, will be apparent to the reader; we
must restrict ourselves here only to the specific field of interest
in the present context. We shall endeavour to keep language and arguments as plain as the subject really is; recourse to abstract formalism is often a disguise more convenient to the author than to the
reader. We bagin therefore by reminding the game with which it all
started. Take any integer positive numbers, and apply to them the rules of arithmetics, with the restrictions that only the direct opera-
tios, sum and multiplication, be allowed, the inverse ones, substrac-
tion and division, forbidden; define furthermore the sum and the product of any two digits as follows

$$a + b = \max\ (a,b)$$
$$a \times b = \min\ (a,b) \qquad (1)$$

We may thus "multiply" any two such numbers, e.g. 736 and 491

```
      736 x                          491 x
      491 =                          736 =
      ─────                          ─────
      111                            461
     736                            331
    434                            471
      ─────                          ─────
    47461                          47461
```

We find that multiplication (and addition) thus defined are always commutative for such "numbers".

It would be an easy matter to demonstrate that, provided the "single digit operations" (1) are meaningful, one can operate in the same way on objects (subtraction and division being of course barred), such as vectors, matrices, etc., obtaining additivity and commutativity whenever they hold in arithmetics.

These "numbers" or "strings" of digits, with the operations (1), form clearly a commutative semi-ring. As in arithmetics each "digit" plays two different roles: one intrinsic to it ("cardinality"), the other ("position") relative to the string in which it belongs. The next remark is that standard set theory treats only intrinsic properties of sets. If in (1) we interpret + as "union" $\lor$ and x as "intersection" $\land$, we can immediately transport all that was said thus far to "strings of sets", or "composite sets", "C-sets" for short.

Operating on C-sets as before, with $\lor$ and $\land$ in place of + and x in (1) (a,b denote now the "simple" sets of which C-sets are strings, as the digits in the former example), one has "C-calculus": a commutative semi-ring which permits, from some given C-sets, to generate any number of other C-sets. Inverse operations are neither possible nor required in this context: only direct ones are permissible; one may perhaps see, though, advantages in being able to express in this way long lists of specifications in terms of some few basic ones.

An example of C-operation of special relevance for our present purpose is the following. Consider a segment S partitioned in segments a_1, a_2, a_3, ..., a_k; this partition $A = a_1 \, a_2 \, ... a_k$

$$\vdash\!\!\frac{\quad}{a_1}\!\!\vdash\!\!\frac{\quad}{a_2}\!\!\vdash\!\!\frac{\qquad\qquad}{\qquad a_k}\!\!\dashv$$

Consider now the same segment partitioned in a different way $B = b_1 \, b_2 \, ... b_L$

$$\vdash\!\!\frac{\quad}{b_1}\!\!\vdash\!\!\frac{\quad}{b_2}\!\!\vdash\!\!\frac{\qquad\qquad}{\qquad b_1}\!\!\dashv$$

Consider now A and B as C-sets: the elements of each partition, or string, are "simple" sets; C-multiplication of A and B gives

$$A \times B = B \times A = a_1 \, a_2 \, ... \, a_k \times b_1 \, b_2 \, ... b_L = C = c_1 \, c_2 \, ... \, c_p$$

and it is immediate to verify that the simple sets of the product are obtained, in order, by joining on the segments the terminal points of both partitions A and B.

The C-product of two partitions gives thus the refinement of one by the other: C-calculus is the natural way of composing partitions, or coverings. In fact, the same property holds true in any number of dimensions. (Apostolico et al., 1978). This is the key property of C-calculus as regards its application to Pattern Recognition.

2) Our interest in an approach of this type to Pattern Recognition originates from the instinctive feeling of the physicist when confronted with problems for which a vast number of approaches is proposed, some indeed of remarkable ingenuity and power, but none of general (at least in some sense) applicability: is there some philosophy, or method, that may be applied to all problems of this sort, even if,of course, with less abundance of results than ad hoc techniques will undoubtly provide? Does one need a language for thinning, one for shrinking, one for counting, one for studying textures, one for retrieving objects against a background, and so on? or may we, perhaps, let "patterns" speak for themselves, changing the pattern itself into something algebraic or numeric, out of which, several, if not all, questions may be answered through essentially a single basic algorithm? This is, of course, a "träumerei"; but the search for "laws",rather than "rules", is a professional deformation for which a physicist need not apologize, although he better be - as we certainly are- duly apologetic about results achieved.
Having expressed (not certainly justified) our motivation, we shall substantiate it with a typical instance. Granted a priori that a major crime of Pattern Recognition is the preliminary reduction of a (say) 2-dimensional image into pixels, and that we must so proceed because we are much less bright than a fly or a frog, we find that a rather peculiar situation then arises. Parcelling a picture into pixels (with tones of grey, or colour) is, logically, a parallel process, out of which we can gather the more information, the finer the grid whose windows generate "homogenized pixels" (from each pixel only averages are taken). Suppose now that the same grid is rigidly shifted, over the picture, by a fraction of its window side; we may proceed as before, and obtain some other amount of parallel information. The question arises: can we use both informations, the one from the first and the one from the second grid partitioning, to get a better, more detailed information on the picture? Since we are taking only averages from each pixel, each time, the answer is no (unless, of course, we perform some mathematical acrobatics): one of the two readings has to be thrown away.
It would be nicer, one might feel, if there were a way of performing readings from the grid such as to permit to combine in a natural way the readings of both grids to obtain a more refined information on the picture (as might have been gathered by using a finer grid to begin with). If one can handle this situation, conceivably it may then be possible to use several times (serially)a single coarser grid, read out of it the (parallel) information obtained by shifting the whole grid by one step, and so on. The use we intend to do of C-cal-

culus is aimed at answering just this question. The "reading" from a grid (of a suitable sort) becomes per se a C-set; two C-sets from different positions of the grid can be C-multiplied; this will give finer information, and so on.

3) Under "suitable" circumstances (to be defined explicitly in the sequel) this procedure can be carried through to the extreme limit of perfect reconstruction of the original picture (as digitized at the finest possible level: e.g. with a $2^{10} \times 2^{10}$ grid for the original, it may be reconstructed by covering it stepwise with, say, a $2^3 \times 2^3$ grid). During this process many things which one does with specific tecniques, such as contour extraction, contrast enhancement, feature extraction, etc., can be performed by interpolating in it steps with "answer" questions of this sort and become part of the algorithm.
But the application of C-calculus will often fail; the original image may not be thus reconstructed. There is an element to be considered, which was before ignored through the adjective "suitable": the size of the window. It is a feature of our approach that the critical size, below which total reconstruction of the picture is impossible, is determined by the structure of the picture itself, and is not a matter of guesswork or trial and error.
One can arrange readings, and ways of analyzing them, from grids having sizes appropriates to constitute in fact filters that see some wanted features and are blind to others. Typically, consider a saucer on a chessboard: things can be arranged so as to see only the saucer or only the chessboard (with a hole); or a specific component of a texture, ignoring all others, or suppress some noise, etc. Such filtering does not smear out or enhance; it gives at worst an intended contour to the saucer, as is natural when working with grids.
A study of this filtering process from the point of view of rigorous mathematics has not been undertaken yet, again on the physicist's view that such studies are always possible on no matter what subject, but that it is preferable first to test whether the subject is worth the effort.
At this stage a wealth of tools becomes available, about which it is better to keep a critical than an enthused view. Most times the practical problems at hand require only partial answers for their solution, like distinguishing between given printed characters. Considerations of this nature are somewhat systemized by using one such tool, which, not surprisingly, call C-matrix; it yields useful informations in several situations of interest, we shall exhibit if mostly through examples.

CONVERGENCE AND FILTERING

1) Our main tool in the application of C-calculus, to Pattern Recognition will be, as was said at the end of section 1-1, the C-multiplication of two partitions. A and B of an N-dimensional domain

$$A = a_1 \ldots\ldots\ldots a_k$$
$$B = b_1 \ldots\ldots\ldots b_L$$

which yields $\quad C = A \times B = B \times A = c_1 \ldots\ldots\ldots c_p$

i.e. is the refinement of A by B, or viceversa, with elements
$c_1 \, c_2 \ldots c_p$

The same approach can be used regardless of the number of dimensions of the pattern to be studied. We shall consider, for the sake of simplicity and for specific relevance to P.R., only one- and two-dimensional patterns (e.g. graphs and pictures); we shall also consider only one additional dimension, which may e.g. denote levels of greyness, discretized or not (with colors, one may add as many dimensions as distinct ones are considered, etc.).
We start with one-dimensional patterns, as it is immediate to visualize in this case the procedure. We restrict our attention to "grids", i.e. to partitions of the abscissa x into segments, for simplicity,of equal lenght, the "windows".
Thus, consider the graph of Fig. 1, where the ordinate y denotes greyness (or intensity of sound, or local pitch...).
Discretize now the x coordinate with a grid G, of window w; change the graph into a sequence of rectangles by substituting the portion of graph corresponding to a given window w_h with the rectangle which projects upon x into w_h and upon y into the segment having as upper and lower extrema the maximum M_h and the minimum m_h reached by the graph within w_h (no matter where, or how many times). We change thus the graph into a string of rectangles.

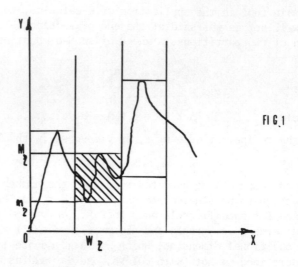

A C-set: a partition of a graph in a string of quadruples.

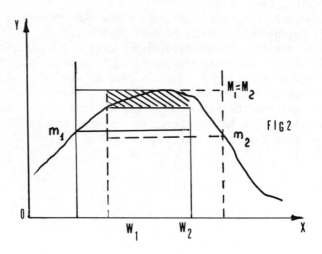

A product of the elements of two C-sets.

The ordered sequel of all these rectangles is the C-set determined
from the graph by partitioning the x-axis with the given grid.
We may now proceed as before, after shifting the grid by a step $l < w$.
Denoting with indices 1 and 2 the two C-sets thus obtained, we have,
with an obvious notation:

$$C_1 = R_{1,1} \,, \ldots \ldots, R_{1,k}$$

$$C_2 = R_{2,1} \,, \ldots \ldots, R_{2,k}$$

$$R_{i,h} = \left[w_{i,h} \; ; \; m_{i,h} \,, \, M_{i,h} \right]$$

We may now define the product of two simple sets $R_{1,h}$ and $R_{2,L}$ as the
intersection of the rectangles just defined, i.e.

$$R_{1,h} \times R_{2,L} = \begin{cases} \phi \text{ iff } W_{1,h} \wedge W_{2,L} = \phi \\[2ex] (W_{1,h} \wedge W_{2,L}); \max \left[m_{1,h}, m_{2,L} \right], \min \left[M_{1,h}, M_{2,L} \right] \end{cases}$$

In other words: instead of attaching to each window w one value, say
the average of y in it, we take two, m_h and M_h; the difference
$M_h - m_h = \Delta_h$ is known as the dynamic of the graph in w_h.
This modification is sufficient to carry out our prposed program, because now it is evident that $C_1 \times C_2$ represent a finer partition of
some strip within which the graph-line is contained, as is shown in
Fig.2.
Consider now any rectangle of the C-set $C_1 \times C_2$; its base is
$w_{1,h} \wedge w_{2,h}$, the height is $y_h = \min.(M_{1,h}, M_{2,h}) - \max (m_{1,h}, m_{2,h})$.
Is thus evident that the dynamic of the graph in it is:

$$\Delta (w_{1,h} \wedge w_{2,h}) \leq y_h, \text{ which reduces}$$

$$\Delta (w_{1,h} \wedge w_{2,h}) = y_h \quad \text{if the graph is monotonic}$$
$$\text{in } w_{1,h} \vee w_{2,h}.$$

This remark is essential in order to study under which conditions iterated C-multiplication of C-sets obtained by shifting a given grid
will reproduce the given graph to maximum permissible accurancy (that
of the original graph, which was supposed digitized at some finer level).
The criterion of convergence to be satisfied for total reconstruction
of the original graph, or parts of it, must clearly be the following:
convergence is achieved wherever one obtains, at the hth iteration,

$m_{i,h} = M_{i,h}$ over the corresponding w_i's. One may substitute to this criterion the weaker one (especially if the ordinate is not discretized) that $M_{i,h} - m_{i,h} < \varepsilon$, prefixed, small as convenient.

The formalization of this procedure is straightforward; the interested reader may reproduce it by himself, or refer to some previous paper.(Apostolico et al.,1977).

For equally spaced grids (it would be only a matter of convenience to relax or change this condition at any wanted step of the procedure), there is a very simple formula which determines whether overall convergence is guaranteed: this will be the case if, and only if:

$$(2) \qquad\qquad w \leq \frac{D}{2}+1$$

where D denotes the smallest distance between a minimum and a maximum of the graph. The proof is given in(Apostolico et al.,1977). The same formula applies also in two (or more) dimensions if we now read w to mean the side of the square window, D the euclidean distance in the plane between such extrema.

2) We can now change our viewpoint. Instead of shifting the grid, obtaining and multiplying the ensuing C-sets, etc., we ask what this procedure will finally yield at a given, fixed point on x-axis. The answer is that, regardless of the order in which these operations are performed, the final values which are associated with any given point are the highest minimum and the lowest maximum that are seen when the window w moves on an interval of lenght 2w - 1, centered at that point. The discussion of this point, which is related of course to (2) is in ref.(Apostolico et al., 1977). Of special interest is the case in which (2) is violated. Our procedure will not reconstruct then the original pattern, but produce a new pattern, which suppresses all those details of the original one which could be retrieved only by respecting (2). In other words, the procedure will act now as a filter (C-filter (Caianiello et al., 1978). A trivial, intuitive example will convince us of this fact. Suppose that we wish to study in this way the before mentioned chessboard. Operating with a (square) grid whose window is smaller than the case of the chessboard will readily reconstruct the chessboard. If, however, the window is larger than the case, no matter how we move the grid we shall always find m = 0, M = 1 (say) in any window: convergence is impossible. It is then a trivial matter to arrange things so that in the first case our procedure reconstructs the chessboard, in the second it yields a total blanc: the chessboard is filtered away. If now we have a saucer on the chessboard, we shall be able to retrieve only the saucer, obliterating the chessboard background; likewise, one can proceed with textu-

res (Caianiello et al., 1979): it is possible to see an object ignoring a textural background, or viceversa, to extract only some relevant textural elements. Many variations are possible on this theme
(Galloway, 1978). One can keep, thus, a window which satisfies (2)
but accept only dynamics within given thrsholds; or play both with
window size and threshold.
The next part illustrates a computational tool that can be extracted
any given pattern, the "C-matrix": it gives automatically optimals
criteria for window and threshold size, and can be useful in the study of several classical problem of P.R.

C-MATRIX

1) Consider a pattern F in any number N of dimensions (for the sake
of illustration we restrict here N = one or two), and consider only
one of some K "attributes" of interest, e.g. the level of greyness
(which we may suppose now digitized). An N-dimensional grid of (square) windows generates, as we have seen, a C-set in N + 1 (K = 1) space; C-multiplication of all C-sets obtained by displacing (according
to some rule) the grid ever the pattern yields, after a suitable number of iterations, a pattern F, which will <u>coincide</u> with F if condition (2) is respected, differ from F otherwise. This process we have
called C-filter; as much, it might deserve <u>per se</u> mathematical inve-
stigation. Our interest here is rather with concrete ways of exploi-
ting the <u>typical new feature</u> of C-calculus, that of <u>permitting either</u>
<u>"precise" measurements of</u> a <u>whole through serial composition</u> (C-mul-
tiplying of <u>"coarser" partial parallel measurements</u>) (each, a C-set
from the grid), or <u>"filtering operations"</u>. "Precise" and "coarse" are
to be understood as in physics. We have found profitable, for this
purpose, to introduce a mathematical object which (for any N, K = 1)
is always 2-dimensional: the C-matrix.

2) We define the C-matrix. Its element c_{hk} has as row label h (=2,3,
4,....) the <u>linear size</u> of the window w_h of the scarning grid G_h
(C-calculus will be more useful the larger can be kept the minimum h
needed for a given analysis); the <u>column</u> label k (= 0, 1, 2, ...)
denotes the possible values of the dynamic K = M - m as read
through w_h. The grid G_h scans the pattern according to some criterion
(in two dimensions, the best has proved to run down the main diagonal)
by one step at a time ("1" means the original digitizing window, if
any, or simply the "resolving power" of the system); G_h has thus
h(= $\sqrt{2}$ h , square grid h, linear) scanning positions; any value k of
the dynamic is registered $P_{ik}^{(6)}$ (= 0, 1, 2, ...) times in the windows, for each position i=1, .., h of the grid G_h. In conclusion

$$c_{hk} = \sum_{i=1}^{h} p_{ik}^{(h)} \qquad\qquad (3)$$

The building of the C-matrix seems, from the definition just given, a such more imposing task than it actually is. In fact, the operations that lead to c_{hk} are performed in parallel for k = 0, 1, 2, ... so that the C-matrix is built one row at a time, or in one piece with suitable hardwere; also, the procedure has to be started from the bottom row, i.e. largest w_h, and it becomes an obvious matter to im- plement the algorithm with devices that suppress the need to explore, moving towards smaller h, territories where, e.g.k,=0 (uniform grey- ness) for a larger h. Nor need one proceed through the full sequence h_{max}, h_{max} - 1, h_{max} - 2, ..., 2: large jumps may be made.

An element c_{ij} of the C-matrix tells us thus: if it vanishes, that the value j of the dynamic of the pattern can never be seen through windows of size w_1 ; if not, how manytimes that is seen by no matter which window w_1. It is easy then to read from the C-matrix many features of the pattern; e.g. if only $c_{i,0}$ = 0, all i, the pattern is a plauteaux, of constant gryness throughout: the max i for which $c_{i,o} \neq 0$ is the width of the largest plateaux; a highest-slope of a (1-dimensional) signal shows as the sequel $c_{ij} \neq 0$, j max, for each i.

3) CONTOUR EXTRACTION

This is a; relevant step in every problem of P.R., with a wide li- terature and a large number of techniques available: gradients and threshold, thinning, joining or separating of broken or interpenetra- ting pieces, template matching, etc.(Roberts, 1965; Hall et al.,1976; German et al., 1977).

We can extract contours with the following role. Consider the first among the columns of the C-matrix, let it be the column h,in which the elements c_{ij} go through a maximum, at some value i. Take the corresponding window w_i as element of the grid of a C-filter, given by C-multiplication of C-sets whose simple sets vanish if smaller than the (hyper) rectangles w_i x h (i.e. h is a threshold on dynamic)

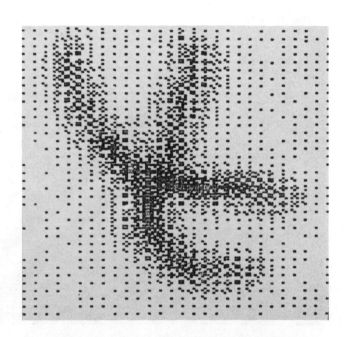

Fig. 3
human chromosome

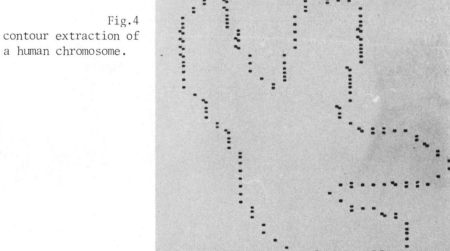

Fig.4
contour extraction of
a human chromosome.

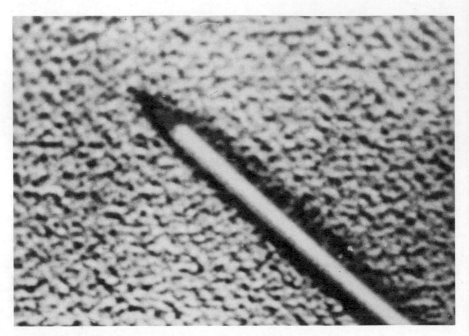

Fig. 5
A pencil on a natural texture

Fig. 6
The application of our filtering method.

SEGMENTATION

This subject, which includes discrimination aginst a background, is the object of much literature, and can be carried to deep contextual and grammatical analysis.
A simple approach to it through C-calculus is obtained by fixing an iterative procedure which again uses data read from the C-matrix. Details can be found in ref.(Feng et al., 1976; Galloway, 1978; Weszka et al., 1979).
Comparison with other algorithms (Feng et al., 1976; Galloway, 1978; Weszka et al., 1979) was made; it appears that thresholds come out of the C-matrix and do not have to be guessed, and that computation time is here less than with RAG, LAG, PT.

FEATURE EXTRACTION

We refer for details to ref 's (Deutsch, 1955). Neurophysiological modeling, Gestalt and invariance requirement: (Deutsch 12) have suggested an algorithm with concentric window so that the inner one acts as "excitatory", the annulus around it as "inhibitory". As before, all relevant parameters are read from the C-matrix. Our experimental results show that C-calculus, as it is, can be adjusted to higher degrees of definition if desired, because it mimics basic neuronal mechanism.

TEXTURES.

The analysis of textures, both per se and as backgrounds, is almost a science within a science; see, e.g. Gibson 195o, Koehler 1975, Haralick 1973). Our views on this subject do not belong to this short summary of our work; more than in other tonics of P.R. we must remind that "percepta" are "phenomena", in the sense of Kant, quantum mechanics or the Vedas, to which the noumenon" and the "observer" equally concur. We wish only to report here, in conclusion, that C-calculus has proved especially "natural" in this context, leading to ready and elementary classification, analysis and discrimination.
We refer the reader to previous works Gisolfi et al., 1980); some examples in this are reported. It is the "chessboard and saucer" game we were mentioning earlier, which is easily implemented through C-calculus into algorithmic simulations which may be rather close in principle to the actual operation of neural tissues.

1) Apostolico A.,Caianiello E.R.,Fischetti E.,Vitulano S. C-calculus: an elementary approach to some problems in Pattern Recognition. Pattern Recognition n.5 1978.
2) Apostolico A.,Vitulano S. A image transform, in Informatik-Fach berichte n.8 Springer Verlag 1977.
3) Brodatz P. Textures, Dever, 1966
4) Caianiello E.R. A calculus for hierarchical system, Proc. First Int. Joint Conf. on Pattern Recognition, Washington, 1973.
5) Caianiello E.R.,Gisolfi A.,Vitulano S. A technique for texture analysis using C-calculus. Signal Processing n. 1,1979.
6) Deutsch J.A. A theory of shape recognition, Brit. J. Psych. 46,
7) Caianiello E.R.Gisolfi A.,Vitulano S. A method of filtering biomedical specimens, Proc. The Int. Conf. of Cybernetics on Society. Tokyo, 1978.
8) Dinstein I. Haralick R.M., Textural features for image classification. Proc. IEEE trans.of System, man and Cybernetics, n.6, 73
9) Feng U.Y. Pavlidis T., Feature generation for syntactic Pattern Recognition, IEEE trans. Comput. n. 12.
10) Galloway M., Texture analysis using gray level run lenghts. Comput. Graphics Image Process n.2.1978.
11) German F.V., Clowes M.B., Finding picture edges through collinearity of feature point. IEEE trans. Comput. n. 24.
12) Gibson J.J., The perception of the visual world. Houghton 1950.
13) Gisolfi A. Mlodkowsli M. Vitulano S. A method for classifying and filtering textures. Progress in Cybernetics and System Research, Hemisphere Pub. Washington, 1980.
14) Hall E. Frei W. Invariant features for quantitative scene analysis Univ. Southern California. 1976.
15) Kohler W. La psicologia della forma. Feltrinelli 1975.
16) Roberts L.G. Machine Perception of three dimensional solids. M.I.T. Press, 1965.
17) Weszka J.S. Nagel R.N. A threshold selection technique. Trans. Comput. 23; n. 12.

FEATURE SELECTION FOR AUTOMATIC [*]
WHITE BLOOD CELLS CLASSIFICATION

A.De Gloria and G. Vernazza

Sibe, Istituto di Elettrotecnica
V.le F.Causa 13, 16145 Genova, Italy

ABSTRACT

Starting from a sample size of 265 normal cells plus 120 pathological
cells, two algorithms for feature selection have been implemented:
the first is based on divergence computation, while the second is
based on the Bhattacharyya distance.
The five most important parameters among 92 are selected for each
classification node; a preliminary hypothesis of gaussian
distribution for each feature has been introduced and a simplified
method, called "matrix increment", for increasing the feature-space k
to the k+1 size has been adopted.
Results are shown in table and grafical form according to functions
with an upper bound for error classification.

INTRODUCTION

Many are the advantages related to Automatic White Blood Cell
Classification (WBCC); in particular, we recall:
- reduction of statistical errors
- saving of human work
- possibility to find natural classes
- relation between structural and functional properties
Two different approaches can be taken: the first is based on flow
systems, while the second is based on static systems.
Flow systems are characterized by high analysis speed (thousands of
cells per second), they analyze the scattering of a laser beam across
the cell; consequently, related features are obtained by taking into
account the cell as a whole. Static systems are characterized by low
analysis speed (some tens of cells per minute); typically, they
employ a TV camera and related features can be associated with
individual parts of the cell.
Available commercial systems are not entirely satisfactory,
particularly as regards discrimination among pathological cells, even
if continued efforts toward increasing their availability are being
expended.

MATERIALS

The data acquisition process has been carried out in our laboratory by

[*]
This work is supported by CNR (Consiglio Nazionale delle Ricerche).

147

a static system, ACTA 500 (F.Beltrame et al. 1980).
A standard Mey-Grumwald-Giemse method has been used as colouring
technique; every cell has been analyzed at 64 grey levels, employing
two standard Kodak filters (Wratten 22 and Wratten 44).
The sample size was 265 normal cells (grouped into 5 classes) and 120
pathological cells (grouped into 2 classes) (table 1).

TABLE 1. Cell classes

Class		Cell number	type
Neutrophils	N	64	normal
Eosinophils	E	54	"
Basophils	B	32	"
Lymphocytes	L	61	"
Monocytes	M	54	"
Blasts	BL	60	Pathological
Promyelocytes	P	60	"

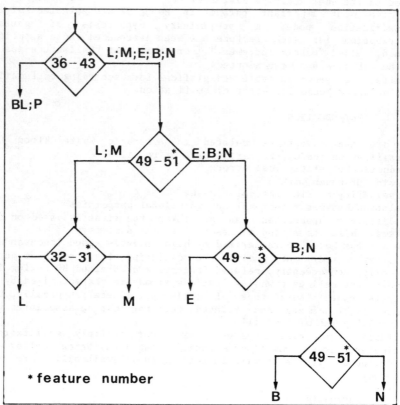

Fig. 1. Basic structure of a classification logic tree.

For each cell, 92 features have been derived, with the following splitting:
- 30 densitometric features
- 15 geometric   "
- 30 colorimetric   "
- 17 histogram derivation (pixels vs. grey levels) features.

In Appendix 1, a detailed list of the considered features is presented, which takes into account many features suggested in the literature (Mui and Fu, 1980).

A logical tree (dicotimization procedure) has been considered as classification process. This structure , shown in Fig.1, is based on 5 nodes.

Although various structures of classification trees can be used, we have considered this one according to classical cytological super-classes.

METHODS

As a preliminary hypothesis, a normal distribution for each feature in each node has been considered then two different approach for features selection have been taken (K. Fukunaga, 1974); the first is based on divergence analysis, and the second on the Battacharyya distance.

If we denote by $\underline{x}$ the pattern vector, by ω_1 and ω_2 two classes, and by $p(\underline{x}/\omega_1)$ the conditioned probability, the divergence value is given by:

$$D = \int_S p(\underline{x}/\omega_1)\ln(p(\underline{x}/\omega_1)/p(\underline{x}/\omega_2))dx + \int_S p(\underline{x}/\omega_2)\ln(p(\underline{x}/\omega_2)/p(\underline{x}/\omega_1))dx$$

where S is the existing field of x, while the Battacharyya distance is:

$$B(1/2) = -\ln \int_S (p(\underline{x}/\omega_1)p(\underline{x}/\omega_2))^{1/2} dx$$

As is known an upper bound (ε_u) for error classification according to Bayes's method can be obtained (Chernoff bound):

$$\varepsilon_u = (p(\omega_1)p(\omega_2))^{1/2} e^{-B}$$

where $p(\omega_1)$ and $p(\omega_2)$ are the probabilities of each class.

The above relationships need to be modified adequately in the case of normal distribution. An approximate evaluation of ε_u for S can be obtained by Marill's diagram (Marill et al. 1963).

In order to select the best set of features in M-space, starting from N features, one should consider all possible combinations (M/N) and select the feature set where a maximum D or B is achieved.

Since this procedure requires a long process time, a simplified method has been adopted.

This method, called "matrix increment", is based on the following steps:
1) For each feature, selected among N, compute D and B and select the

best one according to the corresponding maximums D and B.

2) Add to each of the previously selected features any feature, among N-1 for each pair, compute the related D and B values: the total number of pairs is N-1.

3) Select the maximums D and B, so as to obtain the next best feature in space 2.

4) Go to 2 and continue to complete features ordination.

A complementary approach could be based on "matrix decrement", in this case, all N-1 feature combinations among N are considered at the beginning of the process, and minimum D and B reductions are obtained by subtracting a new feature during each step.

The matrix increment procedure can be implemented on small computers, without any particular "time problems" or "precision", if a small number of ordered features (e.g.5,) are considered; while, in the case of the "matrix decrement" procedure, high dimension matrices (N x N) are considered from the beginning procedure, high dimension matrices (N x N) are considered from the beginning; consequently, some problems might arise concerning the implementation of this procedure on small computers.

Both methods are not entirely correct; in fact, the best k-npla of features could not always be derived from an extension of the (K+1)-npla of features or from a reduction of (K+1)-npla of features. However, we have taken this easy approach on account of its simplicity, and the relevant results are quite satisfactory.

RESULTS

The table 2 gives the results obtained for each node; usually, 2-3 features for each node could be sufficient, since a "saturation" effect is achieved rapidly.

Node 3 (L/M), instead, presents higher errors; as a consequence, new kinds of features should be computed.

D and B results are in sufficiently good agreement, the most frequent parameters are 26-27-33-49-51-89. A typical behaviour of D and B vs. selected features is shown in Fig.2.

DISCUSSION

Our results generally agree with similar investigations reported in the literature (J.F. Preston Jr., 1980), even if, in this preliminary situation, we have considered some different features and very few pathological classes.

More classes should be considered; in this case, according to our experience, texture parameters would become more important for pathological classes; therefore, new texture parameters should be introduced; besides, the sample size should be increased. It is possible to select features without using any gaussian hypothesis: we need only to evaluate the measure of the differentiating power of the set of features according to the Nearest-Neightbour classification rule (A. Jozwickk et al., 1981).

This new method is presently under development and results will be compared with those described above.

TABLE 2. Results with D and B values for each node and an error upper bound esimation (ε_u).

	DIVERGENCE FEATURES	D	ε_u	BHATTACHARYYA FEATURES	B	ε_u
1st	36	255	5	26	1.826	8.1
N	" 43	1327	2	" 51	3.906	1.0
O	" " 26	1399	"	" " 36	5.161	0.3
D	" " " 53	2066	"	" " "23	6.345	0.09
E	" " " "12	2755	"	" " " " 29	7.139	0.04
2nd	49	1686	2	49	1.685	9.3
N	" 51	9990	"	" 76	3.030	2.4
O	" " 26	23889	"	" " 33	4.128	0.8
D	" " " 11	29175	"	" " " 54	5.121	0.3
E	" " " " 54	35405	"	" " " " 77	8.175	0.01
3rd	32	18	25	38	0.948	19.4
N	" 31	62	"	" 13	1.575	10.4
O	" " 89	70	"	" " 89	1.985	6.9
D	" " " 88	134	"	" " " 88	2.534	4.0
E	" " " " 82	175	20	" " " " 33	2.534	3.0
4th	49	11355	2	49	2.161	5.0
N	" 3	21897	"	" 27	3.363	1.7
O	" " 25	29933	"	" " 24	5.010	0.3
D	" " " 79	38787	"	" " " 23	5.980	0.1
E	" " " " 31	53827	"	" " " " 44	6.994	0.05
5 th	49	1695	2	49	1.686	9.3
N	" 51	10635	"	" 74	3.704	1.2
O	" " 25	34347	"	" " 75	5.515	0.2
D	" " " 89	52275	"	" " " 27	6.723	0.06
E	" " " " 44	78177	"	" " " " 91	7.785	0.02

152

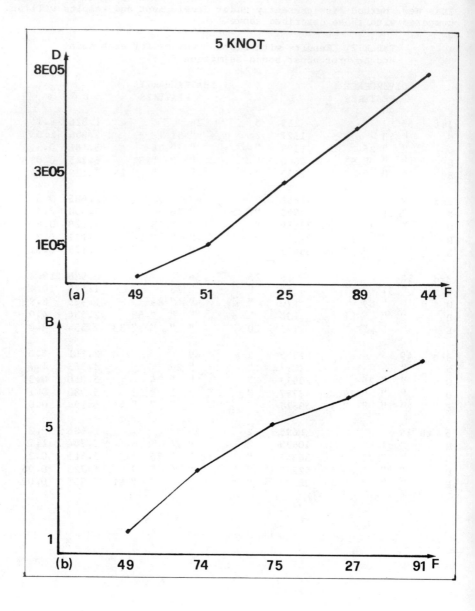

Fig. 2. Typical behaviour of D (a) and (b)
vs selected features..

APPENDIX 1

Feature description
1- Nuclear IOD in white light.
2-   "   "   " Wratten 22 filter.
3-   "   "   "   "   44   "
4-   "   AOD " white light.
5-   "   "   " Wratten 22 filter.
6-   "   "   "   "   44   "
7- cytoplasm IOD in white light. -
8-   "   "   " Wratten 22 filter.
9-   "   "   "   "   44   "
10-   "   AOD " white light.
11-   "   "   " Wratten 22 filter.
12-   "   "   "   "   44   "
13- cell IOD in white light.
14-   "   "   " Wratten 22 filter.
15-   "   "   "   "   44   "
16-   " AOD " white light.
17-   "   "   " Wratten 22 filter.
18-   "   "   "   "   44   "
19- N.U.
20- N.U.
21- N.U.
22- Contrast in W22 between nucleus and cytoplasm.
23-   "   " 44   "   "   "   "
24- Features 23/22 ratio.
25- Contrast between W22 and W44 on the cytoplasm.
26-   "   "   "   "   "   "   " nucleus.
27- Features 26/25 ratio.
28- Features 12/11 ratio.
29-   "   6/5   "
30-   "   29/28   "
31- Nuclear area.
32- Nuclear perimeter.
33- Nuclear form factor.
34- Cytoplasm area.
35- Cytoplasm perimeter.
36-   "   form factor.
37- Cell area.
38-   " perimeter.
39-   " form factor.
40- features 31/37 ratio.
41-   "   34/37   "
42- Malinowska nuclear form factor.
43-   "   cell   "   "
44- N.U.
45- N.U.
46- N.U.
47- N.U.
48- Nuclear barycentre in W22: x

154

49- Nuclear barycentre in W22: y
50-   "   "   " W44: x
51-   "   "   " " : y
52- Nuclear intensity
53- Nuclear colour
54- Nuclear average area using 3 filter
55- N.U.
56- N.U.
57- Cytoplasm barycentre in W22: x
58-   "   "   " " : y
59-   "   "   " W44: x
60-   "   "   " " : y
61- Cytoplasm intensity
62-   "   colour
63-   "   average area using 2 filter
64- N.U.
65- N.U.
66- Cell barycentre in W22: x
67-   "   "   " " : y
68-   "   "   " W44: x
69-   "   "   " " : y
70- Cell intensity
71-   "   colour
72-   "   average area using 2 filters
73- Nuclear average grey level.
74-   "   "   pixel value
75-   "   variance
76-   "   Skewness moment
77-   "   Kurtosis moment
78-   "   energy
79-   "   entropy
80- Cytoplasm average grey level
81-   "   "   pixels value
82-   "   variance
83-   "   Skewness moment
84-   "   Kurtosis moment
85-   "   energy
86-   "   entropy
87- Cell average grey level
88-   "   "   pixels value
89-   " variance
90-   " Skewness moment
91-   " Kurtosis moment
92-   " energy
93-   " entropy

REFERENCES

Beltrame, F. et al., 1980. Analysis system for absorption, fluorescence and phase contrast studies opf cell images. "nd Annual Conf. of the IEEE Eng. in Medicine and Biology Society, 58.

Brenner, J.F., and Gelsema, E.S., et al., 1974. Automated classification of normal and abnormal leucocytes. J. Hist. Cyto., Vol.22, 496-697.

Fukunaga, K., 1974. Introduction to statistical pattern recognition, pp 270-285. New York Academic press.

Jozwick, A., and Wasyluk, H., 1981. A method of features selection and its application to diagnosis of liver diseases. in press.

Marill, T. et al., 1963. On the effectiveness of receptor in recognition system. IEEE Trans. Inf. Theory 11-27.

Mui, J.K. and Fu, K.S., 1980. Automated classification of nucleated blood cells using a binary tree classifier. IEEE Trans. on PAMI, 5 429.

Preston, K.Jr., 1980. Automation of the Analysis of Cell Images. Analitical and Quantitativa Cytology, vol.2, N.1, 1-14.

SURFACE DETECTION ALGORITHM IN THREE DIMENSIONAL COMPLEX SPACE

S.   Impedovo, A.M. Fanelli ,A. Franich

Physics Institute, University of Bari
Via Amendola 173, 70126 BARI, ITALY.

ABSTRACT

The three-dimensional surface detection is a problem of great interest today $[1] \div [5]$.

An extension to a three-dimensional complex space of Sobel's contour following algorithm $[6]$ is proposed here.

Results produced by the algorithm as applied to the detection of
hand-written numeral classes $[7] \div [10]$ are also reported.

INTRODUCTION

We are concerned here with a three-dimensional complex space and a
method for detecting boundaries in this space is proposed.

The discrete complex space is mapped in a three-dimensional array
of three-dimensional blocks of points as shown in section 1. In section 1 the nature of the boundaries is specified too.

The method proposed in section 2 is an extension to the three-dimensional complex space "$\underline{C}^3$" of Sobel's boundary detection algorithm
$[6]$.

In section 3, a test of the method is carried out in the Fourier
Descriptors $[7]$, $[9]$ space to select the hand-written numeral class
frontier $[8]$.

Sec. 1) COMPLEX SPACE REPRESENTATION

In this paper a limited and discrete sub-set " $DL(\underline{C}^3)$ " of the
complex space $(\underline{C}^3)$ is considered.

In the following the polar coordinate system is used.

Let us assume that

$$DL(\underline{C}^3) = \left\{ (d_{12}, d_{13}, d_{14}) \right\} ;$$

where for each j=2,3 and 4; it results that:

$$|d_{1j}| \in [0, pP] ; \quad \begin{array}{l} p= \text{module quantum }, \\ P= \text{number of module quantization levels,} \end{array}$$

and

157

158

$\angle(d_{1j}) \in [0, qQ] = [0, 2\pi]$; q= argument quantum
Q= number of argument quantization
levels.

A limited and discrete sub-set of $\underline{\underline{R}}^6$ space can be represented in a real discrete three-dimensional space $(\tilde{d}_{12}, \tilde{d}_{13}, \tilde{d}_{14})$ by means of the transformations:

$$(|d_{1j}|, \angle d_{1j}) \longrightarrow (|d_{1j}| \cdot Q + \angle d_{1j}) , \quad \forall j=2,3,4. \tag{1}$$

(see fig. 1).

The canonic isomorphism between $\underline{\underline{C}}^3$ and $\underline{\underline{R}}^6$, together with the former transformations allow to investigate the $DL(\underline{\underline{C}}^3)$ set taking into account only a three-dimensional array of PxPxP blocks each one consisting of Q pages of QxQ points (fig. 2).

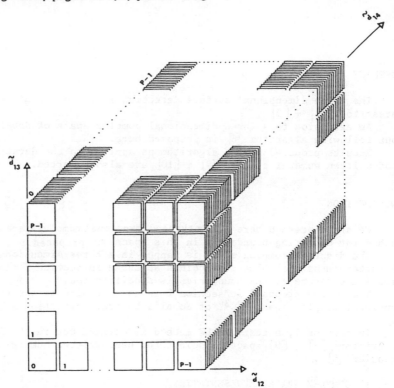

fig.1 Representation of PxPxP blocks in
the space of the terns (d_{12}, d_{13}, d_{14}) .

Because of our pattern recognition orientation, we refer to the objects in the $DL(\underline{\underline{C}}^3)$ set as "classes".

Generally each class is a hypersurface consisting of a set of surface each one enclosed in a block.

A class is here defined as the set of all the points in $DL(\underline{\underline{C}}^3)$ specified by the $\mathcal{H}$ property.

In this paper the $\mathcal{H}$ property is a boolean function

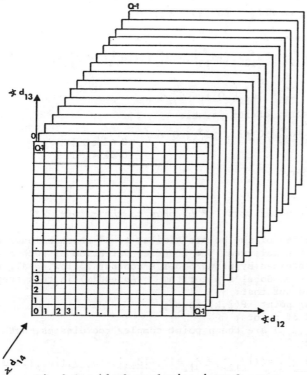

Fig.2 One block explosion into Q pages
each consisting of QxQ cells.

$$\text{DL.}(\underline{C}^3) \longrightarrow \left\{ 0,1 \right\}$$

The points having $\mathcal{H}(z)=1$ are considered inside a class, those with $\mathcal{H}(z)=0$ are outside of it. Only compact and simple connected classes are considered here, in order to detect each class by means of its frontier. The points belonging to the same class will be regarded as similar.

The order relation regarding the set of points belonging to a page of a block, as defined in fig. 3, will be used in the following to select the class frontier. This relation enables the frontier to be selected by computing the function in a minimal number of points. The algorithm shown in the next section allows to detect the contour by computing the $\mathcal{H}$ function only on the class frontier and on a few other inner points which are necessary to reach the frontier.

To detect the intersection of the class frontier with a plane in a block, Sobel's contour following algorithm is used.

Sec. 2) ALGORITHM.

Let us consider the $z_o^* \equiv ((\sphericalangle |d_{12}^{o*}|, \sphericalangle d_{12}^{o*}), (|d_{13}^{o*}|, \sphericalangle d_{13}^{o*}), (|d_{14}^{o*}|, \sphericalangle d_{14}^{o*}))$ point belonging to $DL(\underline{C}^3)$ so that $\mathcal{H}(z_o)=1$.

1)) $z^*=z_o^*$ is assumed

$$z^* \equiv ((|d_{12}^*|, \sphericalangle d_{12}^*), (|d_{13}^*|, \sphericalangle d_{13}^*), (|d_{14}^*|, \sphericalangle d_{14}^*)).$$

2)) The plane

$$\widetilde{d}_{14} = |d_{14}^*| \cdot Q + \sphericalangle d_{14}^* \tag{2}$$

and the matrix of its points:

$$\left(|d_{12}^*| \cdot Q + i, \quad |d_{13}^*| \cdot Q + k \right) \qquad \begin{array}{l} 0 \leqslant i \leqslant Q-1 \\ 0 \leqslant k \leqslant Q-1 \end{array} \tag{3}$$

are considered

Comment
It must be noted that z^* belongs to the matrix (3)

3)) The sub-class of the points similar to z^* which belongs to the matrix (3) is now selected. The frontier detection of such a sub-class can be obtained by using Sobel's contour following algorithm[6].
In the use of Sobel's algorithm (Appendix) in this step, it must be pointed out that:
a) The starting point $P(i,k)$ is z^*;
b) G is a grid of points;
c) if (d_{12}, d_{13}, d_{14}) are the p point complex coordinates, both the transformations:

$$T\left[P(\sphericalangle d_{12}, \sphericalangle d_{13})\right] = ((|d_{12}|, \sphericalangle d_{12}+1), (|d_{13}|, \sphericalangle d_{13}), (|d_{14}| \cdot \sphericalangle d_{14})) \tag{4}$$

and

$$N_d\left[P(\sphericalangle d_{12}, \sphericalangle d_{13})\right] = ((|d_{12}|, \sphericalangle d_{12}+\lambda), (|d_{13}|, \sphericalangle d_{13}+\mu), (|d_{14}|, \sphericalangle d_{14})) \tag{5}$$

give points neighbour to P ;
d) the operator "f" used here is the $\mathcal{H}$ function.

Comment
Each $\mathcal{L}$ line of matrix (3), which starts from z^* and closes itself in one of its points, is a set of points belonging to the z^* class if and only if it consists of points so that $\mathcal{H}(z)=1$ for each of them.
Being the class of z^* compact and connected it follows that also the points of the surface limited by the $\mathcal{L}$ line represent points which belong to the z^* class. Thus the sub-class can be defined by selecting the outer closed line of the points having $\mathcal{H}(z)=1$ (the frontier).

4)) The surface limited by the $\mathcal{L}$ line is filled [11] and the elements of this surface are arranged in order using the relation reported in fig. 3.

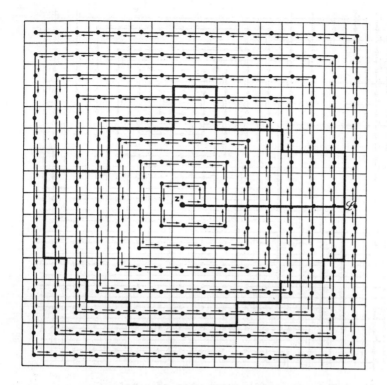

fig.3 Order relation on the points in the
matrix (3). z^* is at the matrix center.
The heavy line $\mathscr{L}$ represents the frontier.

Comment

It must be noted that since (3) is a spherical matrix, closed both in respect to the x-axis and to the y-axis, the order can be defined independently of the position of z^* (fig. 4).

5)) The region frontier which includes the matrices having at least one point z with $\mathscr{H}(z)=1$ is determined.

Sobel's algorithm can again be used in this step pointing out that:

a) G is now a grid of matrices, each corresponding to a pair of modules and consisting of QxQ points.

b) The starting point P(i,k) is now the matrix including z^*.

c) If

$$P(|d_{12}|,|d_{13}|) \equiv (|d_{12}| \cdot Q+i, |d_{13}| \cdot Q+k) \quad \begin{array}{l} 0 \leqslant i \leqslant Q-1 \\ 0 \leqslant k \leqslant Q-1 \end{array} \tag{6}$$

is one of these matrixes, then

$$T[P(|d_{12}|,|d_{13}|)] = ((|d_{12}|+1) \cdot Q+i, |d_{13}|Q+k)_{\begin{array}{l} 0 \leqslant i \leqslant Q-1 \\ 0 \leqslant k \leqslant 0-1 \end{array}} \tag{7}$$

is the positive versus x-axis translation matrix operator, and for each direction " $d(\lambda,\mu)$ ",

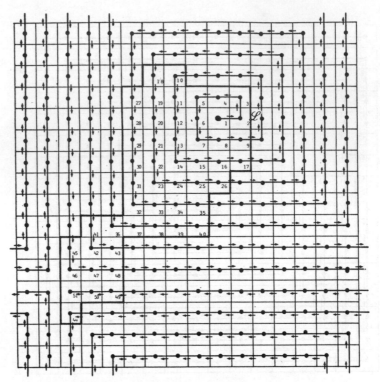

fig.4 The matrix (3) order when z*is not
      central. The order of the elements
      inside the class is defined by the
      numbers.

$$N_d\left[P(|d_{12}|,|d_{13}|)\right] = ((|d_{12}|+\lambda)\cdot Q+i,(|d_{13}|+\mu)\cdot Q+k\,)_{0\,\leqslant\,i\,\leqslant\,Q-1} \qquad (8)$$
$$0\leqslant K\leqslant Q-1$$

represents the P neighbour matrix in direction d.
d)   In this step the "f" function is the discrimination between
empty (including at least one point z having $\mathcal{H}(z)=1$) and non-empty
matrixes.

Comment
    *It must be observed that for each matrix, the new "f" applica-
tion recalls the computing of the former steps 3)) and 4)). Since
step 3)) uses Sobel's algorithm, it is necessary both to define a
starting point "z* " similar to z_o^* and to use the $\mathcal{H}$ function.*
    *If $N_d\,P(|d_{12}|,|d_{13}|)$ (respectively $T\left[P(|d_{12}|,|d_{13}|)\right]$ is the
processing matrix, the point set, which is the projection of the
ordered sub-class of all the points included in the matrix
$P(|d_{12}|,|d_{13}|)$) and belonging to z*class can be considered. The new
starting point z*is that of the projection set having $\mathcal{H}(z)=1$ in
the order in step 4)) .*

6)) The surface limited by the frontier selected in step 5)) is filled[11]. This means that for each pair of modules $(|d_{12}|, |d_{13}|)$ belonging to this surface, the set of all points belonging to the z_0^* class should be determined.

The execution of this step on the grid "G" mstrixes is developped starting from the matrix including z_0 and following the order stated in fig. 3.

Comment

To detect each set by using step 3)) a starting point "z^*" similar to z_0^* must be defined. To do this the same procedure shown in the comment of step 5)) can be used.

7)) Let $\bigsqcup \Lambda$ be the union of the sub-classes selected in step 6)). The elements of each Λ are ordered following the order relation of fig. 3. The Λ sub-classes are ordered on the matrixes grid in the same way. Furthermore, each point similar to z_0^* can be labelled with a (ρ, σ) order pair, where ρ is the plane curve position in the σ-th matrix.

If (ρ', σ') and (ρ'', σ'') are the pairs of two distinct points, the following definition will be true:

$$((\rho', \sigma') < (\rho'', \sigma'')) \iff ((\sigma' < \sigma'') \vee (\sigma' = \sigma'' \wedge \rho' < \rho'')) \tag{9}$$

through this order relation the $\bigsqcup \Lambda$ becomes a order set and thus it can be represented by the family:

$$(z_\nu) \quad 0 \leqslant \nu \leqslant (\sum \text{Card}(\Lambda)) - 1 \tag{10}$$

8)) The new points

$$z = z_\nu + u_i = ((|d_{12}|, \sphericalangle d_{12}), (|d_{13}|, \sphericalangle d_{13}), (|d_{14}|, \sphericalangle d_{14})) + ((0,0), (0,0), (0,1)) =$$
$$= ((|d_{12}|, \sphericalangle d_{12}), (|d_{13}|, \sphericalangle d_{13}), (|d_{14}|, \sphericalangle d_{14} + 1)). \tag{11}$$

which belong to the plane of equation:

$$\breve{d}_{14} = |d_{14}| \cdot Q + \sphericalangle d_{14} + 1 \tag{12}$$

are considered.

These points are generated, following the order of formula (10), until a new point having $\mathcal{H}(z) = 1$ is selected. Let us call this point z^* and return to step 2)).

Since $\sphericalangle d_{14}$ is a periodic function this procedure may be executed at most Q times and thereafter step 9)) will have to be executed.

If no point has $\mathcal{H}(z) = 1$, then $u_i = -u_i$ is assumed and the present step is repeated restarting from the plane

$$\breve{d}_{14} = |d_{14}^{\circ *}| \cdot Q + \sphericalangle d_{14}^{\circ *} \tag{13}$$

This is done until a new plane including no point having $\mathcal{H}(z) = 1$ is obtained.

Comment

This step gives a new set:

$$(z_\nu) \quad 0 \leqslant \nu \leqslant (\sum \text{Card}(\Lambda)) - 1 \tag{14}$$

which is the union of families like the one in (10). Each family corresponds to one $\sphericalangle d_{14}$ value.

9)) The families of union (14) are naturally ordered according to their generation. Following this order, for each point z in (14),the corresponding

$$z=z+U \qquad (15)$$

where $U= ((0,0),(0,0),(1,0))$, can be computed. This is done until a point z, having $\mathcal{H}(z)=1$ is detected. Such a "z" point is assumed as the starting point in repeating the former steps from 1)) to 8)) in order to select the new points similar to z_0^* and included in the block corresponding to $|d_{14}| = |d_{14}^*| + 1$.

This procedure must be repeated until either a block whithout points z similar to z_0^* or the last block corresponding to $|d_{14}|=P$ is selected. The same will be done also for the blocks having $|d_{14}|$ less than $|d_{14}^{o*}|$ until either a block without points z similar to z_0^* or the first block corresponding to $|d_{14}|=0$ is selected.

Sec. 3) EXPERIMENTAL RESULTS.

Some experiments have been carried out to detect the classes of the hand-written Arabic numeral.

If $z_o(t)$ is a hand-written numeral, $z_0^*(t')$ can be calculated [10].

The operator

$$\text{IDFT} \circ \mathcal{F}_{(M=4)} \circ \text{DFT} \circ \mathcal{S} \qquad (16)$$

where
-) $\mathcal{S}$ is a sampling function with a sampling period carefully chosen [7] ;
-) DFT is the Discrete Fourier Transform [13] - [14] ;
-) $\mathcal{F}_{(M=4)}$ is a five point rectangular window low-pass digital filter [15] ;
-) IDFT is the Inverse Discrete Fourier Transform;
allows the reconstruction of a band limited discrete plane curve z_0^*:

$$z_0^* = \text{IDFT} \left[\mathcal{F}_{(M=4)} \left[\text{DFT} \left[\mathcal{S} \left[z_0^*(t') \right] \right] \right] \right] \qquad (17)$$

which represents the same numeral [10] of the original sample $z_0^*(t)$.

The set of all the band limited discrete plane curve like z_o is here denoted by F^*.

It may be shown that F^* is a Hilbert space [8].

The plane curves which belong to the z_0^* class should now be detected. This can be done by selecting only the z_0^* class frontier since F^* is a Hausdorf space and the z_0^* class is simple connection one.

Such a frontier is generally a hypersurface consisting of a three-dimensional closed surface array and each surface is allocated inside a block similar to the one in fig. 2.

If

$$(c_0^{o*},c_1^{o*},c_2^{o*},c_3^{o*},c_4^{o*}) = \mathcal{F}_{(M=4)} \left[\text{DFT} \left[\mathcal{S} \left[z_0^* (t') \right] \right] \right] \qquad (18)$$

is the quintuple of the $z_0^*(t')$ first five Fourier coefficients, a sampling version of the z_0^* class can be obtained by means of the algorithm in the former section.

For this purpose the quantized value of the z_o^* sample Fourier Descriptors tern (d_{12}^{o*}, d_{13}^{o*}, d_{14}^{o*}) [10] must be computed.

Then let us set
$$z^*=z_o^* \quad \text{e.g.} : \quad (d_{12}^*, d_{13}^*, d_{14}^*)=(d_{12}^{o*}, d_{13}^{o*}, d_{14}^{o*}).$$

It must be noted that the $(d_{12}^*, d_{13}^*, d_{14}^*)$ tern, corresponds to a tern of pairs:
$$((|d_{12}^*|, \sphericalangle d_{12}^*),(|d_{13}^*|, \sphericalangle d_{13}^*),(|d_{14}^*|, \sphericalangle d_{14}^*))$$
while the integers in this tern are also used to address the z^* in the complex space of the ($\overset{\smile}{d}_{12}.\overset{\smile}{d}_{13},\overset{\smile}{d}_{14}$) tern.

Furthermore it must be pointed out that the "f" function used in step 3)) of the former algorithm is the hand-written numeral recognition function carried out by a human recognizer using an interactive system consisting of a pdp 11/70 computer with a Tesak display on line.

Instead the "f" function used in step 5)) is the discrimination between empty and non-empty matrixes, where a non-empty matrix is now one including at least one plane curve recognized by man as z_o^* and an empty matrix is one that includes no plane curves recognizable as z_o^* . Obviously also the "f" function at hand is carried out by a human recognizer who uses the same interactive system.

In fig. 6 the sub-class of the numeral "6" (see fig. 5) including the z_o^* sample is shown.

The intersection of the hyper-frontier of the numeral three class with the plane:
$$\overset{\smile}{d}_{14} = |d_{14}^{o*}|\cdot Q + \sphericalangle d_{14}^{o*} =55$$
is reported in fig. 7.

fig.5

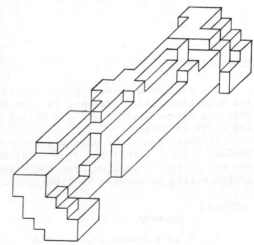

fig.6 The sub-class frontier including the numeral six in fig. 5 .

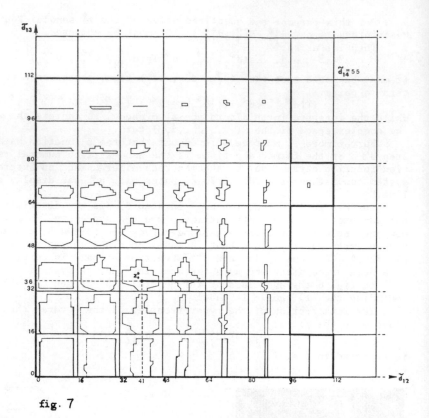

fig. 7

CONCLUSIONS

The algorithm here proposed starts from a point which is inside the detecting class. However, in many other applications, such a point is not accessible and a starting point z_o^* that is out-side the class is taken.

In these cases the same algorithm may be used changing the boolean value 0 with 1 and viceversa; however in the last case, since the class size is smaller than the relative space, a more expensive preprocessing to check a frontier point is necessary.

APPENDIX
-Comment on the use of Sobel's algorithm-

Let G be a square grid of elements $P(i;k)$ where (i,k) is the P element pair of Cartesian coordinates.

The P point has eight neighbours each with $(i+\lambda, k+\mu)$ coordinates where the integer λ and μ can assume the value -1, 0 and +1.

Using the method proposed by H. Freeman[11] the eight neigbours of each element can be achieved by means of eight vectors having origin in P and terminus in each of these neighbour elements. The vectors

fig.8 Sobel's algorithm flow chart.

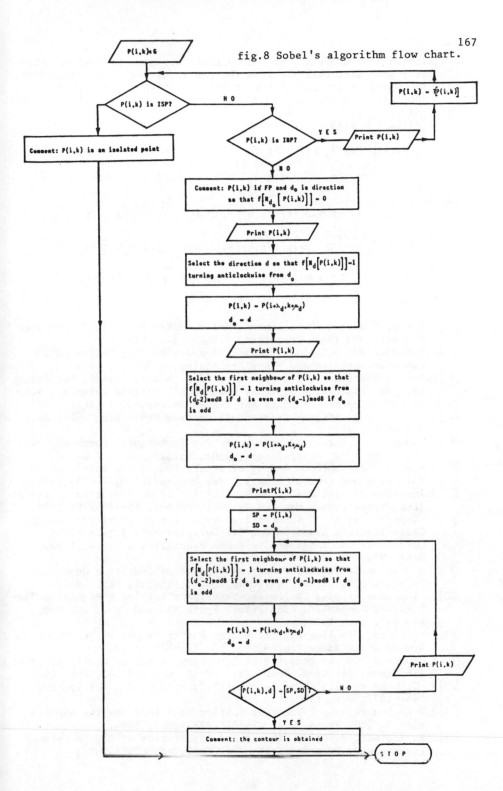

are denoted with numbers from one to eight assigned to them in anti-clockwise direction starting from the positive x-axis. A conventional addition modulo eight is defined on the set of these vectors.

The following translation operators are used in Sobel's algorithm (fig. 8) .

1°) $T\left[P(i,k)\right] = P(i+1,k+0)$, is the translation on the P(i.k) right element.

2°) $N_d\left[P(i,k)\right] = P(i+\lambda_d,k+\mu_d)$ is the translation on the element neighbour P(i,k) in the direction d (λ_d,μ_d).

Furthermore the following definition are also used in the same algorithm:

Def.a) INner Point (INP)
$$(P(i.k) \text{ is INP}) \Leftrightarrow (f\left[P(i,k)\right]=1 \wedge \forall d=1,\ldots,8:f\left[N_d\left[P(i,k)\right]\right]=1)$$

Def.b) Isolated Point (ISP)
$$(P(i,k) \text{ is ISP}) \Leftrightarrow (f|P(i,k)|=1 \wedge \forall d=1,\ldots,8:f\left[N_d\left[P(i,k)\right]\right]=0)$$

Def.c) Frontier Point (FP)
$$(P(i,k) \text{ is FP }) \Leftrightarrow (f|P(i,k)|=1 \wedge \exists d=1,\ldots,8 \ni' f\left[N_d\left[P(i,k)\right]\right]=0)$$

REFERENCES

[1] H.K.Liu; "Two and Three-dimensional Boundary Detection". Computer Graphics and Image Processing.6, 123÷134, 1977.

[2] G.T.Herman and H.K.Liu; "Dinamic Boundary Surface Detection". Computer Graphics and Image Processing.7,130÷138, 1978.

[3] E.Artzy, G.Frieder and G.T.Herman; "The theory, Design, Implementation and Evaluation of Three-Dimensional Surface Detection Algorithm". Computer Graphics and Image Processing. 15,1÷24, 1981.

[4] R.Gordon et al.;"Image Reconstruction from Projection". Sci.Am.; 233,56÷68, 1975.

[5] L.S.Davis. "A Survey of Edge Detection Techniques" Computer Graphics and Image Processing 4, 248÷270,1979.

[6] I.Sobel; "Neighborhood Coding of Binary Images for Fast Contour Following and General Binary Arrey Processing 8,127÷135,1978.

[7] S.Impedovo et al.; Real Time Recognition of Hand-Written Numerals". IEEE Trans. Syst., Man and Cyber., SMC 6-2,145÷148,Feb. 1976.

[8] S. Impedovo et al. " Interactive System for Hand-Written Numeral Classification Based on Fourier Descriptors". International Conference on "Image Analysis and Processing". Pavia, Italy, Oct. 1980.

[9] G.H.Granlund; "Fourier Preprocessing for Hand-Written Character Recognition". IEEE Trans.,Comp..,C.21,195÷201, Feb. 1972.

[10] S. Impedovo et al.; "A Fourier Descriptor Set for Recognizing Non-Stylized Numerals". IEEE Trans. Syst. Man and Cyb., SMC 8÷8, 640-645, Aug. 1978.

[11] T.Pavlidis; "Filling Algorithms for Raster Graphics". Computer Graphics and Image Processing. 10, 126÷141. 1979.

[12] H.Freeman; "On the Encoding of Arbitrary Geometric Configurations". IRE Trans. Electron. Comp. Vol. EC-10, pp. 260÷268, Feb. 1961.

[13] W. Cochran et àl.; "What is the FFT?". Proc. IEEE, Vol.55, 10, 1664÷1677, Oct. 1967.

[14] J.W.Cooley et al.; " The Fast Fourier Transform and its Application ". IEEE Trans. Educ. E-12,1,27÷34,Mar. 1969.

[15] L.R. Rabiner, B. Gold; "Theory and Application of Digital Signal Processing", Prentice-Hall, Inc. Englewood Cliffs, N.J.

NONPARAMETRIC ESTIMATION OF CLASSIFICATION ERROR PROBABILITY

J Kittler

Technology Division, SERC Rutherford Appleton
Laboratory, Chilton, Didcot OX11 0QX, U.K.

INTRODUCTION

The ultimate goal in designing machine pattern recognition systems
is to achieve recognition performance which is either comparable
to that of human beings or, at least, acceptable in view of all
the benefits automation affords.

There are two complementary measures of performance of recognition
systems: the classification error probability, and the reject
rate. Classification error is incurred when the recognizer
incorrectly assings a pattern belonging to one class to some other
class. Pattern rejection occurs when the available information is
not adequate for the recognizer to make a decision with a sufficient
degree of confidence.

When talking about machine pattern recognition the problems that
spring to mind are the classical applications in medicine, remote
sensing, character recognition, speech recognition, etc. These
problems are basically high level tasks which define the role
and specifications for the machine pattern processing system.
However, in the design of the system, one often encounters many
lower level tasks which arc also pattern classification problems,
although they are not normally considered as such. For instance
the problems of thresholding and edge detection fall in this
category at the lowest processing levels. Similarly, the problems
of primitive extraction for syntactic pattern recognition, at the
next higher processing level, are decision making problems of
classification nature. Ideally, all these lower level problems
should also be solved with the above criteria being used as figures
of merits. The estimation of these indices of performance is
therefore a very important problem.

There is a close relationship between error and reject probabilities
and in principle one could obtain an estimate of, say the reject
probability from the knowledge of the error probability. Also the
approaches to estimating error probability can be adapted for reject

probability estimation. Thus we shall concentrate herein on problems of error probability estimation only. Furthermore, for the sake of simplicity we shall restrict the discussion to the case where the reject option is not activated.

There are basically two kinds of classification error that are of interest to the pattern recognition community. First of all there is the Bayes error, or in other words, the minimum achievable error, representing the limit of excellence beyond which it is impossible to go (Devijver and Kittler 1982). The second quantity of interest is the actual error of a particular classification system which characterizes the system's future performance (performance on new data drawn from the same distribution as the one that generated the data used for the system design) (Kittler, 1980).

As measures of the achievable and actual performance, both error probabilities have important applications in feature selection and extraction (Fukunaga, 1972, Devijver and Kittler, 1982). But this common application area is not their only shared characteristic. Both errors are notorious for being difficult to estimate. While the Bayes error estimation can sometimes be obviated by replacing the Bayes error with other criteria that are more readily amenable to numerical evaluation, there is no substitute for the system error estimation.

It should be noted that the distinction between the Bayes error and the system error is not as clear cut as the above Aristotelian classification might imply. For instance, if the decision rule of an actual classification system is optimal, then the system error will be identical with the Bayes error. Admittedly, this ideal situation is rather unrealistic. However, quite often the decision rule of an actual pattern recognition system will be asymptotically optimal, that is the rule's suboptimality will be the result of the small sample size of the design data set. If the design set size was infinite, then the decision rule would become optimal. For such a decision rule the system error can be considered as an estimate of the Bayes error. A typical example of this category of decision rules is the discriminant function for normally distributed classes.

The distinction between these two kinds of error however becomes clear when the form of the decision rule of an actual pattern recognition system is constrained by simplifying assumptions so that the rule cannot approach optimal performance even in the large design sample case. These assumptions are usually imposed by computational or engineering considerations. For instance, if the classes are non linearly separable in the observation space, yet a linear discrimin-ant function in this space is assumed, the resulting (actual) decision rule will not be asymptotically optimal and its performance will bear no relation to the Bayes error.

The problem of estimating classification error probability has received considerable attention first in the context of parametric distributions (John, 1961, Okamoto, 1963, Smith 1947 , Toussaint, 1974) and lately in the context of nonparametric distributions (Highleyman,

1962, Lachenbruch, 1967, Cover, 1969, Toussaint, 1974, Fukunaga and
Kessel, 1973, Fukanaga and Hostetler, 1975, Lissack and Fu, 1974,
Garnett and Yau, 1977, Chen and Fu, 1977, Kittler and Devijver, 1980,
1981, 1982). In the latter case in particular, the suggested
approaches vary widely from the empirical error count method
Highleyman, 1962) to the use of a Parzen probability density function
estimator (Lissack and Fu, 1974).

In this paper we shall concentrate on a very important approach
this range of nonparametric methods, which is based on the k-nearest
neighbour method of estimating conditional error probabilities. This
method was first suggested by Cover (1969). Later, (1973) notable
contributions were made by Fukunaga and Kessel (1973) and Kittler and
Devijver (1980, 81., 82). Herein an attempt is made to present the k-nearest
neighbour approach to classification error probability estimation in
a unified manner, covering both the Bayes error and system error
estimation. The empirical error count estimator is shown, in this
framework, to be a special case of the k-nearest neighbour approach
(with k=1). Finally, finite sample size effects on the described
estimation method are discussed.

SYSTEM ERROR ESTIMATION

Let $\underline{x} = [x_1, x_2, ..x_n]^T$ be a multivariate random pattern vector which
is to be classified into one of m possible classes ω_i, i=1,2,...m.
Suppose further that $P(\omega_i)$ is the a priori probability of occurence
of class ω_i and that the conditional probability density of pattern
vector $\underline{x}$ given class ω_i is $p(\underline{x}|\omega_i)$. (For the sake of generality,
the conditional probability distributions of $\underline{x}$ will be considered to
be nonparametric.) Unclassified patterns then have the mixture
density

$$p(\underline{x}) = \sum_{i=1}^{m} p(\underline{x}|\omega_i) \, P(\omega_i) \qquad (1)$$

Suppose we are given a decision rule $d(\underline{x})$ which partitions the
domain of realization of the random variable $\underline{x}$ into m distinct
regions Γ_i, i=1,2,..,m, associated with classes ω_i, i=1,2,..m,
respectively.

An unknown pattern vector $\underline{x}$ is then assigned to class ω_i if $\underline{x}$ belongs
to region Γ_i, i.e.

$$\underline{x} \rightarrow \omega_i \text{ if } \underline{x} \, \epsilon \, \Gamma_i \qquad (2)$$

For each $\underline{x} \, \epsilon \, \Gamma_i$ the classification error $r(\underline{x})$ incurred by the
decision rule is given by

$$r(\underline{x}) = 1 - P(\omega_i|\underline{x}) \qquad (3)$$

where $P(\omega_i|\underline{x})$ is the a posteriori probability of class ω_i conditioned
on $\underline{x}$. Using the Bayes formula, $P(\omega_i|\underline{x})$ can be calculated as

$$P(\omega_i | \underline{x}) = \frac{p(\underline{x} | \omega_i) P(\omega_i)}{p(\underline{x})} \tag{4}$$

The unconditional classification error e, which is of interest here, is then obtained by taking the expectation of $r(\underline{x})$, i.e.

$$e = \int r(\underline{x}) \, p(\underline{x}) \, d\underline{x} \tag{5}$$

As in practice neither the conditional error $r(\underline{x})$ nor the mixture density function $p(\underline{x})$ are known, we wish to estimate the unconditional error probability e with the aid of an infinite set $X_T = \{\underline{x}_j\}$ of classified samples. An estimate $\hat{e}$ of error e can be obtained as

$$\hat{e} = \frac{1}{L} \sum_{j=1}^{L} \hat{r}(\underline{x}_j) \tag{6}$$

where L is the number of test samples $\underline{x}_j$ drawn from X_T for this purpose, and $\hat{r}(\underline{x}_j)$ is an estimate of the conditional error $r(\underline{x})$ at the point $\underline{x}_j$. As the class conditional probability density functions are assumed to be nonparametric, a nonparametric method of estimating $r(\underline{x})$ must be employed. We could estimate $r(\underline{x})$ indirectly via estimating, for instance, the density functions in (4).The a priori class probabilities $P(\omega_i)$ could be inferred from the proportion of samples belonging to class ω_i in a mixture sample set drawn from X_T.

A more appropriate way, which is also of greater interest in the context of this paper, is to adopt the k-nearest neighbour approach to estimating the a posteriori probabilities on the left hand side of (4) directly. Given a point $\underline{x}_j$ and its k-nearest neighbours from among the points in the mixture set X_T(or k-1 neighbours if the label of $\underline{x}_j$ is also considered) the a posteriori probability $P(\omega_i | \underline{x}_j)$ can be estimated as

$$\hat{P}(\omega_i | \underline{x}_j) = \frac{k_i}{k} \tag{7}$$

where k_i is the number of these neighbours belonging to class ω_i.

From (3) and (7) it follows that for $\underline{x}_j \in \Gamma_i$ the conditional error $r(\underline{x}_j)$ can be estimated by

$$\hat{r}(\underline{x}_j) = \frac{\tau}{k} \tag{8}$$

where τ is given as

$$\tau = k - k_i \tag{9}$$

In other words, τ is the number of nearest neighbours to $\underline{x}_j$ belonging to other classes than the one associated with the region containing point $\underline{x}_j$.

Under the assumption of infinite set X_T, the distribution $\hat{r}(\underline{x})$in (8) is binomial with the expected value equal to $r(\underline{x})$. Thus $\hat{r}(\underline{x})$ is unbiased and so is the estimate $\hat{e}$ of the unconditional error probability given in (6). This can be seen by taking the expected value of $\hat{e}$ over all possible sets of k nearest neighbours and sets of sample points of cardinality L

$$E_L \{F_k \{e\}\} = E_L\{\frac{1}{L} \sum_{j=1}^{L} E_k \{\hat{r}(\underline{x}_j)\}\} =$$

$$E_L\{\frac{1}{L} \sum_{j=1}^{L} r(\underline{x}_j)\} = e \qquad (10)$$

The variance of the estimator $\sigma^2\{\hat{e}\}$ is defined

$$\sigma^2(\hat{e}) = E_L \{E_k \{(\hat{e}-e)^2\}\} \qquad (11)$$

Substituting for $\hat{e}$ from (6) and utilising (10) the right hand side of (11) can be arranged as

$$\sigma^2(\hat{e}) = \frac{1}{L^2} E_L \{\sum_{j=1}^{L} E_k \{\hat{r}^2(\underline{x}_j)\}\} - \frac{e^2}{L} \qquad (12)$$

Note that since $\hat{r}(\underline{x})$ is distributed binomially with parameter $r(\underline{x})$, its variance $\sigma^2(\hat{r})$ is known to be

$$\sigma^2\{\hat{r}(\underline{x})\} = \frac{1}{k} r(\underline{x}) [1-r(\underline{x})] \qquad (13)$$

Thus the term under summation operator in (12) becomes

$$E_k \{\hat{r}^2(\underline{x}_j)\} = \sigma^2\{\hat{r}(\underline{x}_j)\} + r^2(\underline{x}) =$$

$$\frac{1}{k} r(\underline{x})[1+(k-1)r(\underline{x})] \qquad (14)$$

and substituting this result in (12) we find

$$\sigma^2(\hat{e}) = \frac{1}{L^2} E_L \{\sum_{j=1}^{L} \frac{1}{k} r(\underline{x}_j) [1+(k-1)r(\underline{x}_j)]\} - \frac{e^2}{L} \qquad (15)$$

Denoting the variance of the conditional error r by $\sigma^2(r)$, i.e.

$$\sigma^2(r) = E_L \{(r-e)^2\} \qquad (16)$$

(15) can be rewritten as

$$\sigma^2(e) = \frac{e(1-e)}{kL} + \frac{k-1}{kL} \sigma^2(r) \qquad (17)$$

To summarise the estimation of error probability e involves drawing from X_T a set of L test samples $\underline{x}_j, j=1,2,\ldots L$. For each sample $\underline{x}_j$ we find k-1 nearest neighbours in X_T and estimate the conditional error $\hat{r}(\underline{x}_j)$ following (8). Error estimate $\hat{e}$ is then defined by (6)

It is interesting to note that when k=1 the conditional error $\hat{r}(\underline{x}_j)$ will take on values

$$\hat{r}(\underline{x}_j) = \begin{cases} 0 & \text{if for } \underline{x}_j \varepsilon \Gamma_1 \text{ we have } \underline{x}_j \varepsilon \omega_i \\ 1 & \text{if for } \underline{x}_j \varepsilon \Gamma_i \text{ we have } \underline{x}_j \notin \omega_i \end{cases} \qquad (18)$$

It has been shown elsewhere that while $\hat{r}(\underline{x}_j)$ in (18) is an estimate of the conditional classification error, it can also be considered as an estimate of the unconditional error e, but in this case having the binomial distribution with parameter e. As $\sigma^2(\hat{e})$ in (17) is inversely proportional to k, the variance of the estimator for k=1 will be large. However the main advantage of setting k=1 is that we do not have to search for nearest neighbours of $\underline{x}_j, j=1,2,...L,$ for then k-1=0. Thus to obtain an estimate of the conditional (or unconditional) error we simply compare the class label of $\underline{x}_j$ with the class associated with the region containing $\underline{x}_j$, that is with the class assigned to $\underline{x}_j$ by the decision rule (2). This particular procedure is the well known empirical error count method.

So far we have assumed that the partitioning of the observation space (and the associated decision rule) is independent of the set X_T in general, and of the means of estimating the conditional classification error in particular. As a result of this independence the error estimator in (6) has the advantage of being unbiased. While it is perfectly realistic in many cases to assume that the space partitioning is independent of X_T, there are situations where this assumption cannot be satisfied and one of these will be considered in the second part of the next section. First, however we shall introduce the problem of Bayes error estimation.

BAYES ERROR ESTIMATION

Let us consider the problem of estimating the minimum achievable classification error (the Bayes error), e_B, incurred by the Bayes decision rule defined as

$$\text{assign } \underline{x} \rightarrow \omega_i \text{ if } P(\omega_i|\underline{x}) = \max_j P(\omega_j|\underline{x}) \qquad (19)$$

This rule partitions the observation space into regions Γ_{Bi} satisfying

$$P(\omega_i|\underline{x}) = \max_j P(\omega_j|\underline{x}) \qquad \forall \, \underline{x} \varepsilon \Gamma_i \qquad (20)$$

As pointed out earlier, our problem lies in the fact that we do not know the a posteriori class probability functions $P(\omega_i|\underline{x})$. Consequently, the regions Γ_{Bi} associated with this optimal rule cannot be determined but only estimated.

Suppose we have available another infinite set of observations on $\underline{x}$, denoted by X_D. Then we can use this set to estimate functions $P(\omega_j|\underline{x})$. Using the estimator in (7) based on k' nearest neighbours drawn from X_D, we can obtain $\hat{P}(\omega_i|\underline{x})$ and the corresponding partition

$\overset{\sim}{\Gamma}_{Bi}$, i=1,2...m. Although the expected value of the estimate $P(\omega_i|\underline{x})$ is unbiased, this property does not extend to the function $\max\limits_{j} \tilde{P}(\omega_i|\underline{x})$ i.e.

$$E_K\{\max_{j} \tilde{P}(\omega_j|\underline{x})\} \neq \max_{j} P(\omega_j|\underline{x}) \qquad (21)$$

As a matter of fact the unconditional classification error $\tilde{e}$ corresponding to partition Γ_{Bi},Vi, cannot ever be less than the minimum error e_B, i.e.

$$\tilde{e} > e_B \qquad (22)$$

Consequently, the expectation of its estimate $\hat{e}$ in (6) will also satisfy

$$E_L\{ \hat{e} \} > e_B \qquad (23)$$

and by analogy to (17) the variance of $\hat{e}$ will be

$$\sigma^2(\hat{e}) = \frac{\tilde{e}(1-\tilde{e})}{kL} + \frac{(k-1)\sigma^2(\tilde{r})}{kL} \qquad (24)$$

Here $\tilde{r}$ is the conditional classification error corresponding to the particular (sub-optimal) realisation $\overset{\sim}{\Gamma}_{Bi}$ of the optimal space-partition Γ_{Bi}, i=1,2...m.

At this point it should be absolutely clear which estimation procedure the above statistical properties correspond to. We draw a set of L test sample points $\underline{x}_j$ from X_T. For each $\underline{x}_j$ we draw k' nearest neighbours from X_D to identify the region containing $\underline{x}_j$. We then draw additional k-1 nearest neighbours to $\underline{x}_j$ from X_T and note their labels in order to estimate τ in (9). This process is repeated for all $\underline{x}_j$ in L and an estimate $\hat{e}$ is then obtained following (6).

Should any of the realizations of pattern $\underline{x}$ in the set of L be identical with any of those observed earlier, say $\underline{x}_r$, then the class associated with the region containing $\underline{x}_r$, determined earlier, would be used for such a point. More specifically, suppose

$$\underline{x}_s = \underline{x}_r \qquad r < s < L$$

and

$$\underline{x}_r \; \varepsilon \; \overset{\sim}{\Gamma}_{Bi}$$

Then we would also consider $\underline{x}_s$ to belong to region $\overset{\sim}{\Gamma}_{Bi}$, i.e. $\underline{x}_s \varepsilon \overset{\sim}{\Gamma}_{Bi}$.

An alternative possibility is to relax the above sampling procedure in the sense that for each $\underline{x}_j$ we find a unique realization of the class associated with the region containing this point. Thus even in the above situation we would draw a new set of k' nearest neighbours to $\underline{x}_s$ from the set X_D and determine the corresponding region containing it. The resulting strategy reflects more closely normal sampling practices.

This procedural change however, has a profound effect on the variance of the estimator $\hat{e}$ and possibly also on its bias (with respect to the optimal error). Now in addition to variance (24), we shall have the contributory effect of the region Γ_{Bi} varying for all distinct realizations of the test pattern vector $\underline{x}$ even when identical values are assumed. Thus, given $\underline{x}$, the region $\overline{\Gamma}_{Bi}$ containing it will be a random variable with m possible outcomes. The probability distribution of $\hat{\Gamma}_B$ conditioned on $\underline{x}$ is a function of the multi-nomial probability distribution over the joint events that can arise when k' observations are made on a random variable with m possible outcomes the probability of each outcome being $P(\omega_j|\underline{x})$. The probability distribution of Γ_B is difficult to evaluate and here we shall be content simply with the conjecture that the variance of the latter error estimation procedure is larger than that of the former one.

In conclusion, the above approach to the Bayes error estimation suffers from a number of drawbacks. First of all we need an extra data set to estimate the Bayes optimal boundaries between classes. Second, the variance of the Bayes error estimator is relatively large. Third, the error estimator has inherent pessimistic bias (with respect to the Bayes error). Last but not least, the procedure is computationally involved, requiring that, for each test sample point, two data sets are searched for nearest neighbours. In the following, an alternative method for estimating the Bayes error will be considered.

Let us partition the observation space into regions $\hat{\Gamma}_{Bi}$ using the same data set as the one employed for estimating the conditional error probability, namely set X_T. The regions $\hat{\Gamma}_{Bi}$ are defined so that

$$\hat{P}(\omega_i|\underline{x}) = \max_j \hat{P}(\omega_j|\underline{x}) \quad \underline{x} \in \hat{\Gamma}_{Bi} \qquad (25)$$

where $\hat{P}(\omega_j|\underline{x})$ is the k- NN estimate of the j-th class a posteriori probability conditioned on $\underline{x}$ given in (7). Thus here the conditional error estimate in (8) is simply

$$\hat{r}(\underline{x}) = 1 - \max_j \hat{P}(\omega_j|\underline{x})$$
$$= 1 - \max_j \frac{k_j}{k} \qquad (26)$$

In the m-class case the probability distribution of $\hat{r}(\underline{x})$ is defined by the multinomial probability distribution over the joint events that can arise when k observations are made on a random variable with m possible outcomes. This distribution is difficult to handle but it can be conjectured that $\hat{r}(\underline{x})$ is an optimistically biased estimate of the conditional Bayes error $r_B(\underline{x})$. This becomes apparent when one realizes that $\hat{r}(\underline{x})$ for instance, will never take values greater than $(m-1)/m$.

The distribution is more manageable when m=2. It has been shown (Fukunaga and Kessel, 1973) that

$$E\{\hat{r}(\underline{x})\} = \sum_{j=1}^{k/2} \frac{1}{j} \binom{2j-2}{j-1} [P(\omega_1|\underline{x})P(\omega_2|\underline{x})]^j \qquad (27)$$

Noting that

$$P(\omega_1|\underline{x}) \; P(\omega_2|\underline{x}) = r_B(\underline{x}) \; [1-r_B(\underline{x})] \qquad (28)$$

we can write

$$r_B(\underline{x}) = \frac{1}{2} - \frac{1}{2} \sqrt{1-4P(\omega_1|x)P(\omega_2|x)} \qquad (29)$$

The MacLaurin series of (29) gives

$$r_B(\underline{x}) = \sum_{j=1}^{\infty} \frac{1}{j} \binom{2j-2}{j-1} [P(\omega_1|\underline{x}) \; P(\omega_2|\underline{x})]^j \qquad (30)$$

Comparing (27) with (30) we see that

$$E\{\hat{r}(\underline{x})\} < r_B(\underline{x}) \qquad (31)$$

Thus $\hat{r}(\underline{x})$ is indeed an optimistically biased estimate of $r_B(\underline{x})$. Consequently, estimate $\hat{e}$ of the unconditional Bayes error e_B is also optimistically biased, i.e

$$E_L\{\hat{e}\} = \sum_{j=1}^{k/2} \frac{1}{j} \binom{2j-2}{j-1} E_L \{[P(\omega_1|\underline{x})P(\omega_2|\underline{x})]^j\} < e_B \qquad (32)$$

The variance $\sigma^2(\hat{e})$ can be shown to be (Fukunaga and Kessel, 1973)

$$\sigma^2(\hat{e}) = \frac{E_L\{\hat{e}\} \; (1-E_L\{\hat{e}\})}{L} - \frac{(k-1)e_B}{2kL}$$

To summarise, this latter Bayes error estimation procedure involves drawing a set of test samples $\underline{x}_j, j=1,2..L$ from X_T. For each $\underline{x}_j$ we find its k-1 nearest neighbours and determine the class receiving the majority vote from the k patterns (including $\underline{x}_j$).

The conditional error $\hat{r}(\underline{x}_j)$ is then estimated according to (26) and substituted in (6) to find unconditional error estimate, $\hat{e}$.

FINITE SAMPLE SIZE EFFECTS

The statistical properties of the estimators discussed above are only asymptotic, that is they hold when sets X_T and X_D are of infinite size. In practice when X_T and X_D are finite, many assumptions that have been made, either explicitly or implicitly, break down. First of all, nearest neighbours to an arbitrary point $\underline{x}$ will no longer assume the same value as $\underline{x}$. Instead, they will be drawn from a finite neighbourhood of $\underline{x}$ over which functions $P(\omega_i|\underline{x})$, $V\underline{x}$, vary. As a result, the probability distribution of $\hat{r}(x)$ will not be a function of the binomial/multinomial distribution but instead it will be mixed binomial/multinomial. This and some other effects have been discussed by Kittler and Devijver (1982).

Second, and probably even more serious effect, is that estimates $\hat{r}(\underline{x}_j)$, $j=1,2...L$, cease to be statistically independent. Among the $k-1$ nearest neighbours to point $\underline{x}_j$ there may be points which are also among the $k-1$ nearest neighbours to other test samples. Apart from some initial experimental studies this effect has not yet been properly investigated.

The only exception where the assumptions made do not qualitatively change even when X_T is finite is the k=1 case in (18). Thus the statistical properties of the error estimator $\hat{e}$ in this situation remain valid. Naturally k=1 cannot be used in the case of the second Bayes error estimator, for $\hat{r}(\underline{x}_j)$ in (26) would always assume zero value. This clearly shows the tendency of the estimator to underestimate the true error probability.

COMMENTS AND CONCLUSIONS

There are a number of other aspects, such as those relating to efficiency of data utilization, that should not be overlooked. These arise, for instance, when the same data must be used for the design of a pattern classifier (decision rule) and then for the estimation of its error. This particular problem has been addressed in Kittler (1982). Also the question of cardinality of set X_T in relation to k and L is very important, expecially because of the contradicting views on the required size of X_T (Fukunaga and Kessel, 1973, Kittler 1982). However these questions lie beyond the scope of this paper, and in any case, further work will be needed before they can be conclusively answered.

The main purpose of this paper was to discuss the k-nearest neighbour approach to classification error estimation in a unified manner. The discussion covered both the recognition system error estimation and the Bayes error estimation. The empirical error count has been shown to be a special case of this nonparametric error probability estimation approach.

REFERENCES

Chen, S., and Fu,K.S., 1977 Nonparametric Bayes risk estimation
for classification. IEEE Trans.on Systems, Man and Cybern., Vol
SMC-7, pp. 651-656

Cover, T., 1969. Learning in pattern recognition.In Methodologies
of Pattern Recognition (s. Watanabe ed). pp. 111-132, New York:
Academic Press.

Devijver, P.A., 1978. Nonparametric estimation of feature evaluation
criteria. In Pattern Recognition and Signal Processing (C.J. Chen.
Ed.) Noordhoff.

Devijver, P.A., 1978. Nonparametric estimation by the method of
ordered nearest neighbour sample sets. Proc. 4th IJCPR, pp. 217-223
Kyoto, Japan.

Devijver, P.A., and Kittler, J., 1982. Pattern Recognition: A
statistical approach. Prentice Hall International, London

Fukunaga, K., 1972. Introduction to statistical pattern recognition.
Academic Press, New York.

Fukanaga, K., and Hostetler, L., 1975. k-nearest neighbour Bayes
risk estimation. IEEE Trans. Inf. Theory Vol. IT-21, pp. 285-293.

Fukunaga, K., and Kessel, D., 1973. Nonparametric Bayes error
estimation using unclassified samples. IEEE Trans. Inf. Theory,
Vol.IT-19, pp. 434-439.

Garnett, J M., and Yau, S.S., 1977. Nonparametric estimation of the
Bayes error of feature extractors using ordered nearest neighbour
sets. IEEE Trans. Comput. Vol C - 26, pp. 46-54.

Highleyman, W.H., 1962. The design and analysis of pattern recognition experiments. Bell Syst. Tech. J., Vol. 41, pp 723-744.

John, S., 1961. Errors in discrimination. Ann. Math.Statist. Vol.
32, pp. 1125-1144.

Kittler, J., 1980. Computational problems of feature selection
pertaining to large data sets, in Pattern recognition in practice.
(L.N. Kanal and E.S. Gelsema, eds.), pp. 405-414, North Holland,
Amsterdam.

Kittler, J., 1982. On the efficiency of data utilization in system
error estimation. Proc. 6th IJCPR, Munich

Kittler, J., and Devijver, P.A., 1980 The probability distribution
of conditional classification error. IEEE Trans. on Pattern
Recognition and Machine Intelligence, Vol. PAMI-2, pp. 259-261.

Kittler, J., and Devijver, P.A., 1981. An efficient estimator of pattern recognition system error probability. Pattern Recognition, Vol. 13, pp. 245-249.

Kittler, J., and Devijver, P.A., 1982. Statistical properties of error estimators in performance assessment of recognition system. IEEE Trans. on Pattern Vol. PAM1-4, pp. 215-220.

Lachenbruch, P.S., 1967. An almost unbiased method of obtaining confidence intervals for the probability of misclassification in discriminant analysis. Biometrics, Vol. 23, pp.639-645.

Lissack, T., and Fu, K.S. 1974. Error estimation in pattern recognition via L∞ - distance between posteriori functions. IEEE Trans. Inf. Theory, IT-22, pp. 34-45.

Okamoto, M., 1963. An asymptotic expansion for the distribution of the linear discriminant function. Ann. Math.Statist. Vol. 34., pp. 1286-1301.

Smith, C.A.B., 1947. Some examples of discrimination. Ann. Eugen., Vol 18, pp. 272.

Toussaint, G.T., 1974. Bibiography on estimation of misclassification. IEEE Trans. Inf. Theory, Vol. IT-20, pp. 474-479.

HIGH LEVEL LANGUAGES FOR CLIP4

G.P. Otto and D.E. Reynolds

Image Processing Group, Department of Physics and Astronomy,
University College London, Gower Street, London WC1E 6BT

ABSTRACT

The design and implementation, with some examples of the use,
of two high level languages for image processing on the CLIP4
cellular array processor are discussed.   One of the languages is
based on C (a compiled block-structured language similar to Pascal),
and the other is based on POP-2 (an interactive block-structured
language mainly used in Artificial Intelligence research).

1. INTRODUCTION

We are going to discuss two high level languages, IPC and POPX,
which have been developed for image processing on the CLIP4 cellular
array processor.   Both languages are designed to encourage parallel
algorithms so that programs take full advantage of CLIP4 multiprocessor architecture.   Although many languages have been developed
for image processing(Duff, 1981), and several are designed to be
suitable for parallel processors   e.g. Uhr (1981), Levialdi (1981),
IPC and POPX are notable because they are amongst the few high level
languages which have been used for doing image processing on an
array processor.

As these languages are designed primarily for use on CLIP4, we will
quickly summarize the CLIP4 hardware.   Fuller descriptions can be
found in Duff(1978a) and Fountain (1981a).

2. BACKGROUND - CLIP4

CLIP4 is a Single Instruction stream, Multiple Data stream (SIMD)
computer, consisting of a 96 x 96 array of binary processors, each
connected to its nearest neighbours only, with 35 bits of memory per
processor.   The array is controlled by a purpose-built 16 bit
processor, which has its own memory in which the programs are stored.
Each element of the array is identical, and each cell carries out the
same operations at the same time.

Usually, pictures are loaded into the array from a camera or video-tape so that each pixel of the picture corresponds to one cell of the array. The interconnections in the array can be switched so that the array forms either a square (8-connected) or a hexagonal tessellation of the picture.

CLIP4 forms a complete computer, but apart from the video I/O the only I/O facility is a paper-tape reader, so for program development at least it is connected to a PDP-11/34. The PDP-11/34 acts like a more sophisticated controller, providing facilities like disc storage for programs and images, and peripherals such as printers and a magnetic tape drive.

CLIP4 has its own machine code and assembly language, CAP4 (Wood,1979). However, we developed higher level languages for CLIP4 because:

(1) It takes a long time to write large or complex programs in assembly code, and modifying them (which is frequent during program development) requires great care.

(2) The array memory of CLIP4 is rather limited for grey level processing, which makes it necessary to dynamically allocate memory for images. Doing this manually is very time-consuming and error-prone.

3.   OUTLINE OF IPC

IPC (Image Processing C) is, as its name implies, an adaptation for image processing of a language called C, (Kernighan, 1978a). Many conventional high-level languages provide most of the facilities required by a language for driving CLIP4, so it was natural to adapt an existing language for this. Rather than write a complete compiler from scratch, we decided to adapt an existing compiler. This implied that the language could not compile into CLIP4 machine code (in its first implementation at least), as we did not have a compiler for a machine with a similar instruction set, but this was out-weighed by the fact that we could concentrate more on the image processing features of the language. So the language was implemented as a program in the PDP-11/34 driving subroutines in CLIP4.

C is a general-purpose, block-structured language similar to Pascal or Algol 60. It has modern control flow and data structures, a versatile set of operators and standard functions, and good I/O facilities.

Apart from general east of use, C had several advantages: it is easy to produce programs in (separately compiled) modules, it provides good bit-manipulation facilities and it appeared easier to adapt the C compiler than any other we had available.

IPC is fundamentally C with a large subroutine library and a few extra syntactic constructions.

The features which we have added to C are:

3.1 A data-type for images

As images are the main type of data being handled in IPC, it was natural to provide a special data-type to make this easier. Because the image data stays in CLIP4, all that needs to be recorded in the PDP-11/34 is the address(es) of the data in CLIP memory and some information about what that data represents (e.g. unsigned or 2's complement signed numbers).

Rather than fix the precision to which images are stored (e.g. 8 bits/pixel) we allowed the image type to be of any precision. This means that, for example, an image whose pixels all have values between 0 and 31 would be stored as 5-bit numbers. Since CLIP4 is an array of binary processors, with memory which is addressed in bits, it does not require much extra effort to make routines handle images of any precision, and it significantly reduces the memory required in many algorithms. This method of reducing the memory used is more flexible than the alternative of having several image types of fixed precision (e.g. binary, grey, double), mainly because it is simpler to cope with overflow (when adding numbers, for example), since routines can easily increase the precision of the result if necessary.

3.2 Dynamic CLIP memory allocation

Manual allocation of memory for images is very time-consuming and tedious, but simple to automate. Dynamic (run-time) memory allocation is essential to make full use of the (rather limited) array memory. IPC has subroutines to do this allocation, and, if necessary, to swap images to and from secondary memory (disc, at present).

3.3 A subroutine library

A subroutine library provides the basic arithmetic, boolean, I/O, and filtering operations for images, and a range of other useful functions.

Externally, these all look like standard C subroutines, but they manipulate the data in CLIP according to the information in the image structure.

For example, "mult(im1,im2)" will multiply the data in CLIP associated with im1, with the data associated with im2, putting the result in another area of memory (allocated by the memory allocation routines) and returning (in IPC in the PDP-11) an image structure noting the address, precision, sign etc. of the result.

These standard subroutines automatically do any memory re-allocation required, and take care of the possible permutations of precision and sign in the data, so that all images can be treated as though they are stored as high precision signed numbers.

3.4 An image assignment operator

The subroutine library is, in general, arranged so that it returns its result in a separate image, thus permitting nested function calls. To complement this facility, there is an image assignment operator "$=", which effectively copies the data in the image on its right-hand side to the image on its left-hand side.

e.g. cube $ = mult (im, mult(im, im);

(The symbol "$=" was chosen because it was completely distinct from any legitimate C construction, but still resembled an assignment operator).

3.5 An interactive display system

Since, in practice, it is very difficult to devise and implement algorithms which work perfectly first time, it is very convenient to have some interactive facilities for examining images.

In IPC, the basic facilities are provided by the "command" subroutine. Whenever this subroutine is executed, a prompt is given at the user's terminal and he can then interactively display images, or portions of images, on a display monitor or on a V.D.U., or print copies on a hard copy device.

The images can be referred to by name, and the user can list and get information on all images which have data associated with them at that stage of the program, or he can just examine absolute memory addresses, or files of images on disc.

The user can also, if he chooses, gain access to many other interactive facilities (such as POPX) from any "command" subroutine.

3.6 Facilities to drive CLIP4 directly

If, for efficiency, someone wishes to code part of his algorithm in CLIP4 assembly code, he can either write in IPC, using the CLIP4 array operations, or write in CAP4 and link the resulting subroutine(s) to his IPC program.

3.7 Other features

We do not have the space to discuss the finer points of IPC here (Reynolds, 1981a), but two other features worth mentioning are the flag to set hexagonal or square connectivity in the array, and a data-type for 3 x 3 binary masks.

4. EXAMPLES OF IPC PROGRAMS

A few examples will give a better idea of what IPC is like in practice.

One simple problem is that of finding the centroid of a binary image. By using a subroutine called "ramp", which generates an image consisting of a ramp of numbers starting from zero and increasing by one grey-level per pixel in a given direction across the array, we can easily generate the x or y co-ordinates at each point, and hence calculate the position of the centroid. The full program is:

```
/*
 * Example of IPC - find centroid of binary image
 */

# include        <clip.h>            /* defines images etc. */

main( )
{
        image   object;            /* declare variables */
        float   area, x, y;        /* floating point */

        openclip ();               /* initializes CLIP4 */
        setname(object);           /* initializes image variables*/

        object $=inpics(1);        /* take binary picture from
                                                        camera */

        area = (float) volume         /* find area of object */
                    (object);
                /* "(float)" converts the integer returned by "volume"
                                        to floating point */

        x = (float) volume(ands(ramp(dirc{8},7),object)) / area;
                                /* find x-coord of centroid */

        y = (float) volume(ands(ramp(dirc{6},7),object)) /area;
                                /* find y-coord of centroid*/
        printf("Centroid of object is at %4.1f, %4.1f \n",x,y);

}
```

"ands" is a generalization of the boolean "and" which returns an image equal to the first argument where the second argument is non-zero, and zero elsewhere; "volume" returns the sum of all the pixels.

It is sometimes convenient to be able to try various operations on an image quickly and easily. We have a "menu" program for this purpose, where functions specified by one or two letter mnemonics are applied to the "current" image and the result is displayed and becomes the new "current" image. This is essentially a greatly extended and more sophisticated version of the following:

```
/*
 * Example of IPC - simple menu program
 */
```

```
# include        <stdio.h>            /* defines I/O package */
# include        <clip.h>             /* defines images etc.*/

main ()

{

    image   current, backup;          /* declare variables */
    int     ch, ch2, radius;

    openclip ();                      /* initializes CLIP4 */
    setname(current, backup);         /* initializes image variables */

    backup $= current $= setnum(0);        /* clear images */

    do  {

            printf(">")               /* prompt */
            ch= getkey();             /* get character from keyboard */
            if (ch == '/'){

                    current $= backup;      /* go back to previous
                                                    image */
            }else {
                    backup $= current;      /* update backup image */
                    switch (ch) {
                    case 'i' :
                        printf("Take picture from camera \n");
                        current $= inpics (6)
                        break;
                    case 'C' :
                        command();   /* examine images in more
                                                    detail */
                        break;
                    case 'e' :
                        break;              /* exit from program */
                    case 'm' :
                        ch2 = getkey(); /* get 2nd character */
                        switch (ch2) {
                        case'f' :
                            printf("Median filter, 3 x 3");
                            current $= medn8 (current);
                            break;
                        case 'l' :
                            printf ("Median filter,radius=");
                            scanf("%d", & radius);
                            current $= median(current,radius);
                            break;
                        default:
                            printf("??");
                        }
                        break;
```

```
            default:
                     printf("??");

            }
      }
      display (current);              /* display result*/
      putchar('\n');
 } while (ch != 'e');

}
```

The main difference between this and the full "menu" program
(apart from the number of functions) is that in the full program the
user can easily save and restore (named) images, as well as working
on the current image.   Nevertheless such programs are rather
limited in scope, and a complete language (such as POPX) would be
used for more extensive interactive work.

5   COMMENTS ON IPC

Parallel algorithms are encouraged because images are always
treated as an object, rather than as a collection of pixels.
Although you can write algorithms which are inherently serial in IPC,
it is much easier to express them in a manner which takes advantage
of the parallelism of CLIP.

We adapted an existing (serial) language because we needed many of
the facilities it could provide (e.g. control structures, I/O, and
file manipulation), and because it had a similar basic structure to
the one that we wished to have.   This meant that we could take
advantage of the vast amount of experience embodied in such languages,
and by adapting an existing compiler, increase the amount of effort
we could put into the special features of the language.

IPC is, in its present version, implemented largely by means of
subroutines (in the PDP-11 and/or CLIP) rather than as features of
the compiler itself.   This is very convenient when developing a
language, as it is simpler to modify subroutines than compilers.
Now that IPC is more settled, it could be tidied up in several minor
ways by improving the compiler itself.   For example, the initial-
ization of the CLIP and of the image types could be done automatically, removing the need for "open-clip" and "setname" calls; and the
standard operators such as "+", "*", "<" could be extended to images,
so that arithmetic and boolean expressions involving images could be
expressed in the normal way.

In IPC, a given instruction is executed on <u>every</u> <u>pixel</u> <u>of</u> <u>an</u> <u>image</u>,
so that it is not directly possible to perform an operation on only
<u>part</u> of an image.   This does not restrict algorithms as they can be
expressed using subroutines which conditonally select areas of images.
For example, we can calculate the sum of the x co-ordinates of an
object by

        sigma _ x = volume (ands(ramp(dirc{8},7),object));

("ramp(...)" generates the x co-ordinates of each point of the array, and "ands" is an extension of the boolean "and" - see above).

This form of expression is natural for some algorithms, but rather awkward for others, so future versions of IPC would incorporate control structures such as a "parallel if" construction, which would execute a statement (or compound statement) at each pixel only if some condition were true at that pixel (see, for example, Uhr (1981a) and Levialdi (1981a).

IPC has the high level language attributes of ease of use and read-ability. It is not, however, very portable. This is partly because it allows the use of CLIP4 machine code instructions, and it is biased towards CLIP4's architecture in several minor ways. For example, IPC does not provide simple facilities for serial process-ing of images. Clearly IPC could be extended to cure this problem. This does not remove a major difficulty: efficient algorithms often have to reflect features of the hardware on which they are implemen-ted . Thus, unless we are prepared to accept inefficiency (sometimes very great inefficiency), algorithms will not usually be portable between computers which have greatly differing architect-tures even if the languages in which they are expressed are! Since there are very few machines with a similar architecture to CLIP, we decided that the extra effort required to make IPC truly portable was not worthwhile, especially as any serial algorithms can be easily expressed in C, of which IPC is a superset.

The current IPC implementation is reasonably efficient (for programs which do a lot of grey level processing, an IPC program is comparable in speed to a CLIP4 assembler program), but it is rather inefficient when doing many functions which require just one or two CLIP instructions. This is due to the time required to gain access to CLIP from a user's program in the PDP-11 (about 1 ms at present); this overhead could be reduced, but the only complete cure would be to compile into CLIP4 machine code.

6. POPX

POPX is an interactive language for image processing on CLIP4. It is developed from POP-2 Burstall (1977a) and Clocks (1979a). which is a block-structured interactive language mainly used in Artificial Intelligence research. Although POP-2 is somewhat different from C, POPX is very similar in spirit to IPC, and the differences which exist are almost entirely due to the differences between the original languages. Thus, the main difference is that POPX is an inter-active language, while IPC is compiled. The only other notable difference is that the operators in POPX have been extended to act on images, so that, for example, you can use expressions like "im1 + im2 /im3". So, rather than repeat much of what we said above, we will just give some examples of POPX. For a fuller description of POPX see Burstall (1977a) and Reynolds (1981b).

First something very simple:

```
: varsim pic;                    ! declare variables!
: inpic(6) >> pic;               ! take in 6 bit picture from camera!
: volume(pic) / (96.0 * 96.0) =>    ! now find average grey level!
43.20
:
```

":" is the prompt by the computer, ">>" assigns the value of the
(image) expression on the left-hand side to the right-hand side, and
"=>" prints the value of an expression.

Now let us find the edges in "pic", using an operator ("^^") which
replaces the value at each pixel by the maximum value in the local
neighbourhood:

```
: varsim edges;
: ^^pic - pic >> edges;        ! large values give strong edges!
: edges > 2 >> edges;          ! now threshold to give binary image!
:
```

Note that the comparison between"edges" and 2 returns a binary
image which is one where the condition is true.

Now, to find the centroid of an object (compare the IPC example
above):

```
: varsim object;                 ! declare variables!
: vars area x y;
: inpic(1) >> object;        ! take 1 bit (binary) picture from camera!
: volume(object) -> area;
: volume(ramp(dir8,7) & object) / area -> x;
:                              ! "&" is the operator for "ands" !
: volume(ramp(dir6,7) & object ) / area - > y;
: x =>                          ! x co-ordinate of centroid !
53.45
: y =>                          ! y co-ordinate of centroid !
64.52
:
```

The operator "->" is normally used to assign the value of the
expression on the left-hand side to the variable on the right-hand
side, but "->>" is used for images so that the data in CLIP is
copied as well as the data in the PDP-11 describing the image. When
">>" is used instead of "->>", it displays the result as well as
doing the assignment.

Another simple example is given by this function for finding the
hexagonally connected skeleton of an object:

```
! Example of POPX - thinning subroutine!
```

```
clipfn mythin in => out;   ! declare function name, input and output
                                                            variables!
vars mask i;                      ! declare local variables!
varsim current old;
        setmask( { 1 1          ! set up thinning mask - the last !
                   x x x         !  variable specifies that hexag-
                                                            onal  !
              0 0 }, 1) ->  ! connectivity is to be used        !
                      mask
        in ->> current;         ! take copy of input!
        0 ->> old;
        until volume(old /= current) < 0.5 then  ! repeat until no
                                                            change!
            current ->>old;
            forall i 1 1 6;  ! for all six (hex) directions...!
                  thin(current, mask) ->> current;
                            ! remove points where mask fits !
                  mask <| 1 ->mask;   ! rotate mask once !
            close;
        close;
        current ->> out;

end;
```

which is used just like any other function, as in

```
: varsim in out;
: inpic(1) >> in;
: mythin(in) >> out;   ! now "out" contains the skeleton of "in" !
:
```

7. DISCUSSION

An important feature of IPC and POPX which has not yet been emphasized is that the implementation, and use, is severely constrained by the limited memory per pixel.   Although there is a reasonable quantity of memory overall, one penalty of doing calculations in parallel is that much more memory is used for workspace (see, for example, Marks (1980).   Thus the memory available to each processor is more significant to the programmer than the total memory, and although the cost of memory is dropping, it is notable that even the largest array processors built or being planned at present(Danielsson,1981a) have much less memory per processor than modern serial computers.

We would have preferred to have just one language, rather than two. There is sometimes a need for an interactive language (which led to POPX), but we could not produce an interactive language which is fast enough for large CLIP programs, so we produced IPC for situations where speed of execution was important.   In fact, IPC is used far more than POPX at present, because

(1) the difference in execution speed is very noticeable for large programs,

(2) the simple interactive facilities (e.g. "command" subroutine and

"menu"programs) provided with IPC (and written in IPC) are adequate for most purposes,

(3) The time required for compiling programs is usually far out-weighed by the time needed to plan and type them in,

(4) and most people prefer to use just one language, even if another might be somewhat better for some purposes.

8. CONCLUSION

IPC and POPX have almost completely replaced CLIP4 assembly code for programming CLIP4, and are now being used on a variety of problems including general pattern recognition, 3-D reconstruction, texture analysis and computer tomography. High level languages for cellular array processors like CLIP4 can be produced, with relatively little effort, by adapting existing serial languages.

9. ACKNOWLEDGEMENT

This work was supported by the Science and Engineering Research Council.

REFERENCES

Burstall, R.M., Collins, J.S., and Popplestone, R.J.,(1977). Programming in POP-2, University Press, Edinburgh.

Clocksin, W., (1979). The Unix POP-2 System, Dept. of Artificial Intelligence, University of Edinburgh.

Danielsson, P.E. and Levialdi, S., (1981). "Computer Architectures for Pictorial Information Systems", Computer Vol. 14(11), pp.53-67.

Duff, M.J.B., (1978). "Review of the CLIP image processing system", Proc. National Computer Conference, pp.1055-1060.

Duff, M.J.B. and Levialdi, S., (1981). Languages and Architectures for Image Processing, Academic Press, London.

Fountain, T.J., (1981). "CLIP4 : Hardware Manual", Report : 81/1, Image Processing Group, Dept. of Physics and Astronomy, University College London.

Kernighan, B.W. and Ritchie, D.M. (1978). The C Programming Language, Prentice-Hall, Englewood Cliffs, New Jersey.

Levialdi, S. et al.,(1981). "On the design and implementation of PIXAL, a language for image processing", pp.89-99 in Languages and Architectures for Image Processing, (Edited by M.J.B. Duff and S. Levialdi),Academic Press, London.

Marks, P. (1980). "Low-Level Vision Using an Array Processor", Computer Graphics and Image Processing Vol. 14, pp.281-292.

Reynolds, D.E., (1981). "POPX User Manual". Report: 82/3, Image Processing Group, Dept. of Physics and Astronomy, University College London.

Reynolds, D.E., and Otto, G.P., (1981). "IPC User Manual", Report: 82/4, Image Processing Group, Dept. of Physics and Astronomy, University College London.

Uhr, L., (1981). "A language for Parallel Processing of arrays, embedded in PASCAL", pp.53-89 in Languages and Architectures for Processing (Edited by M.J.B. Duff and S. Levialdi), Academic Press, London.

Wood, A., (1979). CAP4 User's Manual, Image Processing Group, Dept. of Physics and Astronomy, University College London.

A STRUCTURAL APPROACH TO RESTORATION AND VECTORIZING OF DIGITIZED ENGENEERING DRAWINGS.

U. Cugini
Istituto di meccanica, Sezione Disegno Macchine
Politecnico di Milano, Italy

P. Micheli
I.F.C.T.R. — C.N.R. di Milano, Italy

P. Mussio
I.F.C.T.R. — C.N.R. di Milano, Italy

0. ABSTRACT

An approach to the solution of the problem of the restoration and vectorization of digitized engineering drawings is presented.
The presented procedure is based on the knowledge of the graphical and procedural rules underlying the conception and realization of the drawing. The implemented system allows to restore and describe the original drawing in terms of vector and in a relational description, so that it could be reproduced using stroke devices or stored and managed in a traditional graphic data base.

1. INTRODUCTION

For quite some time in the field of drafting the use and economic advantages offered by computer aided drafting and design systems (1) (2) has been shown to the industrial world. The ever increasing development of graphic systems and lower costs enlarges its field of application. These systems mainly allow to use the techniques and advantages typical of data bases especially regarding the possibility of updating or modifying already recorded data. A great problem is that up to now no cheap solution has been found for filling this data base with all the information essential to the engineering drawings, especially in handling the archives already in existence in a certain industrial context at the moment of introducing the drafting system (3) (4). The importance of this problem, especially in the mechanical industries, where the size of these archives has a magnitude of tens of thousands drawings is easily understandable.

This work is done with a partial financial support from C.N.R. under contract n. 78.01587.07 and n. 79.02483.07.

2. SPECIFIC CHARACTERISTICS OF THE PROBLEM

In a technical drawing the image is formed by well defined sets of graphic strokes (straight lines, circumferences, arcs, curves, alphanumeric strings, graphic symbols) with graphical properties which are also well defined (solid lines of different thickness, dashed or dotted lines, crosshatched areas). This set of strokes can be seen as an alphabet in a graphical language. Elements of the alphabet are related to each other according to very precise rules of both geometrical and topological type. In fact the conventional language used in technical drawing is a formalized language as far as both graphical ortography and syntax following well-specified rules.

During the recognition and synthesis phases of the graphic entities composing the drawing, the strategy and recognition methodology can be oriented towards the research of a well defined set of prototypes.

A contextual analysis can certify the correctness or incorrectness of recognized structures. At higher synthesis level, that of the description of a drawing for two-dimensional closed figures and logic operators (11), the fact that the technical drawing is the representation of real objects (mechanical parts, buildings, plants, etc.) allows us to define the contextual interpretation rules derived from the typical characteristics of the objects which the drawing itself may represent. But the documents to be delt with have a wide spectrum of variation with regard to the characteristics of the graphic signs (pencil, pen, ...), the contrast between the drawing and the background and the presence of noise (marks, dirt creases, support imperfections, etc.).

3. APPROACH FOLLOWED AND MOTIVATIONS

A general consideration should be stated before any technical comparison between the two well known possible approaches: the use of a line follower system directly producing a compact vectorial description of the drawing or the scanning of the image which produces a map of the drawing in terms of grey level codes, which are then processed with a restoration algorithm.

The digitization problem of technical drawings, as serious as it may be, should be delt with only once by the company which has decided to automatize its own management production of technical drawings. In fact the new drawings will presumably be produced by CAD instruments and therefore directly into an automatically handling form. It is then difficult that the machines acquired for this task will be used again in spite of their undoubtedly high purchasing cost.

On the contrary, obviously the programs run on a general purpose computer which is not necessarily used only for this function. For this reason a software approach has been chosen, and in this paper we will be dealing with a specific work phase of our method: the phase of the synthesis of the description of the original drawing from the digitized image.

In summary the problem was to construct an instrument to transform the raster image, as obtained by a scanner , into a synthetic description of the original drawing.

The drawing is described in terms of its user defined structures: regions (rectangles, arcs, polygons , etc.); relations among regions.

The description may be in two forms: a vectorial form which is represented by a numerical array and is often called synthetic or numerical or internal; an expanded or external or person-to-person, or machine-to-person comunication form, which is described in a proper subset of a natural language (fig. 10b, 11b).

This description interpreted by suitable programs has to: allow the regeneration of the original drawing; allow its storage and updating in a graphic data base.

The software tool is designed and implemented with a priori knowledge of the language with which the drawings have been constructed. The problem can be restated in the following form: starting from digitized data, it is necessary to obtain an appropriate computed description of the original symbolic drawing in terms of data, data structures, and algorithms. The analysis process is carried out in different stages. After a pre-elaboration stage the numeric matrix obtained from the digitization, is transformed into a binary matrix.

Points belonging to the original drawing and some types of noisy points (tab. 1, point A) are set to one (that means accepted as meaningful). Before starting the real restoration phase, the set of vertices, which is a proper subset of points that forms the boundary, is individuated in the binary matrix.

These points, properly codified (14), are grouped into subsets. These sets are the input to the restoration phase (tab. 1, point B).

The identification of structures and their grouping into meaningful images in the goal language, is made by means of a structural analysis that starts from morphological characteristics of the input data.

In the binary matrix, each stroke of the original drawing results into an area (a connected set of marked points). A segment is transformed into a nearly linear path whose

edges are lines often interrupted by steps; an arc is
transformed into a path very similar to a part of
annulus, that lies between two nearly concentric curved
edges, which approsimate two noisy circles.
These observations suggest to study the different paths
in the binary image, and to build up an associated
suitable data structures, which will hold the information
related to each path.
In this procedure, strong hints about the nature of the
strokes, that have generated the paths, are collected and
allow a final classification of the paths, the
individuation of its geometrical properties and its
relations with other geometrical entities.
The implementation of this procedure needs a distributed
information collection: in each step new informations are
obtained ,while those derived from previous stage may be
confirmed, modified or deleted. In a first phase, an edge
description approach is followed. The contour of each
connected set of marked points is analysed, and useful
structures are identified, such as possible arcs or
rectilinear edges, while those structures which cannot
exist in the conventional goal language are eliminated or
corrected.
In the second phase, the recognized edge structures are
examined and composed; so that admissible classification
of the path and of their relation is indicated.
In the third phase, the classification of path and its
relations are used to identify sets of vertices, which
are the basis for the geometrical properties estimation
of the classified entities.
The entire process is carried out through different
levels of analysis: topologycal, geometrical, contextual
analysis.
The first level finds hints about the existence of
possible entities by means of their morphological
characteristics, the following ones confirm the validity
and the coherence of the previously obtained results,
resolving the existing conflicts. This way allows to
overcome doubtful cases in complex situations: when there
are no structural elements which allow the discrimination
among different entities (16).

4. FROM THE DIGITIZED IMAGE TO THE BLACK/WHITE IMAGE

A digitized image is affected by two kinds of noise:
accidental and systematic.
The first one is caused by the digitization of unwanted
signs appearing on the starting document, such as stains
or support imperfections.
The second one is due to the sampling and quantization

effects. In the first step the raster image is transformed into a black and white one, filtering away the accidental noise. To this aim:
- the data coming from different images are normalized
- the data are compressed so the required memory is reduced
- the first type of noise (accidental) is eliminated
- the coloured digitized image is transformed into a black and white one, applying a thresholding function. This function maps points assigned to the classes of interest into 1 (marked points), and those belonging to non-significant classes to 0.

Fig. 1a, 1b, 1c, and 2 show the original technical drawings. Fig. 3 shows fig. 2 after this first phase.

5. FROM A BINARY IMAGE TO STRINGS OF USEFUL CODES

In this second step an existing instrument for the processing and analysis of binary pixels representations of digital images from different sources (Remote sensing , astronomy) was used (14).

Points in the binary image are mapped into a decimal number ranging from $0 \leqslant C \leqslant 255$ by means of the following relation $C = \sum_0^7 v_i \cdot 2^i$ where v_i is the binary value of the point adjacent to point in hand in the position i (fig. 4).

It has been demonstrated (15) that a binary image can be reconstructed and described from the set S of triples $<C_j , X_j , Y_j >$ associated to the vertices where X_j and Y_j are the coordinates of the vertex and C_j is the associated code. This set is then subdivided into subsets of triples S_i. Each S_i describes the contour of simple or multiple connected set of marked points. Each S_i is stored as nx3 matrix. It can be noted that simple connected sets of marked points are derived by the digitization of simple figures such as isolated segments, dashed lines or crosses. These signs can be easily detected at this stage of the process. Their characteristics are then computed and the associated data cancelled from the set of codes.

Fig. 5 shows the state of the restoration image after this phase. Two kinds of systematic noise not yet removed at this stage, are shown.

6. THE RESTORATION PROCESS

A production system is used to get a vectorial description of the image. A production system (PS) allows to explore single characteristic patterns in the data to reach the user-defined goal.

A production system is made of three basic components:
a) the set of data to be examined.

b) a set of rewriting rules (RW) . Each rule is a pair of an antecedent and a consequent (or of structure and action). The antecedent is a structure which is searched for in the data, while the consequent is an indicator of the activities that must be carried out as a consequence.

c) the interpreter which controls the recognition of the antecedent part of the rule in the data, carries out the esecution of the recognized rule and reports the result.

The set of data is made up of the sets of triples (C_j , X_j , Y_j) related to the vertices and by any other information collected during the restoration process. For clarity we associate to the numerical codes of the vertices alphabetical symbols (fig. 8b) so that the antecedent of the rules can be described by a string of characters called seed. For each object at the beginning of the process the external and internal contours are subsequentely analysed.

In a second stage, the information obtained from the contours study, are compared, so that bidimensional strokes are recognized.

At last, the line drawing is restored to filiform state.

Fig. 6a shows a detail of the fig. 2.

Fig. 7 , 8 and 9 show the restoration process. The details of the process are described in the following paragraphes and resumed in Tab. 1.

7. RESEARCH OF CONTOUR STRUCTURES AFFECTED BY CHARACTERIZING NOISE (Tab. 1, point C11)

Some elementary geometrical structure (arcs and inclined segments), when digitized, results in a path, whose contour is affected by a characterizing noisy sequence of vertices, which is strong hints about the nature of the original strokes (fig. 3). The aim of this first step is the recognition of the elementary geometric structures, the storing of related informations and the elimination of unnecessary triples. The configurations of the noise structures ,which a preliminary study of data has proved necessary for individuation of arcs and segments, are the antecedent in this step. The associated seeds are searched for in the set describing the contour of each object. The interpreter fires the functions which realize the actions, associated to the found seeds. Each function examines the contour Si in hand and verifies the existence of the searched structure. If the structure exists the function stores its characteristics, deletes the triples grouped in the structures from the set Si and inserts in their place a triple $<m, n, p>$ which identifies

the structure and where it is stored. In any case the function notifies to the interpreter the results of the actions.
For example, the characteristic seed of an arc from $90°$ to $180°$ is the following: NGPH
Seed identification in the contour string , describing the external contour of the largest object in fig. 6a, causes the firing of the consequent function A1 (fig. 6b). A1 examines the codes of neighbouring points in the contour. If it finds a sufficient number of points, so that an arc may exist, a geometrical control is requested. If the control is successful, the triples grouped into the arc, are stored together with the recognized characteristics in a matrix called CURVES, while in Si are replaced by an identifying flag (fig. 7a).

8. ELIMINATION OF THE NOISY STRUCTURES DUE TO THE BORDER EFFECT (Tab. 1, point C12)

At this stage , the triples in sets Si are descriptions of not yet classified vertices or flags of the recognised structures.
Fig. 6a shows the presence of step-wise structures, which, by their dimensions, are not allowed in a conventional technical drawing (shown with an arrow in fig. 6a). Well-defined substrings of simbols, identifying these structures, can be chosen as seeds in RW rules.
The consequent functions check for the geometrical congruences of the structures. If the congruence conditions are satisfied, the triples associated to the noisy points are erased from the set Si.
This phase is subdivided into three parts:
 -elimination of the triangular noisy configurations;
 -elimination of the quadrangular noisy configurations;
 -elimination of the step-wise noisy configurations.
Fig. 7a visualizes the first external contour found in the image examined after the recognition of the arc. Fig. 7b,7c,7d show the various steps for the elimination of the three noisy configurations in the external contour. Fig. 8 summarizes the situation of the object at this point of the restoration.

9. RECOGNITION OF THE LINEAR STRUCTURE NOT YET FOUND (Tab. 1, point C13)

Boundary subsets, which appear as horizontal, vertical, $45°$ and $135°$ inclined segments are then detected, because they are now described by sets of only meaningful vertices , which appear as regular structures when drawn (see fig. 8). The only examination of the code allows to

classify the segment in six classes: right or left
horizontal, upper and lower vertical, right and left
inclined.

10. PUTTING TOGETHER FACING STRUCTURES (Tab. 1, point
C21)
An object can be described as set of subsets, which are
paths. In fig. 8 the object can be described by
recognizing linear and curved paths. In this phase, the
recognized subsets of the contours, are grouped when they
bound the same structures. For example the right boundary
with the left of a vertical stroke, or the exterior with
the interior boundary that delimitate an arc. The phase
is subdivided into two steps:
a) pairing of the horizontal, vertical, oblique (45 and
   135) segments.
b) pairing of the arcs and possible curves.
Regarding point b), particular attention must be paid to
those boundaries which can be classified both as noisy
inclined segments or short arcs. We call them possible
arcs: p.a. The pairing of the arcs and of the p.a. is
done analysing the data contained in the matrix 'CURVES'.
In this phase the conflict 'p.a. or oblique segment' may
be resolved comparing the structures found on the
opposite sides of the same path if at least one of the
two structures is not doubtfully classified (fig. 9, fig.
8).

11. GROUPING OF PAIRED STRUCTURES (Tab. 1, point C22)
In this stage we will group the classified paths that
probably were generated by a single geometric stroke.
This is the case of the set of linear paths groupable in
a single path or the set of arcs that form a single
structure (fig. 8, segment A, B, C). Furthermore, areas
which were genereted by digitization of crossings,
vertices, points of contact and, for what regards the
curved strokes, points of tangency or points of fillet
are recognized. The paths converging in the areas are
stored in matrices. For example, to individuate the
crossings we rely on the codes that characterize the
oblique segments of 45° and 135° having coordinates
defering by one or segments that have not been paired in
the previous phase. Fig. 9 shows relationships and
individuated structures at the end of this phase in the
image of fig. 8. As in the previous phases , here again
the information collected during the aggregation are
used to resolve doubtful classifications of structures.
As an example, if two p.a. where coupled together, they
form unclassified path (u.p.). If this u.p. is followed,

but not directly connected, with some classified structure, u.p. is classified in the same class of this structure. As example if a doubtful arc matches with an undoubtful arc, then the two paths are grouped into one arc.

12. REDUCTION TO FILIFORM STRUCTURES (Tab. 1, point C31)

At this point of the restoration process, a binary image can be generated and it will be composed by a set of marked points, forming different paths. Contours of these paths have been smoothed. Subsets of the contours of these paths have been interpreted as segments, arcs, circles (eg. fig. 7d the set of points $<\underline{HQ}>$ is a segment). Elements from the subsets have been put together, when they are the two possible boundaries of the same stroke (e.g. fig. 7d the two sets $<\underline{HQ}>$ and $<\underline{GG}>$ are paired). Tokens have been coupled if at least one element in the first set forms a possible structure with one element of the second one. (e.g. the $<\underline{HQ}, \underline{GG}>$ and $<\underline{SI}, \underline{SH}>$ are grouped into a linear path). Each resulting structure is a candidate to become a filiform structure.

To transform such entities into filiform ones, the method of minimum least squares has been applied to all the vertices attributed to each specific set. Fig. 10a shows the graphic output after this step.

13. PARAMETRIC CORRECTIONS (Tab. 1, point C32)

After the phase of reduction to filiform structures the graphical elements are correctly classified and reconstructed one by one. The relations between them are not yet well defined. These relations can be computed using the stored information during the grouping phase. In particular, the informations about the areas in which the paths converge, are antecendent in a p.s., which verifies the possible geometrical relations. As an example we can use the matrix where tangent points are stored to recognize inscribed figures. In this matrix we have stored labels identifying couples of paths, which now belong to an identified stroke. If two figures are inscribed, an appropriate number of paths have been stored in the grouping phase. The system verifies the congruence of the collected relations (see fig. 10b, 10c, 11a, 11b, 12).

14. HINTS ABOUT THE IMPLEMENTATION

Due to the large amount of data to be treated and to the well-defined strategy, phases A and B are implemented by FORTRAN programs. The following steps are implemented using an APL program MODULO (13), simulating a PS interpreter. In each step, tables of antecedent and consequent have been studied, so that the whole computation results in data driven process. It is important to note that the efficiency of the system depends on the correctness, completness and no ambiguity of the rules of the rewriting system, that controls the whole description of the noisy structures. The use of the tables to describe the rules, on the other hand, guarantees the flexibility of the system. Thus, if faced with an unexpected noisy configuration, a new rules is added to the table without modifying any other program. Furthermore the followed approach allows the overcoming of the problem of an unexpected noisy configuration thanks to the gathering distributed information and the numerous checks of plausibility to which every structure has to undergo before the final recognition. This approach has shown its importance in the cases where the use against real data has demonstrated that some seeds were a weak indicator of structures, and/or some consequents were an inappropriate computational tools. In such cases the PS structure allowed a redefinition and/or the introduction of new concepts without affecting neither the general structure nor the other implemented rules in the device.

15. DISCUSSION

As shown in fig. 11a, not all the types of noises have been eliminated at the end of the process. The original drawing shows how the tangents rhombus-circle were purposely drawn imperfectly. In fact, one tends to be geometric (one point of contact), while the other is partially superimposed. The use of this figure had the aim of showing the correction limits reachable with the present set of relations used. We have seen, particularly, how the use of the matrices of the tangents allows to check if an element is inscribed into another one, but not into a pair of other elements. For this reason the remaining bugs seen in fig. 11a are justified. This limit may be corrected using contextual information, obtained by the syntesis of different views that are known to represent the same object. Fig. 12 shows the union of three results of reconstruction of the three views in the same drawing (fig. 1). This step can be the starting point for following levels of analysis which checks and corrects possible incongruences between the views of the same object as described in the conventional language of the engineers, based on the syntesis rules deriving from the formalization of orthographic projection methods of solid objects representation.

REFERENCES
(1) C. Lang: "Achievements in Computer Aided Design",
    information Processing 74, pp. 758-767
(2) J. Hatvany, W. Newman, M. Sabin: "World Survey of
    Computer Aided Design", CAD Journal, vol. 9 n. 2
    April 1977, pp. 79-98.
(3) J. Slutzky: "The Future of Digitizing of Engineering
    Data", in Proceedings of a symposium on the automated
    production storage, retrieval and display of digitized
    engeneering data, Chao Wang ed. Monterey 1977,
    pp. 116-121.
(4) P. Cheng, Chao Wang ed. "Proceedings of a Symposium
    on the Automated Production, Storage, Retrieval and
    Display of Digitized Engineerind Data", Monterey,
    Jan. 1977
(5) D. J. Buscher: "Digital Rapresentations of Engineering
    Drawing Report", HDL-TR-1834, Harry Diamond
    Lab. Adelphi MD, Nov. 1977
(6) Daniel Hochman: "Digitization of microfilm-stored
    engeenering data" in Proceedings of a Symposium on the
    Automated Production Strorage, Retrieval and Display
    of Digitized Engineering Data, P. Cheng, Chao Wang ed
    ed Monterey, Jan 1977 pp. 176-185.
(7) C. F. O'Donnell:"Trends in Hardware and Software for
    Digitized Engeneering Data Systems" in the
    Proceedings of a Symposium on the Automated
    Production, Storage, Retrieval and Display of
    Digitized Engineering Data, P. Cheng, Chao Wang
    ed. Monterey Jan. 1977, pp. 135-138
(8) D. Ruthland: "Automatic line drawing digitization
    using a television scanner" in Proceedings of a
    Symposium on the Automated Production Storage,
    Retrieval and Display of Digitized Engineering Data,
    P. Cheng, Chao Wang ed. Monterey, Jan, 1977pp. 192-194
(9) G. Woetzel: "A fast economic scan to line convertion
    algorithm SIGRAPH '78 Aug. 1978, pp. 125-129
(10)S. Kakumuto, Y. Fujimoto, J. Kawasaki: "Logic diagram
    recognition by divide and synthesis method" in
    "Artificial intelligence and pattern recognition in
    computer aided desig", edited by J. C. Latombe. N. Holland
    1978, pp. 429-450
(11)U. Cugini, M. Dell'Oca, A. Mirioni, P. Mussio: "An interactive
    drafting system based on bidimensional primitives",
    in Proceedings of International Conference on
    Interactive Tecniques in Computer Aided Design,
    Bologna 1978, pp. 321-332
(12)U. Cugini, A. Della Ventura, P. Mussio, A. Rampini: "A
    system for automatic digitization of tecnical
    drawings" in Proceedings of the International

204

Conference on Image Analysis and Processing.

(13)S. Bianchi, A. Della Ventura, M. Dell'Oca, P. Mussio,
A. Rampini: "An APL Pattern Directed Module for
Bidimensional data analysis", APL'81 Conference
Proceedings, APL Quote Quad Vol 12 n. 1 Sept. 1981.
(14)P. Brambilla, A. Della Ventura, P. Mussio, A. Rampini:
"Interactive analysis of dimansional data",
EUSIPCO-80 Signal Processing: THEORIES AND
APPLICATIONS, Lausanne, Switzerland, Sept. 80,
edited M. Kunt, North Holland Publishing Company.
(15)L. F. C. T. R. Internal Report 1980: M. Padula, P. Mussio.
(16)P. Micheli: "TESI DI LAUREA IN FISICA", anno
accademico 1982.

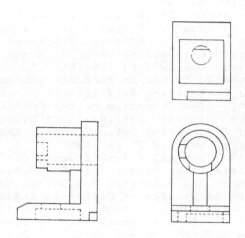

Fig. 1 First original drawing of the three views
of an object

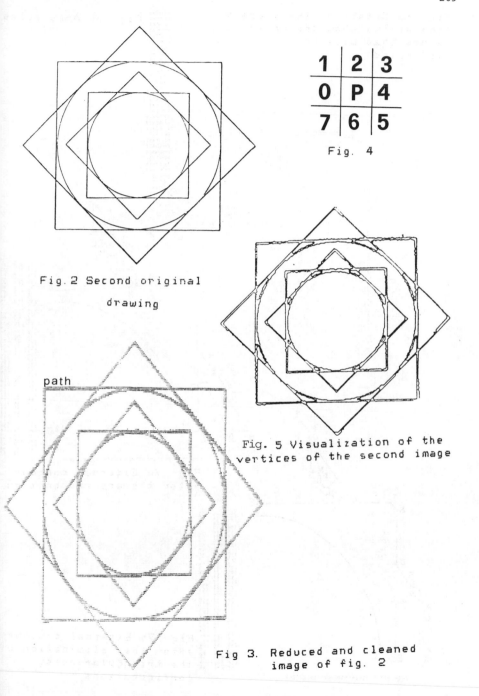

Fig. 2 Second original
drawing

1	2	3
0	P	4
7	6	5

Fig. 4

path

Fig. 5 Visualization of the
vertices of the second image

Fig 3. Reduced and cleaned
image of fig. 2

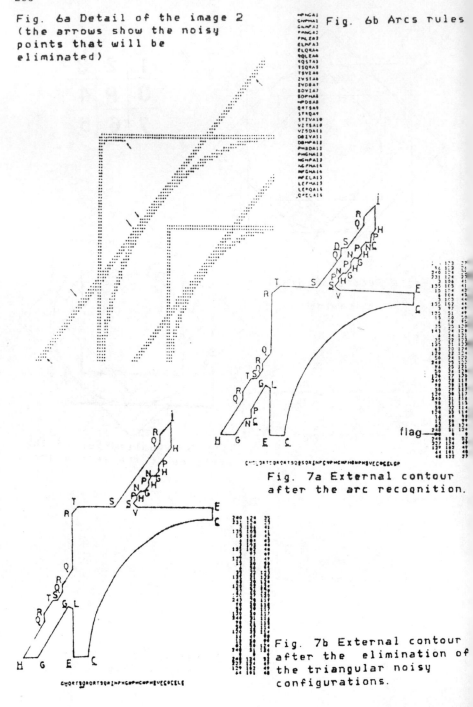

Fig. 6a Detail of the image 2
(the arrows show the noisy
points that will be
eliminated)

Fig. 6b Arcs rules

flag

Fig. 7a External contour
after the arc recognition.

Fig. 7b External contour
after the elimination of
the triangular noisy
configurations.

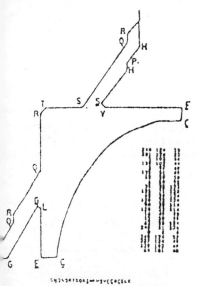

Fig. 7c External contour
after the elimination of
the quadrangular noisy
configurations.

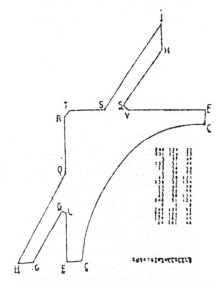

Fig. 7d External contour
after the elimination of
the noisy steps.

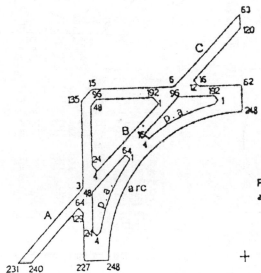

Fig. 8 Contours situation
after the pairing phase.

```
        LIST THE STRUCTURES AND RELATIONS FOUND

THE FOLLOWING VERTICAL SEGMENTS HAVE BEEN PAIRED

PAIR NUMBER  1      3  97  49 135  31  49   WITH    48  54  30  24  34  30
PAIR NUMBER  2    227 124  43 129 102  49   WITH    48  39  30  24 115  30

THE FOLLOWING HORIZONTAL SEGMENTS HAVE BEEN PAIRED

PAIR NUMBER  3     15  50  50   6  50  95   WITH   192  51  92  36  52  52
PAIR NUMBER  4     12  50  99  62  30 124   WITH    96  31  36 192  31 108

THE FOLLOWING OBLIQUE (45 DEGREES) HAVE BEEN PAIRED

PAIR NUMBER  5    231 124  23   3  97  49   COM    240 124  25  54 101  48   0
   0   0   0   0
PAIR NUMBER  6      4  95  31   1  32  93   CON     48  99  30  54  37
 61  16  66  35  96  77  96
PAIR NUMBER  7      6  30  95  53  50 124   CON     16  49  98 120  22
124   0   0   0   0   0   0

THE SEGMENTS AT 135 DEGREES HAVE NOT BEEN PAIRED

MATRIX OF THE POSSIBLE CURVED LINES

 1 1 1 1 1 3 4
 2 3 2 1 2 3 0
 3 4 2 2 2 4 0

MATRIX DESCRIPTION
FIRST COLUMN PROGRESSIVE NUMBER LINES
SECOND COLUMN NUMBER OF THE CONTOURS TO WHICH IT BELONGS
THIRD COLUMN 1 ARCO ,2 POSSIBLE EIGHTH OF CIRCLE, 3 CIRCLES
FOURTH COLUMN NUMBER OF CREATED VARIABLE
FIFTH COLUMN- 1 INTERNAL, 2 EXTERNAL
COLUMNS LEFT OVER NUMBER OF POSSIBLE EIGHTH WHICH CONSTITUTE THE STRUCTURE.

THE FOLLOWING CURVES HAVE BEEN PAIRED
ARC  1 WITH EIGHTH  2 3

THE FOLLOWING PAIRS HAVE BEEN LINED JP

VERTICAL LINING PAIRS 1 2
HORIZONTAL LINING  PAIRS 3 4
45 DEGREES LINING  PAIRS 5 6 7

NUMBER ASSIGNED TO THE TWO DIMENSIONAL SEGMENTS FOUND
 1 CONSTITUTED OF PAIRS 1 2
 2 CONSTITUTED OF PAIRS 3 4
 3 CONSTITUTED OF PAIRS 5 6 7
THE CROSSINGS ARE MADE UP OF THE FOLLOWING SEGMENTS
1 3
2 3
THE VERTICES ARE MADE UP OF THE FOLLOWING SEGMENTS
1 2
THE TANGENTS ARE MADE UP OF THE FOLLOWING LINES
ARC 1 SEGMENT 1
ARC 1 SEGMENT 2
ARC 1 SEGMENT 3
POINTS OF CONTACT HAVE NOT BEEN FOUND
FILLETS HAVE NOT BEEN FOUND
```

Fig. 9 List of the structures and relations found in the examined object.

Fig. 10a Second image after the phase of reduction into filiform structure.

Fig. 10b Final image of fig. 2

```
        FINAL DESCRIPTION IMAGE GS01F2

SQUARE     S1 WITH SIDES

  S11  FROM POINT    30.5 206     TO POINT   209     206
  S12  FROM POINT   209   206     TO POINT   209      47
  S13  FROM POINT   209    47     TO POINT    30.5    47
  S14  FROM POINT    30.5  47     TO POINT    30.5   206

SQUARE     S2 WITH SIDES

  S21  FROM POINT    17.5 124.5   TO POINT   129      13
  S22  FROM POINT   129    13     TO POINT   240.5   124.5
  S23  FROM POINT   240.5 124.5   TO POINT   129     236
  S24  FROM POINT   129   236     TO POINT    17.5   124.5

SQUARE     S3 WITH SIDES

  S31  FROM POINT    30   176     TO.POINT   178.5   176
  S32  FROM POINT   178.5 176     TO POINT   178.5    76
  S33  FROM POINT   178.5  76     TO POINT    30      74
  S34  FROM POINT    30    75     TO POINT    30     176

SQUARE     S4 WITH SIDES

  S41  FROM POINT    57.5 125.5   TO POINT   129      54
  S42  FROM POINT   129    54     TO POINT   199.5   124.5
  S43  FROM POINT   199.5 124.5   TO POINT   128     196
  S44  FROM POINT   128   196     TO POINT    57.5   125.5

CIRCLE C1 WITH CENTRE ON POINT 129.37 125.5 AND RADIUS 79.17
CIRCLE C2 WITH CENTRE ON POINT 128.37 125.5 AND RADIUS 49.57
C1 INSCRIBED IN Q1
C1 INSCRIBED IN Q2
C2 INSCRIBED IN Q3
C2 INSCRIBED IN Q4
```

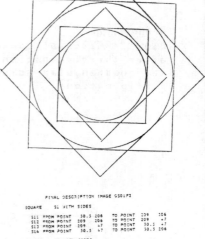

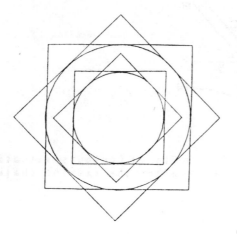

Fig. 10c Description Fig. 10b

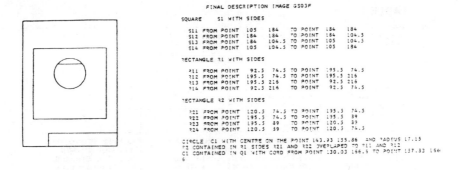

FINAL DESCRIPTION IMAGE GS03F

SQUARE   S1 WITH SIDES

    S11 FROM POINT 105   184   TO POINT 184   184
    S12 FROM POINT 184   184   TO POINT 184   104.5
    S13 FROM POINT 184   104.5 TO POINT 105   104.5
    S14 FROM POINT 105   104.5 TO POINT 105   184

RECTANGLE R1 WITH SIDES

    R11 FROM POINT 92.5 74.5   TO POINT 195.5 74.5
    R12 FROM POINT 195.5 74.5   TO POINT 195.5 216
    R13 FROM POINT 195.5 216   TO POINT 92.5 216
    R14 FROM POINT 92.5 216   TO POINT 92.5 74.5

RECTANGLE R2 WITH SIDES

    R21 FROM POINT 120.5 74.5   TO POINT 195.5 74.5
    R22 FROM POINT 195.5 74.5   TO POINT 195.5 39
    R23 FROM POINT 195.5 39   TO POINT 120.5 39
    R24 FROM POINT 120.5 39   TO POINT 120.5 74.5

CIRCLE C1 WITH CENTRE ON THE POINT 143.93 155.86 AND RADIUS 17.15
R2 CONTAINED IN R1 SIDES R21 AND R22 OVERLAPED TO R11 AND R12
C1 CONTAINED IN Q1 WITH CORD FROM POINT 130.03 166.5 TO POINT 157.33 166.6

Fig. 11a Final view 2

Fig. 11b Description Fig.11a

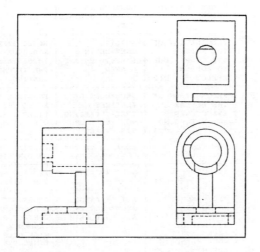

Fig. 12 Final image of fig. 1.

TABLE 1

RESTORATION PHASES		GOAL OF THE PHASE	RECOGNIZED STRUCTURES IN THE BINARY IMAGE	INTERPRETATION OF RECOGNIZED STRUCTURES IN TERMS OF THE ORIGINAL DRAWING
FROM THE DIGITIZED IMAGE TO THE BLACK-WHITE ONE A		PRODUCTION OF COMPRESSED BINARY IMAGE OF LOW NOISE LEVEL		THICKNESS OF LINES
FROM A BINARY IMAGE TO A STRING OF USEFUL CODES B		INDIVIDUATION OF SETS SI OF VERTICES OF THE CONTOUR OF EACH (MULTIPLE) CONNECTED SET OF POINTS	SIMPLE AND MULTIPLE CONNECTED SETS OF POINTS	SIMPLE CONNECTED SETS OF POINTS ARE THE STROKES OF DASHED LINES, CROSSES OR OTHER SIMPLE MARKERS
T H E R E S T O R A T I O N P R O C E S S	CONTOUR RESTORATION C1	RESEARCH OF CONTOUR STRUC-TURES AFFECTED BY CHARACTERIZING NOISE C11	NOISY SEQUENCES OF VERTICES CHARACTERIZING A CURVED CONTOUR OR A LINEAR INCLINED ONE	POSSIBLE ARCS OR INCLINED SEGMENTS ON THE BOUNDARY OF A PATH
		ELIMINATION OF THE NOISY STRUCTURES DUE TO BORDER EFFECT C12	NOISY USER-DEFINED STRUCTURES ARE ERASED	RECOGNIZED STRUCTURES ARE IMPOSSIBLE IN THE TECHNICAL DRAWING
		RECOGNITION OF THE LINEAR STRUCTURES NOT YET FOUND C13	SEQUENCES OF VERTICES CHARACTERIZING NOT YET FOUND STRUCTURES	POSSIBLE SEGMENTS ALONG THE EIGHT COMPASS DIRECTIONS
	PATH RESTORATION C2	PUTTING TOGETHER FACING STRUCTURES C21	SUBSETS OF THE CONTOURS THAT BOUND THE SAME SUBSTRUCTURES	PARTIAL RESOLUTION OF CONFLICT AMONG DIFFERENT CLASSI-FICATION OF THE SAME SET OF POINTS
		GROUPING OF MATCHING STRUCTURES (AND STORAGE OF PATHS CONVERGING IN AREAS) C22	SET OF PATHS GROUPABLE IN A SINGLE PATH	CROSSINGS, VERTI-CES, POINTS OF CONTACT, POINTS OF TANGENCY THAT WILL HELP IN THE FINAL CORRECTION
C	FILIFORM STROKE RESTORATION C3	REDUCTION OF THE INDIVIDU-ATED ENTITIES TO FILIFORM ONES C31	SET OF PARAMETERS WHICH DEFINES THE GEOMETRIC ENTITIES	
		RESETTLEMENT OF GEOMETRIC RELATIONS AMONG RECOGNIZED ENTITIES C32	CROSSINGS, VERTICES, POINTS OF CONTACT, POINTS OF TANGENCY, POINTS OF FILLETS	SET OF VECTORS THAT DESCRIBES THE IMAGES
DESCRIPTION D		PRODUCTION OF FIGURES AND THEIR DESCRIPTIONS		VERBAL AND GRAPHICAL DESCRIPTIONS OF THE ORIGINAL DRAWINGS

PRELIMINARY RESULTS ON AUTOMATIC RECOGNITION OF CADASTRAL MAPS

L. Masera

CSELT - Centro Studi e Laboratori Telecomunicazioni S.p.A.
Via G. Reiss Romoli, 274 - 10148 TORINO (Italy)

ABSTRACT

Automatic conversion of archives of maps from paper support to magnetic support, directly accessable from a computer, is required in a large number of applications. This paper reports preliminary results on a particular problem i.e., automatic recognition of cadastral maps. Some algorithms to solve some parts of this problem are proposed and applied to real cases.

1. INTRODUCTION

Telephone companies, power companies, water distribution agencies, etc., supplying a service based on a network covering an extended land have to solve the problem of management of maps archives: the largest part of this activity is the recording of the modifications made on the network in order to daily update the situation.

Usually these kinds of maps are stratified on many levels of detail; the lowest level represents only the configuration of the land (streets, building, parks, etc.) and at each higher level particular aspects of the network are added.

Figg. 1a, 1b display two different levels of detailing of a map of the italian telephone operating company. The presence of letters, numbers, special symbols, etc. is to be noted.

Since map updating is usually made by means of a lengthy procedure, reduction of this time is strongly desired.

A possible way to speed up the updating procedure is obtained storing the maps into a fast-access computer memory. Inspection and/or correction even from remote terminals becomes possible. Some companies producing graphical/optical systems have always developed reproduction systems and management software that give an effective solution to the previous problems. They are based, however, on the availability of electronic archives representing the maps in a suitable form.

211

212

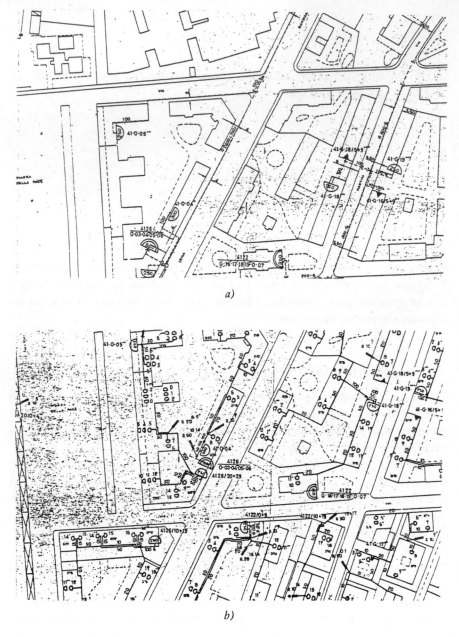

a)

b)

Fig. 1 - Two different levels of detailing of the map of the italian telephone operating
company

The conversion of the archives from paper to magnetic support is an outstanding problem to be solved. The direct conversion by scanning made by facsimile-like apparatus requires a large amount of memory and has a low efficiency in the retrieving and updating operations.

A second solution requires digitizing tables, that permit the information transfer by running a cursor over the map lines.

This solution is practicable only when the amount of maps is not large. If the number of maps to convert is high (hundreds of thousand in the case of the italian telephone operating company) then costs and times justify the introduction of sophisticated pattern recognition techniques.

The paper reports preliminary results on the automatic recognition of the lowest level of map archives, i.e. cadastral maps. An example of such a map is reported in Fig. 2.

The goal is of simulating a machine that gives a computer a simple description of the maps, in such a way that updating, deleting and finding of certain map details is possible.

2. GENERAL DESCRIPTION

The whole procedure can be split in two principal subproblems: the first one is the acquisition and pre-processing and the second one the recognition.

The first part is constituted by:

- Acquisition
- Thresholding
- Possible reconstruction of broken lines.

The second part requires the following operations:

- Region contour following
- Marking of the recognized region
- Extraction and recognition of the objects inside the region.

In the next paragraphs all the phases constituting the entire procedure will be described In detail and some problems encountered will be pointed out.

3. ACQUISITION

Many devices can be used to acquire an image drawn on paper; but for this application a high resolution is of paramount importance. The performance of two different scanning devices was tested and compared: a digital group 3 fac-simile and an optical reader developed and built by CSELT [1].

These devices have about the same scanning resolution i.e. 8 lines/mm and 1728 points/scanned line.

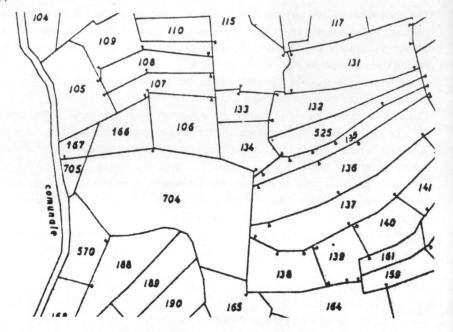

Fig. 2 - An example of cadastral map

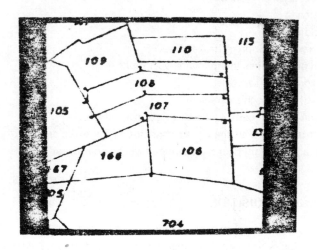

Fig. 3 - A portion of map acquired by means of optical reader

The first apparatus gives in output only a two level digital signal because there is an inner thresholding automatic process based on the measure of the average contrast of the image; the second one, instead, gives 256 gray level digital samples on which it is possible to perform some processing to improve image quality. In Fig. 3 an example of a portion of map acquired by the optical reader is reported.

However, the following operations need a two level image as input, so a thresholding process is involved.

In the next paragraph some problems related to this operation will be examined.

4. THRESHOLDING

The problems related to the thresholding are caused by the sum of the defects of all optical and mechanical devices that constitute the scanning apparatus. There are many algorithms, known in the literature, to get a two level image from a gray scale image [2] and their principal feature is to compensate for non-uniform lighting over the scanned line and the defects of optical systems.

Some experiments of thresholding based on contrast enhancement techniques [3] or local adapting of the threshold level has been made, but these algorithms are too noise sensitive, so an algorithm for only lighting compensation has been choosen; moreover the optical reader does not present relevant distortion to be taken into account.

The algorithm for lighting compensation consist of a measure of lighting on some white scanned lines and for every point the mean value is computed. This value is used as threshold and for every other scanned line the value of lighting is divided, point by point, by the threshold value.

Although the output of the thresholding process is fairly good (see Fig. 4), it is possible to get some lines that are incorrectly broken.

The most important reason of this degradation is due to the possible low quality of the copies of cadastral maps available at the competent offices.

Since line continuity is a necessary condition for the following steps, an algorithm for lines reconstruction must be used.

5. BROKEN LINES RECONSTRUCTION

This phase is split in two steps: the first one of line thinning, the second one of reconstruction.

The first process has been widely studied in the literature [4]. It can be based on the inspecting of many kinds of neighbour: rectangular, squared, exagonal, etc.; we have chosen a squared neighbour, because the best results for our applications were obtained with it.

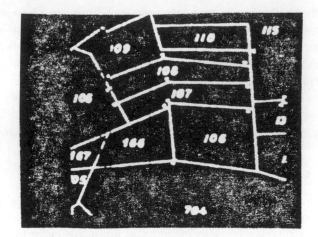

Fig. 4 - Output of thresholding process

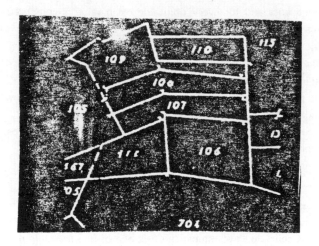

Fig. 5 - Thinned map

The reconstruction procedure is based on detection of all "hanging points", that is the extremal point of the segments of lines.

The detection of these points is made by following the thinned lines and detecting the points where the direction of following is reversed.

In the following step the algorithm, for every hanging point, looks for the nearest non-connected hanging point. The two points are linked if their distance is less then a prefixed threshold. The value of the threshold is strictly related to the resolution of scanning process and it is determined, for the moment, by means of some experimental test on the typical size of the random interruptions.

In case of interruption in a point of crossing lines the algorithm fails, because it is not sensitive to the direction of the lines so it is possible that the pair of nearest points is not the right pair of points to be connected. However, this case is very unlikely, because in the point of crossing lines the graphical strokes are more dense.

In some cases wrong connections between characters written inside the region have been found, but in the following step this defect is corrected.

This algorithm gives right reconstruction in 95% of the cases.

Fig. 5 displays the output of thinning process and the result of reconstruction step is reported in Fig. 6.

In the following paragraph we assume that the closed regions of the map have continuous boundary.

6. RECOGNITION OF A CLOSED REGION

In this application the shape of a region is not important, but it is essential to be able to pick up all the information contained in it.

Therefore the procedure can be divided in the following three steps:
- Contour following
- Colouring
- Detection of inner objects.

Contour following has been widely treated in the literature [5], so it will not be examined in this paper. However, the algorithm used in these tests will be briefly described.

The procedure consists in following clockwise the contour of every region starting from the highest and rightmost black point following a white point.

During the process every pair of coordinates of the touched points are stored and when the starting point and the following two points are reached the process must stop, because otherwise the process would loop.

At the end of this step the bound of a region is fully known by means of the coordinates of its points.

The following step is called "colouring", and consists in marking all white points inside

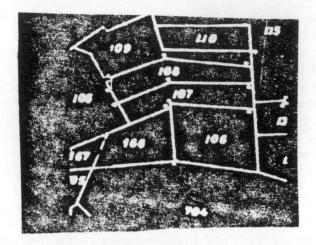

Fig. 6 - Output of reconstruction step

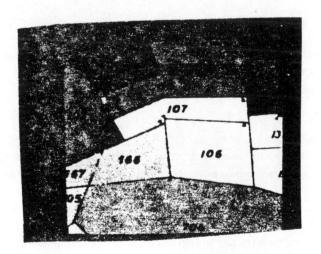

Fig. 7 - Output of colouring process

the region and extracting the objects (characters, symbols) that are encountered during the operations, as explained in the following paragraph.

7. COLOURING AND RECOGNITION STEPS

It is essential to mark in some way the inner points of the recognized region to prevent their subsequent examination.

We call the colouring algorithm developed in our experimental system "by diffusion". It is based on identifying a white point that is surely inside the region and in "colouring" it. Starting from this point all the white points in its neighbourhood will be coloured. The process is repeated for all coloured points and when it is not possible to colour any further point the processing is stopped.

In Fig. 7 the output of the colouring phase is reported; during this phase the wrong reconstruction of lines are corrected and the black points, concerning the inner objects, are marked in a suitable way for further examination in the following step of the recognition.

As said before, inner objects can belong at different classes and although they are of the same category they can be written or drawn in many different ways (e.g. hand written, typed, bended, etc.).

The object are isolated one at a time in a binary matrix, normalised in their size, made straight and oriented in a standard direction. Such a matrix is the input of the symbol recognizer [6], which is based on the feature extraction at high information level such as contours, projections and profiles.

At these features an algorithm to reduce the dimensionality, generally too high, is applied; so that a better efficiency is obtained. Afterwards every symbol is assigned to a class it belongs to, in such a way that the error probability is minimum.

8. CONCLUSIONS

The system described in this paper has been implemented on a Digital PDP 11/60 minicomputer connected with the optical reader and a video interface for displaying. Its performance is good enough considering the fact that it operates on real data and not on "ad hoc" models. This is an important feature, because the greatest part of engagement is dedicated to the compensation of the imperfection related to the data acquisition.

Future development can be:

- detection of bounding marks
- discrimination between streets and regions
- detection of footpaths, represented by means of dashed lines.

REFERENCES

[1] L. Chiariglione, L. Corgnier, G. Ponte, S. Sandri, A. Sciarappa: ATRAS: un sistema di lettura automatica di testi, Elettronica e Telecomunicazioni, To be published.

[2] J.S. Weszdk, A. Rosenfeld: Threshold evaluation techniques, IEEE Transaction on Systems, Man and Cybernetics, Vol. SMC 8, Aug. 78, pp. 622-635.

[3] G. Garibotto, G. Micca: Image processing by a two-component model, Proc. of the 2nd Scandinavian Conference on Image Analysis, Helsinki, June 15-17, 1981, pp. 158-163.

[4] E.S. Deutsch: Thinning algorithm on rectangular, hexagonal and triangular arrays, Comm. of ACM, Sept. 1972, V. 15, n. 9, pp. 827-837.

[5] M. Basseville: Dètection de contours: mèthodes et ètudes comparatives, Ann. Tèlècomunic., V. 134, n. 11-12/79, pp. 559-579.

[6] L. Barp, L. Chiariglione, M. Guglielmo: Estrazione di caratteristiche ed algoritmi di riconoscimento per caratteri manoscritti. CSELT R.T., V. 5, n. 1, Mar. 1977.

Natural Languages

FLEXIBLE PARSING OF DISCRETELY UTTERED SENTENCES

L. Borghesi and C. Favareto

Elettronica San Giorgio - ELSAG S.p.A.
Via Hermada 6 - 16154 Genova - Italy

ABSTRACT

A syntactic-semantic parser of spoken sentences pertaining to a subset of natural Italian Language is proposed here.

Error-free and fast analysis, partial interpretation ability, man-machine dialogue trend, different semantic environment adaptability and natural language usage are its main characteristics. All of these features are supported by a technique of input reliability evaluation. Particular attention is devoted to the description of the internal knowledge representation and of the mechanism that manages, at different points of the analysis, the whole process.

Some examples relevant to the particular semantic domain chosen will be illustrated.

Finally the results following from the analysis of 50 sentences, spoken by 3 different speakers, will be given.

INTRODUCTION

The main problem in such a vocal parser is the lack of certainty on the single items of the input sentence.

In fact the representation of each uttered word, following the recognition stage, is an ordered list of possible interpretations with associated dissimilarity measures.

As a consequence, it is possible to have doubts not only about every single word of the sentence, but also on complete sentence parts. Moreover, irrecoverable recognition errors may require the capability of parsing incomplete sentences.

In fig. 1 a typical parsing input is shown. The input sentence is: TOGLI TUTTO DALLA STANZA (Remove everything from the room).

Each input word is replaced by a complete list of possible alternatives with associated distance scores.

Spoken Sentences: TOGLI TUTTO DALLA STANZA

Parsing Input :

word	dis	word	dis	word	dis	word	dis
TOGLI	32.1	UN	46.4	DALLA	16.7	RAGGIO	42.4
OTTO	34.7	QUANTO	46.8	DAL	19.4	NOVANTA	42.8
DAMMI	34.8	UNA	46.9	AL	20.9	STANZA	42.9
TOGLIERE	35.1	VENTI	47.0	TAVOLO	23.7	QUADRATO	44.1
COSTRUISCI	35.9	OTTO	48.1	.		.	
.		UNO	48.5	.		.	
.		TUTTO	49.5	.		.	
		.					

FIG. 1 EXAMPLE OF A TYPICAL INPUT OF THE PARSER

The first interpretation is not always the correct one and, in
fact, in this example, only TOGLI and DALLA are is the first position.

It is interesting to observe, furthermore, that there are more
than one syntactically correct paths . For example the parser can find
both the actually spoken sentence: TOGLI TUTTO DALLA STANZA and, this
one: COSTRUISCI UN TAVOLO QUADRATO (Build a square table).

An efficient parser must also be able to solve other problems not
strictly connected to a particular kind of input. In fact it should,
of course, achieve fast operations; that requires the ability to mini
mize the number of alternative parses (Woods, 1975).

Furthermore the parser should be designed in such a way as to satisfy the "generality" expectations; that is it should be easily adap
table to any semantic domain at least in the limited semantic domain
cases. Since the parser results should be followed by the execution
of some operation in any practical application it is required that it
produced trusty results and, in particular, that it always included
the right sentence interpretation within all the output ones.

Finally, to allow a graceful dialogue with its users the parser
must be able to analyze also partial sentences (for example elliptical or fragmentary ones), thus making it possible to use naturally
expressed sentences (Hayes et al., 1979).

1 MAIN PARSER'S CHARACTERISTICS

The main features of our parser, that permit to satisfy the above mentioned requirements, are the following:

1) representation of the language in terms of a network whose elements are syntactic groups and syntactic features;
2) definition of a confidence measure of the recognition results and its extension also to groups of words (syntactic groups);
3) adoption of a recursive working strategy which anchors the parsing on the most reliable words in a first step and on the most reliable groups in a second one.

We selected the furnishing of a living room as the discourse domain and we defined a vocabulary of a 116 words.

This vocabulary, although limited, leads to a total number of over 10^5 possible sentences that include commands for constructing or moving pieces of furniture, assignment of labels, definition of unit lengths, inquiries about mutual distances, etc.

1.1 LANGUAGE REPRESENTATION

According to the first point each sentence of the language is described by a sequence of syntactic groups.

These groups are defined as sentence parts with a well precise semantic meaning.

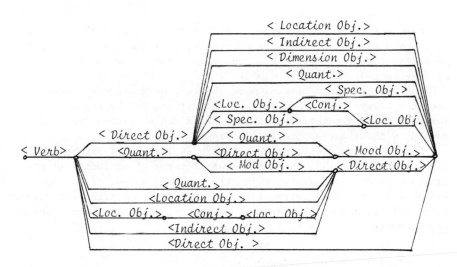

FIG. 2   LANGUAGE REPRESENTATION

226

We defined, for example, the verb, the direct object, the location object, etc.

On the whole we introduced only 9 groups; in our opinion this set of syntactic groups is enough to describe, at a syntactic level, all the possible sentences pertaining to this semantic environment.

In fig. 2 it can be seen how all the sentences of the language can be represented as paths through a network in which every arc corresponds to a syntactic group.

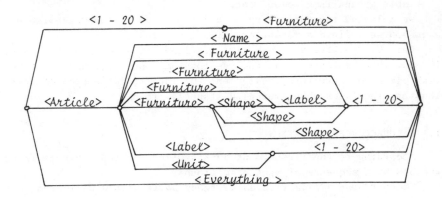

FIG. 3   DIRECT OBJECT REPRESENTATION

Each syntactic group is, in turn, represented by a number of possible word sequences, or, more precisely, of sequences of associated syntactic features. Figure 3 shows, for example, how the direct object is represented.

One feature can represent more than one word and every new word does not always need a new feature definition. So the present vocabulary can be easily increased to a certain degree within the semantic domain, without any change in the grammar.

Obviously the choice of using features instead of vocabulary entries and of describing the sentences in terms of syntactic groups agrees with the need of improving the analysis speed, of making the semantic environment representation oriented to a partial interpretation analysis and of allowing easy adaptability to different semantic environments.

1.2   RELIABILITY EVALUATION

The doubts connected with the vocal input suggested the need for a tool that   measured the goodness of each word recognition. To this

purpose a method to evaluate the reliability of recognition results
was defined (Musso et al., 1981).

By this method every word, in the ordered list, is associated
with a confidence score indicating its probability of being the correct one (see fig. 4).

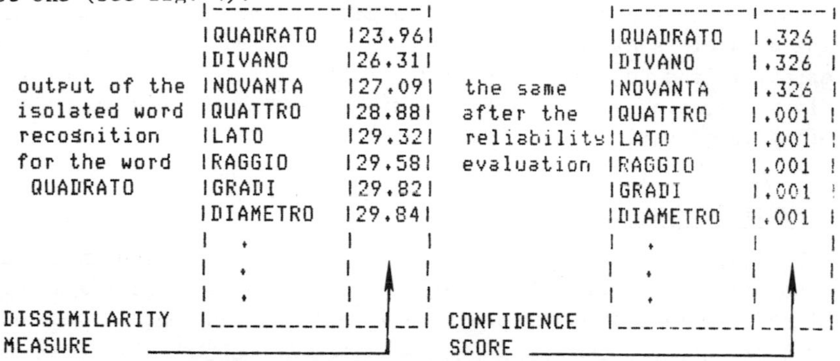

```
                          |-----------|-----|              |-----------|-----|
                          |QUADRATO  123.961|              |QUADRATO  1.326 |
                          |DIVANO    126.311|              |DIVANO    1.326 |
        output of the     |NOVANTA   127.091|  the same    |NOVANTA   1.326 |
        isolated word     |QUATTRO   128.881|  after the   |QUATTRO   1.001 |
        recognition       |LATO      129.321|  reliability |LATO      1.001 |
        for the word      |RAGGIO    129.581|  evaluation  |RAGGIO    1.001 |
           QUADRATO       |GRADI     129.821|              |GRADI     1.001 |
                          |DIAMETRO  129.841|              |DIAMETRO  1.001 |
                          |  .        |    |              |  .        |    |
                          |  .        |  ↑ |              |  .        |  ↑ |
                          |  .        |  | |              |  .        |  | |
    DISSIMILARITY         |_____|__|__|  CONFIDENCE    |_____|__|__|
    MEASURE              _____   SCORE     _____
```

FIG. 4   RELIABILITY EVALUATION

In this way, as described below, the most reliable words of the
sentence can be selected and the parser anchored to them. The same reliability score is also used to evaluate the syntactic groups found
and to decide which, among alternative groups, is the most probable
one.

1.3 ISLAND DRIVEN WORKING STRATEGY

All the operations of the parser are centered around the concept
of reliability score. In fact, in a first step, the parser anchors its
analysis to the most reliable word of the sentence (that we named
"guide word") and searches, both to the right and to the left of it,
for all the syntactic groups that include the features associated to
the guide word. Each of these syntactic groups is named "island".

Not only the first word in the ordered list can be used for this
aim, but sometimes also the second and the third ones are taken into
consideration. For each island a cumulative reliability score, function
of the single word scores, is computed.

The same procedure is then applied to the remaining words until
the whole sentence has been examined and there are no more guide words;
at this point a lattice of island, possibly overlapping, is obtained.

In a second step the parser, in an almost identical fashion as before, searches for the most reliable island (that we named "guide island"), anchoring to it the exploration of the language network to get
a match with one of the possible sentences. When this is not possible,
because of very unreliable recognition of a whole syntactic group, the
partial sentence recovered is proposed in output together with a hypothesis about the missing constituent.

At this point a module for graceful man-machine interaction could be activated, in order to obtain the needed information by means of an appropriate dialogue.

In addition there are some parameters, specifying the number of retained alternatives at various points of the parsing, that allow to control parser's performance both in terms of speed and confidence. These parameters allow the parser to work with different degrees of flexibility and so, they must be carefully selected, according to the application, i.e. according to the risk that can be tolerated when ac cepting an acoustically unclear sentence.

2 RUNNING EXAMPLES

In fig. 5 the main steps of the analysis of a particular sentence are summarized. To make the comprehension easier we report a simulated english example that corresponds to a real italian sentence processed by the parser.

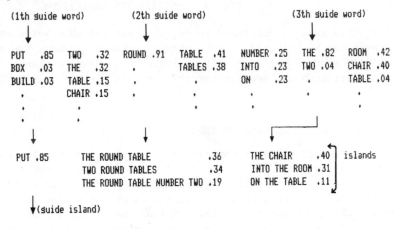

FIG. 5   RUNNING SIMULATED EXAMPLE

The input sentence is: PUT THE ROUND TABLE INTO THE ROOM. In the first step, starting respectively from the 1st, 2nd and 3rd guide word (PUT, ROUND, THE), the parser finds some possible islands with associa ted reliability score. In a second step, starting from the guide is- land the parser searches a match between a path in the language net- work and the islands. The final result is the correct interpretation of the sentence even if there were three recognition errors.

Sometimes the parser outputs are not univocal as in the previous example. In fact, if the reliability score of a whole island is too low, the parser provides an output in which, instead of a detailed word-by-word interpretation, an hypothesis about the type of the missing syntactic group appears as shown in the example below:

PUT<direct object> IN THE MIDDLE OF THE ROOM

If, on the contrary, there are two or more words with approximately the same reliability score and the same syntactic role, then the parser supplies in the output those alternatives with their associated reliability scores and the whole decision will be deferred to a following pragmatic module or dialogue component. For example we can have an output like this one:

PUT THE {TABLE .32} NUMBER TWO IN FRONT OF THE DOOR
       {CHAIR .29}

In fig.6 the main steps of the parsing algorithm are summarized.

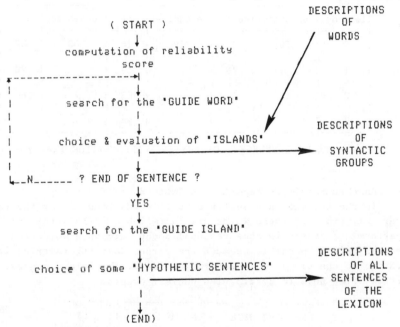

FIG. 6   MAIN STEPS OF THE PARSING ALGORITHM

3   RESULTS

The present parser has been tested on a set of 50 sentences spoken by three different speakers (two males and one female). A poor word recognizer was adopted in order to stress parser's capabilities. We compare in table 1 the parser performances and those of the recognizer alone. For each speaker the first column reports the percent of success of the recognizer alone, i.e. how many times all the words of a sentence were in the first position. The column reports the percent of success of the parser (i.e. how many times the parser was able to interpret the sentence).

Each row corresponds to a case in which there are, respectively, none, 1, 2 and 3 lost islands whose reliability was not sufficient to take any decision.

We want to notice that for the 1st speaker the parser locates the correct sentence in the 92% of the cases and achieves a 96% correct interpretation if it assumes that there is one lost island. For the 2nd speaker these values increase more slowly because of a very unreliable input (10% of success for the regnizer).

However the main result is that the parser never took a decision that did not contain the correct interpretation.

# of lost islands	SPEAKER N. 1		SPEAKER N. 2		SPEAKER N. 3	
	recognizer	parser	recognizer	parser	recognizer	parser
0	30	92	10	10	58	82
1		96		54		98
2				88		100
3				94		

TABLE 1 PERCENT OF SENTENCE RECOGNITION (see text)

Another result is reported in table 2.

In the average each sentence is 11 words long. After the recognizer analysis 7 of these words are unreliable while after the parser performance there is some residual doubt only on 2 words (on the average). This is possible because the parser does not restrict its observation to the single word but looks also at the island context and so it is often able to distinguish unclear events.

AVERAGE SENTENCES LENGTH	11
AVERAGE DOUBT FOR THE INPUT	7
AVERAGE DOUBT FOR THE OUTPUT	2.4
AVERAGE RECOVERY	4.6

TABLE 2 PARSING PERFORMANCE

4   CONCLUSION

We have described a parser of spoken sentences in which the design decisions taken are a necessary step to satisfy the requirements of a voice interactive system.

In fact the choice of using features instead of vocabulary entries and of describing the sentences in terms of syntactic groups agrees with the needs of improving the analysis speed, of making the semantic environment representation oriented to a partial interpretation analysis and of allowing the adaptability to different semantic environments.

Finally we want to notice the characteristics that make this parser oriented to a graceful man-machine interaction. They are its ability to provide in the output more than one choice with its associated reliability score and its ability to interpret also partial input.

The first characteristic, in fact, allows a pragramatic module to make a choice among various alternatives, looking at their reliability score or, if in doubt, to activate a dialogue module which requests the needed information. The second characteristic permits the management of a dialogue in which also elliptical sentences are allowed or, anyhow, the maximum freedom of expression is permitted.

REFERENCES

Hayes, P., Reddy, R., (1979). An anatomy of graceful interaction in spoken and written man-machine communication,
Report CMU-SS-79-144, Carnege Mellon Univ.

Musso, G., Borghesi, L., Favareto, C., (1981), Confidence evaluation for an isolated word recognizer, in 4th F.A.S.E. Proceedings
p. 293-296.

Woods, W.A. (1975), Syntax, semantics and speech, in Reddy D.R. ed.,
Speech Recognition, Academic Press.

AN INTERPRETER OF NATURAL LANGUAGE QUERIES

Leonardo LESMO & Pietro TORASSO

Istituto di Scienze dell'Informazione - Università di Torino
C.so Massimo D'Azeglio, 42 - 10125 TORINO - ITALY

ABSTRACT

This paper describes the structures adopted for representing the syntactic and semantic knowledge sources in a system which interprets queries in natural language issued against a relational data base. The syntax is represented as a partitioned set of pattern-action rules, whereas the semantic knowledge is inserted in form of network into the lexicon; this latter is accessed by semantic check procedures associated with the slots of frames which are instantiated to build the final representation.

A particular attention will be paid to the explanation of the way these knowledge sources interact during the analysis of the command in order to avoid independent translation steps and intermediate representations of the command.

INTRODUCTION

The interpretation of a command in natural language consists in the translation of the surface form of the command into an internal representation suitable to determine the sequence of operations needed to satisfy the command's requests. During the translation process some checks are performed to ascertain that the input command is consistent with the system's knowledge. The constraints imposed on the structure of a sentence have usually been split in syntactic constraints and semantic ones, so that every natural language interpreter needs a syntactic knowledge source and a semantic knowledge source. However, there are significant dissimilarities in the way these knowledge sources are represented and used. By focussing the attention on the way syntax and semantics interact during the translation of the command, it is possible to identify two different approaches (Charniak 81).

A first solution involves a sequentialization of the syntactic and semantic analyses: this means that firstly the system checks the syntactic correctness of the command by parsing it and translates it into an intermediate representation (Woods 78; Harris 78; Konolige 80; Guida & Somalvico 80) normally consisting in one or more parse trees; then the system examines the resulting parse trees to determine for each of them whether it satisfies the semantic constraints, in which case the tree is translated into the final representation.

The most evident disadvantage of this approach concerns the need of building and handling a number of intermediate structures, most of which will be discarded by the subsequent step of the analysis (notice that this will happen even if a semantic inconsistency occurs at the very beginning of the sentence), as pointed out by Konolige (1980).

The alternative approach consists in taking advantage in parallel of the constraints imposed on the command structure by the syntactic and semantic knowledge sources. Such an approach is obviously more flexi ble than the previous one and this flexibility produced a wide variety of solutions, each showing some peculiarities in the representation (and consequently in the way of interacting) of the two   knowledge sources (Schank, Lebowitz & Birnbaum 79; Rieger & Small 81; Wilensky 81; Arens 81; Sidner et al. 81).

The approach of directly translating the input command into the fi nal representation has been adopted in the construction of the system we have developed; this system is characterized by a separation of the syntactic and semantic knowledge sources, but they cooperate heavily during the translation process.

The system, whose overall organization is described in Lesmo, Magna ni & Torasso (1981), is devoted to the interpretation of queries in Italian language issued against a relational data base containing med ical information. The final representation of the command consists in a set of frame instantiations linked together and it may immediately be interpreted as a sequence of algebraic operations on the data base.

The system uses four different knowledge sources: syntactic KS, se mantic KS, lexical KS, pragmatic KS.

The syntactic KS is represented by means of a set of pattern-action rules partitioned in subsets called Syntactic Rule Packets (SRP), each of which is associated with a particular constituent and specifies the particular forms it may assume. The analysis is performed left-to-right in a deterministic fashion (Lesmo, Magnani & Torasso 81), where the term "deterministic" is used in the sense proposed by Marcus (1980): in fact the inspection of the pattern parts of the rules and the use of a lookahead buffer allow the system to choose deterministic ally the rewriting rule which must be applied to translate the constit uent. Greater details about the behaviour of the action part of the syntactic rules will be reported in the following.

As regards the semantic KS, it is rather difficult to identify a sin gle component of the system implementing the semantic knowledge.   In fact, the semantic constraints are specified in the form of procedures each of which is associated with a slot of one of the prototype frames. However, those procedures accomplish also part of the translation task and, for verifying the semantic correctness, thay refer to a network which is actually included in the lexical KS (as in Heidorn 78). Also in this case a more detailed description of the semantic procedures will be given below.

The lexical KS includes a dictionary, each entry of which contains a root-ending representation of a word of the domain, its syntactic category and, just in case it is a content word , a pointer to a node of the network mentioned above.

Finally, the pragmatic KS is represented in tabular form and accomplishes two tasks: it allows the system to infer some data which have been subsumed in the surface form of the command and stores information regarding the associations between external terms and real data base objects (e.g. relation names). A more detailed description of both the lexical and pragmatic KS has been given in Lesmo, Magnani and Torasso (1981 b).

FRAME STRUCTURE AND COMMAND REPRESENTATION

As stated above, the final representation of the command consists in a set of frame instantiations linked together. The frames are instantiated under request of the action part of the syntactic rules on the basis of a set of frame prototypes which are defined a-priori. The current version of the system includes five prototype frames: COMMANDFR, CONCEPTFR, ACTIONFR, RESTRICTIONFR and CONSTRAINTFR (°). Each of them corresponds to a different role in the semantic interpretation of the command.

COMMANDFR refers to the operation which has been requested (e.g. listing, averaging, etc.) and contains the specification of the data to operate upon (normally the name of an attribute of a relation).

CONCEPTFR corresponds to what we called a concept, i.e. to a type of entities (individual objects). A concept is associated with a data base relation containing the data relative to the entities of that type (e.g. PATIENT). An individual is usually identified by the value of a particular attribute which is the key of the relation; however, it is possible to select a subset of the existing individuals by specifying some restrictions on the admissible values of one or more attributes.

RESTRICTIONFR instantiations are used for this purpose in that they contain those specifications (attribute name, comparison operator, value) and are linked to instantiations of CONCEPTFR.

Another way of selecting subsets of entities is to specify that the entities to select must be connected to entities of another kind (in general it could be the same one) in a given way. For example, you could want to select all the patients which have performed a given laboratory test (and LABDATA is the concept corresponding to the laboratory tests). These selections are performed by means of JOIN opera

---

(°) In the following we will refer to the instantations of the prototype frames by means of the terms: COMINST, CONCINST, RESTRINST, CONSTRINST, ACTINST. However, they are only shorthands, so that CONCINST should be read as "instantation of CONCEPTFR".

tions. However, the relations which correspond to the two concepts are not joined together directly, but via a connection relation which specifies, by means of a composite key, what entities of the first type are connected to what entities of the other one. These connection relations may contain intersection data (e.g. in the example above the result of the labtests performed by the the patients) and their exist ence is justified by the normal use in natural language of a verb to indicate the kind of association existing between the two kinds of en tities. In the example above the verb is "to perform", a relation PERFORM exists in the data base and in the final representation of the query an ACTINST occurs between the two CONINSTs (one for PATIENT and one for LABDATA).

The last frame prototype is CONSTRAINTFR. It plays the same role as RESTRICTIONFR but its instantiations are linked to ACTINSTs instead of CONCINSTs, in that they specify restrictions on the values of intersec tion data. Even if the structure of CONSTRAINTFR and RESTRICTIONFR are analogous (attribute name, comparison operator, value), two frame pro totypes are needed because of the different checks to perform on the slot values.

As an example, in fig. 1 is reported the structure of CONCEPTFR.

SLOT NAME	SLOT TYPE	CHECK
NAME	EXTERNAL	CHN1
NAME!	INTERNAL	NIL
QUALIF	LINK	NIL
SFECIF	LINK	NIL
BACKACT	REVL	NIL
BACKCOMM	REVL	NIL
CONCCH	CHAIN	NIL

Fig. 1 - The frame prototype CONCEPTFR

The slots composing the frames are of five types:
- EXTERNAL. They contain the actual lexical entries appearing as con tent words in the input command.
- INTERNAL. They concern the internal representation which will be used to access the data stored in the data base relations. They are filled with the translation of the entry contained in the correspond ing external slot or with a value inferred from the context, if the content of the external slot is undefined.
- LINK. They contain pointers to other frame instantiations.
- REVL. They are "reverse links" and are automatically set when the corresponding direct link is set.
- CHAIN. They contain pointers which implement chain of concepts; chains are used to represent set of (i.e. ANDed) conditions.
In CONCEPTFR we have the following slots:

- NAME: it contains the word used in the surface form of the command
  to refer to the concept (if it exists).
- NAME!: it contains the name of the corresponding data base relation.
- QUALIF: it contains a pointer to a RESTRINST (or to the head of a
  chain of them).
- SPECIF: it contains a pointer to an ACTINST specifying the connec
  tion relation which must be joined to the relation whose name is
  stored in NAME!.
- BACKACT: it is a pointer to a preceding ACTINST (it is used if this
  concept is the second one in a JOIN).
- BACKCOMM: it is a pointer to a COMMINST (it is used if the relation
  whose name is in NAME! contains the attribute to operate upon).
- CONCCH: it contains a pointer to another CONCINST (it is used to rep
  resent, for example, "list the patients who performed the hepatic
  biopsy and the BSP").

It is apparent that a link between an ACTINST and a CONCINST (or viceversa) implies a JOIN operation, whereas a link between a CONCINST and
a RESTRINST (as well as a link between an ACTINST and a CONSTRINST) im
plies a SELECT operation on the data base relation referred to by the
corresponding CONCINST (or ACTINST).

A detailed example of the translation of a query and of the use of
the check procedures (only one of them appears in CONCEPTFR) is report
ed in the Appendix.

THE ACTION PART OF THE SYNTACTIC RULES

As stated above, the selection of the syntactic rule which must be
used to translate a constituent is performed by using the pattern part
of the rules composing the Syntactic Rule Packet associated to that
constituent. When the rule has been chosen, its action part is execut
ed; it accomplishes two tasks: describes the composition of the consti
tuent and adds to the final representation of the command the struc
ture which corresponds to the translation of the constituent. Notice
however that such procedures are concerned only with structure build
ing operations (i.e. frame instantiating and linking) and with extern
al slot filling. In fact the task of completing the translation by
filling the internal slots is left to the semantic check procedures
associated with the slots of the prototype frames.

The action part of the rules involve the following imperative state
ments:
- CAT (L): the CAT operation verifies that the current word in the
  lookahead buffer belongs to one of the categories composing the
  list L. If the lookahead buffer is empty or all the words stored in
  it have already been scanned, a request for a new word is issued.
  This request activates a procedure which performs the following oper
  ations: reads a word from the input string, accesses the dictionary
  and stores in the lookahead buffer the lexical entry together with

the associated information (the syntactic category and possibly a pointer to the corresponding node of the network).

- PUSH (C,I): the PUSH operation transfers the control to the SRP asso ciated with the constituent C and specifies that the structure ob tained by translating C must be connected to the frame instantiation I. In other words, a PUSH triggers the procedure which matches the pattern part of the rules belonging to the SRP associated with C against the contents of the lookahead buffer. The result of this match, which may require the input of new lexical items into the lookahead buffer, is the scheduling of the action associated with the chosen syntactic rule.

- POP: is the last operation of each action; its execution involves a return of the control to the action which issued the PUSH.

- CREATE (F,N): the CREATE operation builds a new instantiation of the prototype frame F. When a new instantiation is created, all its slots are empty (so that it is obviously not linked to any other instantiation). N is the local name of the newly created instantia tion, which allows the system to refer to it during the execution of the action which issued the CREATE. Notice that this means that the sole instantiations which may be assessed directly by an action are the ones created by the action itself and the "current instantia tion" (i.e. the second parameter of the PUSH which caused, after the pattern matching step, the execution of the current action); however other instantiations may be reached by travelling the currently ex isting links.

- FILL (S,N,V): it makes the system fill the slot S of the frame in stantiation whose local name is N with the value V (actually N may be a list which specifies the path to be traversed to reach the in stantiation starting from another frame instantiation whose local name is known by the current action). A fundamental side-effect of the FILL operation is the triggering of the semantic check procedure associated with the filled slot. The behaviour of these procedures will be described in the following paragraph, but it is worth notic ing that a FILL may cause the waking up of other procedures which were suspended because of the unavailability of the contents of the just filled slot.

- LINK (N1,S,N2): it fills the slot S of N1 (which must be of type LINK) with a pointer to the frame instantiation N2 (as regards N1 and N2, they may assume the forms described for the parameter N of FILL). The linking of N1 and N2 via S makes the system automatically fill the reverse link of N2 associated with S. As the FILL, the exe cution of a LINK operation may cause the resumption of a suspended check procedure.

- DEL: it deletes the first entry of the lookahead buffer. The DEL op erator is needed since the CAT operator does not consumes the tested lexical item; this allows the implementation of the pattern matching step of rule selection as a sequence of CAT operations. The DEL op eration is applied to function words (e.g. prepositions) because they do not appear in the final representation of the command, where as the content words are deleted from the buffer during the FILL op eration which uses them.

SEMANTIC CHECK PROCEDURES

The semantic check procedures take care of two tasks: they verify that each update of the command representation is semantically consis tent with the structure previously built and they fill as soon as pos sible the internal slots of the partially built interpretation. The semantic consistency is verified by accessing the information stored in form of network in the internal part of the dictionary, whereas the internal slots are filled either by translating the contents of a cor responding external slot or by inferring the value to insert by in specting the context of the slot. Both the deduction of the subsumed data and the translation of the available ones are performed on the basis of the pragmatic KS (for more information see Lesmo, Magnani & Torasso 81b).

Apart from the conditional statement, which allows the system to choose a particular sequence of operations depending on the current situation of the internal representation, the distinctive operations involved in the semantic check procedures are CHECK and SETIS:

- CHECK (E1,E2,R): E1 and E2 are two expressions each of which identi fies a particular slot (EXTERNAL) by specifying a path on the inter nal representation (this path starts from the current frame instan tiation, i.e. that one with which the semantic check is associated). By indicating with V1 and V2 the values of the slots identified by E1 and E2, the CHECK operation verifies that the relation R is de fined in such a way that R(V1,V2) holds. This test is performed by accessing the network part of the dictionary; in fact V1 and V2 are actually content words and CHECK reports TRUE when they are connect ed by an arc labelled with R.
- SETIS (E,L): E is an expression identifying a slot (same as E1 and E2 for CHECK, but in this case the slot type is INTERNAL) and L is a list whose first element is the name of a function mapping a set of slot values (these slots are identified by the remaining items of L) into a value which will be put into the slot identified by E. There fore SETIS is the operation which accomplishes the translation and the inference by using the pragmatic KS.

It is apparent that the possibility of executing a semantic check pro cedure depends on the availability of the values of the slots referred to in the CHECK and SETIS operations occurring in the procedure. Our choice of not deferring the semantic checks until the end of the syn tactic analysis (see introduction) forced us to adopt a demon-like ap proach for the activation of the semantic procedures. In fact the trig

gering of a semantic procedure (remember that it is firstly triggered
by a FILL operation) does not produce its immediate execution; what
really happens is that a copy of the procedure body is stored in a
list of active procedures; this list is examined each time a FILL or
LINK operation is executed, to verify whether one or more active pro
cedures may be executed. It could happen that a procedure is stored
in the list, immediately selected for execution and run until its very
end, but normally some of the slots whose contents are required by a
CHECK and SETIS operation are not yet available. In this latter case,
the procedure is suspended at the position where the unavailable slot
values are required and it is stored again in the active procedure
list together with its suspension point. When no check procedure is
executable, the control is returned to the syntactic procedure which
issued the last FILL or LINK operation.

In the Appendix an example of the translation of an input command
will be reported, together with a partial description of the sequence
of operations performed by the syntactic and semantic procedures.

CONCLUDING REMARKS

The description of the system given above makes apparent that no cen
tral controller guides the operation flow. In fact the semantic check
procedures are triggered when a slot is filled by the syntax, but the
actual time when they are executed is determined by the global status
of the translation process. In an analogous way the syntactic proce
dures are not directly scheduled by anotherprocedure, but a set of pat
tern-action rules is activated and this activation is followed by an
independent selection step which actually chooses the procedure to ex
ecute. It has been shown how this distribution of the control allows
the system to carry on in parallel the syntactic and semantic analyses
of the command even if the two KSs are kept separate.

Another feature of the system, which has not been discussed exten
sively in the paper is the adoption of syntactic categories which are
semantically biased. Even if this approach is not new (Burton 76;
Hendrix 77; Waltz 78), we tried to preserve the possibility of using
the same grammar in other domains, so that our categories are not
strictly correlated with the different lexical items, but with the
role they play in the phrases where they may appear. For instance, the
category NOUN has been split   into CONCNAME, IDENTIFIER, PROPERTY
and ATTRIBUTE in order to have different categories for nouns identify
ing concepts (patient), single individuals (albumine), characteristics
of an individual or a class (age) and intersection data (value - of a
labtest for a patient). The system takes advantage of this distinction
not only to impose more strict syntactic constraints on the structure
of the commands, but also to choose a particular translation for a
noun. Notice, for example, that in order to translate the phrase "val
ue of albumine" a connection relation (PERFORM) must be included   in

the translation to indicate that it is required a specification of the patient(s) whom the phrase is referred to, whereas the phrase "cost of albumine" is self-consistent, so that no connection relation must be included.

The current version of the system (implemented in LISP on a DEC-10) suffers from a number of limitations. Some of them are currently being overcome (for example, the grammar is being extended to cover update commands and yes/no questions), but the most severe difficulties arise from structural problems. Among them is the inability of the system to handle commands which are syntactically ill-formed. In fact the verifi cation of the syntactic correctness and the structure building opera tions are intermixed in the action part of the syntactic rules, thus preventing the system from distinguishing the two different phases; on the other hand, the first of them (verification) should be handled in a more flexible way (see, for example, Hayes and Carbonell 81), to al low the system to perform partial matches (or equivalent operations) to recognize a pattern even if it is not perfectly correct.

REFERENCES

Arens, Y., 1981. Using Language and Context in the Analysis of Text. Proc. 7th Int.Joint Conf. on Artificial Intelligence, Vancouver B.C. pp.52-57.

Burton, R.R., 1976. Semantic Grammar: An Engineering Technique for Constructing Natural Language Understanding Systems. BBN Report No.3453.

Charniak, E., 1981. Six Topics in Search of a Parser: An Overview of A.I. Language Research. Proc. 7th Joint Conf. on Artificial Intelligence, Vancouver B.C., pp.1079-1087.

Guida, G., Somalvico, M., 1980. Interacting in Natural Language with Artificial Systems: the DONAU Project. Information Systems, 5, pp.333-344.

Harris, L.R., 1978. The ROBOT System: Natural Language Processing Ap plied to Data Base Query. Proc. 1978 ACM Annual Conf., pp.165-172.

Hayes, P.J., Carbonell, J.G., 1981. Multi-strategy Construction Specif ic Parsing for Flexible Data Base Query and Update. Proc. 7th Int. Joint Conf. on Artificial Intelligence, Vancouver B.C., pp.432-439.

Heidorn, G.E., 1978: Natural Language Dialogue for Managing an On-line Calendar. Proc. 1978 ACM Annual Conf., pp.45-52.

Hendrix, G.G., 1977. The LIFER Manual. Tech.Note 138, SRI Internat.

Konolige, K.G., 1980. A Framework for a Portable Natural Language In terface to Data Base, in Mechanical Intelligence: Research and Appli cations (ed.Sagalowicz), SRI Final Tech. Report, pp.15-54.

Lesmo, L., Magnani, D. and Torasso, P., 1981. A Deterministic Analyzer for the Interpretation of Natural Language Commands. Proc. 7th Int. Joint Conf. on Artificial Intelligence, Vancouver B.C., pp.440-442.

Lesmo, L., Magnani, D. and Torasso, P., 1981b. Lexical and Pragmatic

242

Knowledge for Natural Language Analysis. Proc. Int. Conf. on Cyber netics and Society, Atlanta GA, pp.301-305.

Marcus, M.P., 1980. A Theory of Syntactic Recognition for Natural Language. MIT Press, Cambridge MA.

Rieger, C. and Small, S., 1981. Toward a Theory of Distributed Word Expert Natural Language Parsing. IEEE Trans. on Systems, Man and Cybernetics, SMC-11, pp.43-51.

Schank, R.C., Lebowitz, M. and Birnbaum, L., 1979. Parsing Directly into Knowledge Structures. Proc. 6th Int. Joint Conf. on Artificial Intelligence, Tokyo, pp.772-777.

Sidner, C.L., Bates, M., Bobrow, R.J., Brachman, R.J., Cohen, P.R., Israel, D., Schmolze, J., Webber, B.L., Woods, W.A., 1981. Research in Knowledge Representation for Natural Language Understanding, BBN Report No. 4785.

Waltz, D.L., 1978. An English Language Question Answering System for a Large Relational Data Base. Comm. ACM, 21, pp.526-539.

Wilensky, R., 1981. A Knowledge Based Approach to Language Processing: a Progress Report. Proc. 7th Int. Joint Conf. on Artificial Intelligence, Vancouver B.C., pp.25-30.

Woods, W.A., 1978. Semantics and Quantification in Natural Language Question Answering, in Advances in Computers, 17 (ed. Yovits), Academic Press, pp.1-87.

APPENDIX

We purport here to make clearer the interaction between syntactic and semantic knowledge sources by showing a detailed example. Let us consider the sentence: QUALI SONO I PAZIENTI CON ITTERO INTENSO CHE HANNO EFFETTUATO LA BIOPSIA EPATICA? (What are the patients with severe jaundice who have performed the hepatic biopsy?); its final representation is reported in fig.2.

Let us follow now the way the system translates the phrase "CON IT TERO INTENSO" (with severe jaundice); its internal representation (part B of fig.2) may be paraphrased as "who show, with a value equal to severe, the symptom whose name is jaundice".

When the system encounters the word "CON", the current situation of the internal representation corresponds to part A of fig.2. When the word "ITTERO" (jaundice) is analyzed, the system remarks that it is not a property of the patients, but an identifier, so that a simple restriction cannot express the condition "CON ITTERO"; for this reason a syntactic routine is entered, which builds the structure B of fig.2 in the following way: the instantiations ACT1, CONSTR1, CONC2 and RESTR1 are created (in this order) and linked each other as shown in fig.2, then CONC1 is linked to ACT1.

After that, a FILL is performed to fill an external slot of RESTR1 with "ITTERO". This FILL operation triggers a semantic check procedure which:

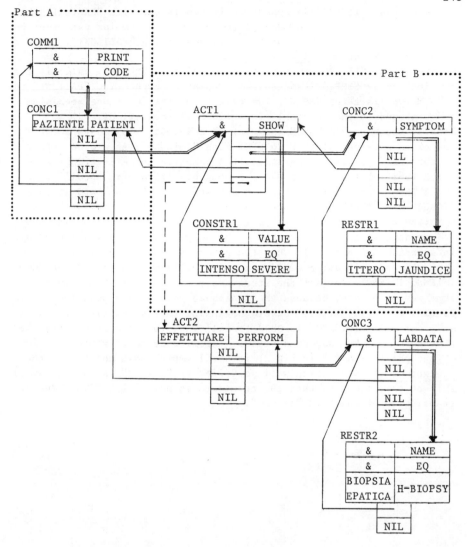

Fig.2 – Final representation of the sentence QUALI SONO I PAZIENTI CON
ITTERO INTENSO CHE HANNO EFFETTUATO LA BIOPSIA EPATICA? (What
are the patients with severe jaundice who have performed the
hepatic biopsy?)

    – & means "undefined", i.e. that the word is subsumed in the
input command

    – ═══➤ indicates a direct link

    – ───➤ indicates a reverse link

    – ----➤ indicates a chain link

- checks that "ITTERO" is semantically consistent with "PAZIENTI" by accessing the network component (notice that a complex path must be travelled to reach the slot of CONC1 containing "PAZIENTI", but all needed links are available);
- infers that "ITTERO" must be translated as "JAUNDICE", which is the "NAME" of a "SYMPTOM" and that the relation connecting "PATIENT" to "SYMPTOM" is named "SHOW". The results of the inference mechanism are stored in the internal slots via SETIS operations.

Finally the word "INTENSO" (severe) is scanned; this causes the filling of an external slot of CONSTR1 with "INTENSO". As a side effect of this FILL operation the associated semantic check is triggered, which verifies that "INTENSO" is a possible linguistic specification of "ITTERO" and infers that its translation is "SEVERE" and it is a "VALUE" of "ITTERO" which appears in the connection relation "SHOW".

Notice that during the analysis of the phrase "CON ITTERO INTENSO" no semantic check procedure has to be suspended, because all needed information is available when the procedures are triggered.

A different situation would arise in the (admissible) case of "CON INTENSO ITTERO". In fact the structure B of fig. 2 is built in the same way as before, because the lookahead technique allows the system to find the word "ITTERO" before beginning the translation of "INTENSO", but when "INTENSO" is used to fill the slot, the associated check procedure must be suspended because the already built representation of the phrase (part B in fig.2) is still empty. This means that the content of the slot which will be filled by "ITTERO" is not yet available at this time, so that the procedure is suspended to wait the translation of the word "ITTERO".

Author Index

Subject Index

248